Ruby Programming

Basic to advanced Concepts

Ruby programming: Basic to advanced concepts

CREDITS

Author

Alban Andahi

Reviewers

Thomas Levy
Eric Simon
Brian Fernando

Lead Technical Editor

Stacy Alexander

Copy Editors

Paul Dukes
Lucas Pierre
Dickey Brian

Acquisition Editor

Joey Kaufman

Project Coordinator

Anita Gabriel

Proofreader

John Mike

Layout Coordinator

Alexia Amanda

Graphics

George Peter

Cover

Mike Wilson

ABOUT THE AUTHOR

Alban Andahi has been a programmer for over a decade. He has written software professionally as a developer, software engineer and systems architect. He has also worked as a contributing factor to many professional books which have emerged top sellers across the globe.

Apart from being a significant figure in the software world, he's also an entrepreneur and a mentor. He can be contacted on Email: authoralbanandahi@gmail.com

ACKNOWLEDGEMENTS

This book would not have been possible without patient help from Stacy Alexander, Anita Gabriel, Alexia Amanda and everyone who helped put this book together. Thanks also whole team Thomas Levy, Eric Simon, and Brian Fernando for such a wonderful job. Thanks also to Paul Dukes, Lucas Pierre, Dickey Brian, Joey Kaufman, George Peters and Mike Wilson.

Special Thanks to my wife for being loving, caring and supportive throughout all my projects. I LOVE YOU. To my son Sean and Daughter Shamim, Daddy Loves you. Thank you for being the inspiration behind every step I make.

Table of Contents

1. OVERVIEW

Ruby is a pure object-oriented programming language. It was created in 1993 by Yukihiro Matsumoto of Japan.

You can find the name Yukihiro Matsumoto on the Ruby mailing list at www.ruby-lang.org. Matsumoto is also known as Matz in the Ruby community.

Ruby is "A Programmer's Best Friend".

Ruby has features that are similar to those of Smalltalk, Perl, and Python. Perl, Python, and Smalltalk are scripting languages. Smalltalk is a true object-oriented language. Ruby, like Smalltalk, is a perfect object-oriented language. Using Ruby syntax is much easier than using Smalltalk syntax.

Features of Ruby

- Ruby is an open-source and is freely available on the Web, but it is subject to a license.
- Ruby is a general-purpose, interpreted programming language.
- Ruby is a true object-oriented programming language.
- Ruby is a server-side scripting language similar to Python and PERL.
- Ruby can be used to write Common Gateway Interface (CGI) scripts.
- Ruby can be embedded into Hypertext Markup Language (HTML).
- Ruby has a clean and easy syntax that allows a new developer to learn very quickly and easily.
- Ruby has similar syntax to that of many programming languages such as C++ and Perl.
- Ruby is very much scalable and big programs written in Ruby are easily maintainable.
- Ruby can be used for developing Internet and intranet applications.
- Ruby can be installed in Windows and POSIX environments.
- Ruby support many GUI tools such as Tcl/Tk, GTK, and OpenGL.
- Ruby can easily be connected to DB2, MySQL, Oracle, and Sybase.
- Ruby has a rich set of built-in functions, which can be used directly into Ruby scripts.

Tools You Will Need

For performing the examples discussed in this book, you will need a latest computer like Intel Core i3 or i5 with a minimum of 2GB of RAM (4GB of RAM recommended). You also will need the following software:

- Linux or Windows 95/98/2000/NT or Windows 7 operating system
- Apache 1.3.19-5 Web server
- Internet Explorer 5.0 or above Web browser
- Ruby 1.8.5

This book will provide the necessary skills to create GUI, networking, and Web applications using Ruby. It also will talk about extending and embedding Ruby applications.

What is Next?

The next chapter guides you to where you can obtain Ruby and its documentation. Finally, it instructs you on how to install Ruby and prepare an environment to develop Ruby applications.

2. ENVIRONMENT SETUP

Try it

We assume you have already set up Ruby Programming environment to execute all the examples at the same time when you are doing your theory work. This gives you confidence in what you are reading and to check the result with different options.

```
#!/usr/bin/ruby -w

puts "Hello, Ruby!";
```

Local Environment Setup

If you are still willing to set up your environment for Ruby programming language, then let's proceed. This book will teach you all the important topics related to environment setup. We would recommend you to go through the following topics first and then proceed further:

- **Ruby Installation on Linux/Unix** : If you are planning to have your development environment on Linux/Unix Machine, then go through this chapter.
- **Ruby Installation on Windows** : If you are planning to have your development environment on Windows Machine, then go through this chapter.
- **Ruby Command Line Options** : This chapter list out all the command line options, which you can use along with Ruby interpreter.
- **Ruby Environment Variables** : This chapter has a list of all the important environment variables to be set to make Ruby Interpreter works.

Ruby Installation on Linux/Unix

Here are the steps to be followed to install Ruby on a Unix machine:

NOTE: Before proceeding, make sure you have root privilege.

- Download a zipped file having latest version of Ruby. Follow **Download Link**.
- After having downloaded the Ruby archive, unpack it and change into the newly created directory:

```
$ tar -xvzf ruby-1.6.7.tgz
$ cd ruby-1.6.7
```

- Now, configure and compile the source code as follows:

```
$ ./configure
$ make
```

- Finally, install Ruby interpreter as follows:

```
$ su -l root # become a root user
$ make install
$ exit       # become the original user again
```

- After installation, make sure everything is working fine by issuing the following command on the command-line:

```
$ruby -v
ruby 1.6.7 (2002-06-04) [i386-netbsd]
```

- If everything is fine, this should output the version of the installed Ruby interpreter as shown above. You may have installed different version, so it will display a different version.

Using yum to Install Ruby

If your computer is connected to the Internet, then the easiest way to install Ruby or any other other RPM is using the **yum** utility. Give the following command at the command prompt and you will find Ruby gets installed on your computer.

```
$ yum install ruby
```

Ruby Installation on Windows

Here are the steps to install Ruby on a Windows machine.

NOTE: You may have different versions available at the time of installation.

- Download a zipped file having latest version of Ruby. Follow **Download Link**.
- After having downloaded the Ruby archive, unpack it and change into the newly created directory:
- Double-click the Ruby1.6.7.exe file. The Ruby installation wizard starts.
- Click Next to move to the Important Information page of the wizard and keep moving till Ruby installer completes installing Ruby.

You may need to set some environment variables if your installation has not setup them appropriately.

- If you use Windows 9x, add the following lines to your c:\autoexec.bat: set PATH="D:\(ruby install directory)\bin;%PATH%"
- Windows NT/2000 users need to modify their registries.
    - Click Control Panel | System Properties | Environment Variables.
    - Under System Variables, select Path and click EDIT.
    - Add your Ruby directory to the end of the Variable Value list and click OK.
    - Under System Variables, select PATHEXT and click EDIT.
    - Add .RB and .RBW to the Variable Value list and click OK.
- After installation, make sure everything is working fine by issuing the following command on the command-line:

```
$ruby -v
ruby 1.6.7
```

- If everything is fine, this should output the version of the installed Ruby interpreter as shown above. You may have installed different version, so it will display a different version.

Ruby Command Line Options

Ruby is generally run from the command line in the following way:

```
$ ruby [ options ] [.] [ programfile ] [ arguments ... ]
```

The interpreter can be invoked with any of the following options to control the environment and behavior of the interpreter.

Option	Description
-a	Used with -n or -p to split each line. Check -n and -p options.
-c	Checks syntax only, without executing program.
-C dir	Changes directory before executing (equivalent to -X).
-d	Enables debug mode (equivalent to -debug).
-F pat	Specifies pat as the default separator pattern ($;) used by split.
-e prog	Specifies prog as the program from the command line. Specify multiple -e options for multiline programs.
-h	Displays an overview of command-line options.
-i [ext]	Overwrites the file contents with program output. The original file is saved with the extension ext. If ext isn't specified, the original file is deleted.
-I dir	Adds dir as the directory for loading libraries.
-K [kcode]	Specifies the multibyte character set code (e or E for EUC (extended Unix code); s or S for SJIS (Shift-JIS); u or U for UTF-8; and a, A, n, or N for ASCII).
-l	Enables automatic line-end processing. Chops a newline from input lines and appends a newline to output lines.
-n	Places code within an input loop (as in while gets; ... end).
-0[octal]	Sets default record separator ($/) as an octal. Defaults to \0 if octal not specified.
-p	Places code within an input loop. Writes $_ for each iteration.

-r lib	Uses *require* to load *lib* as a library before executing.
-s	Interprets any arguments between the program name and filename arguments fitting the pattern -xxx as a switch and defines the corresponding variable.
-T [level]	Sets the level for tainting checks (1 if level not specified).
-v	Displays version and enables verbose mode
-w	Enables verbose mode. If program file not specified, reads from STDIN.
-x [dir]	Strips text before #!ruby line. Changes directory to *dir* before executing if *dir* is specified.
-X dir	Changes directory before executing (equivalent to -C).
-y	Enables parser debug mode.
--copyright	Displays copyright notice.
--debug	Enables debug mode (equivalent to -d).
--help	Displays an overview of command-line options (equivalent to -h).
--version	Displays version.
--verbose	Enables verbose mode (equivalent to -v). Sets $VERBOSE to true.
--yydebug	Enables parser debug mode (equivalent to -y).

Single character command-line options can be combined. The following two lines express the same meaning:

```
$ruby -ne 'print if /Ruby/' /usr/share/bin


$ruby -n -e 'print if /Ruby/' /usr/share/bin
```

Ruby Environment Variables

Ruby interpreter uses the following environment variables to control its behavior. The ENV object contains a list of all the current environment variables set.

Variable	Description
DLN_LIBRARY_PATH	Search path for dynamically loaded modules.
HOME	Directory moved to when no argument is passed to Dir::chdir. Also used by File::expand_path to expand "~".
LOGDIR	Directory moved to when no arguments are passed to Dir::chdir and environment variable HOME isn't set.
PATH	Search path for executing subprocesses and searching for Ruby programs with the -S option. Separate each path with a colon (semicolon in DOS and Windows).
RUBYLIB	Search path for libraries. Separate each path with a colon (semicolon in DOS and Windows).
RUBYLIB_PREFIX	Used to modify the RUBYLIB search path by replacing prefix of library path1 with path2 using the format path1;path2 or path1path2.
RUBYOPT	Command-line options passed to Ruby interpreter. Ignored in taint mode (Where $SAFE is greater than 0).

RUBYPATH	With -S option, search path for Ruby programs. Takes precedence over PATH. Ignored in taint mode (where $SAFE is greater than 0).
RUBYSHELL	Specifies shell for spawned processes. If not set, SHELL or COMSPEC are checked.

For Unix, use **env** command to see a list of all the environment variables.

```
HOSTNAME=ip-72-167-112-17.ip.secureserver.net
RUBYPATH=/usr/bin
SHELL=/bin/bash
TERM=xterm
HISTSIZE=1000
SSH_CLIENT=122.169.131.179 1742 22
SSH_TTY=/dev/pts/1
USER=amrood
JRE_HOME=/usr/java/jdk/jre
J2RE_HOME=/usr/java/jdk/jre
PATH=/usr/local/bin:/bin:/usr/bin:/home/guest/bin
MAIL=/var/spool/mail/guest
PWD=/home/amrood
INPUTRC=/etc/inputrc
JAVA_HOME=/usr/java/jdk
LANG=C
HOME=/root
SHLVL=2
JDK_HOME=/usr/java/jdk
LOGDIR=/usr/log/ruby
LOGNAME=amrood
SSH_CONNECTION=122.169.131.179 1742 72.167.112.17 22
LESSOPEN=|/usr/bin/lesspipe.sh %s
RUBYLIB=/usr/lib/ruby
G_BROKEN_FILENAMES=1
```

```
_=/bin/env
```

Popular Ruby Editors

To write your Ruby programs, you will need an editor:

- If you are working on Windows machine, then you can use any simple text editor like Notepad or Edit plus.
- **VIM** (Vi IMproved) is a very simple text editor. This is available on almost all Unix machines and now Windows as well. Otherwise, your can use your favorite vi editor to write Ruby programs.
- **RubyWin** is a Ruby Integrated Development Environment (IDE) for Windows.
- Ruby Development Environment **(RDE)** is also a very good IDE for windows users.

Interactive Ruby (IRb)

Interactive Ruby (IRb) provides a shell for experimentation. Within the IRb shell, you can immediately view expression results, line by line.

This tool comes along with Ruby installation so you have nothing to do extra to have IRb working.

Just type **irb** at your command prompt and an Interactive Ruby Session will start as given below:

```
$irb

irb 0.6.1(99/09/16)

irb(main):001:0> def hello

irb(main):002:1> out = "Hello World"

irb(main):003:1> puts out

irb(main):004:1> end

nil

irb(main):005:0> hello

Hello World

nil

irb(main):006:0>
```

Do not worry about what we did here. You will learn all these steps in subsequent chapters.

What is Next?

We assume now you have a working Ruby Environment and you are ready to write the first Ruby Program. The next chapter will teach you how to write Ruby programs.

3. SYNTAX

Let us write a simple program in ruby. All ruby files will have extension **.rb**. So, put the following source code in a test.rb file.

```
#!/usr/bin/ruby -w


puts "Hello, Ruby!";
```

Here, we assumed that you have Ruby interpreter available in /usr/bin directory. Now, try to run this program as follows:

```
$ ruby test.rb
```

This will produce the following result:

```
Hello, Ruby!
```

You have seen a simple Ruby program, now let us see a few basic concepts related to Ruby Syntax.

Whitespace in Ruby Program

Whitespace characters such as spaces and tabs are generally ignored in Ruby code, except when they appear in strings. Sometimes, however, they are used to interpret ambiguous statements. Interpretations of this sort produce warnings when the -w option is enabled.

Example

```
a + b is interpreted as a+b ( Here a is a local variable)
a  +b is interpreted as a(+b) ( Here a is a method call)
```

Line Endings in Ruby Program

Ruby interprets semicolons and newline characters as the ending of a statement. However, if Ruby encounters operators, such as +, -, or backslash at the end of a line, they indicate the continuation of a statement.

Ruby Identifiers

Identifiers are names of variables, constants, and methods. Ruby identifiers are case sensitive. It means Ram and RAM are two different identifiers in Ruby.

Ruby identifier names may consist of alphanumeric characters and the underscore character (_).

Reserved Words

The following list shows the reserved words in Ruby. These reserved words may not be used as constant or variable names. They can, however, be used as method names.

BEGIN	do	next	then
END	else	nil	true
alias	elsif	not	undef
and	end	or	unless
begin	ensure	redo	until
break	false	rescue	when
case	for	retry	while
class	if	return	while
def	in	self	__FILE__
defined?	module	super	__LINE__

Here Document in Ruby

"Here Document" refers to build strings from multiple lines. Following a << you can specify a string or an identifier to terminate the string literal, and all lines following the current line up to the terminator are the value of the string.

If the terminator is quoted, the type of quotes determines the type of the line-oriented string literal. Notice there must be no space between << and the terminator.

Here are different examples:

```
#!/usr/bin/ruby -w

print <<EOF
    This is the first way of creating
    here document ie. multiple line string.
EOF

print <<"EOF";                # same as above
    This is the second way of creating
    here document ie. multiple line string.
EOF

print <<`EOC`                 # execute commands
     echo hi there
     echo lo there
EOC

print <<"foo", <<"bar"  # you can stack them
     I said foo.
foo
     I said bar.
bar
```

This will produce the following result:

```
    This is the first way of creating
    her document ie. multiple line string.
    This is the second way of creating
    her document ie. multiple line string.
hi there
lo there
```

```
        I said foo.
        I said bar.
```

Ruby BEGIN Statement

Syntax

```
BEGIN {
   code
}
```

Declares *code* to be called before the program is run.

Example

```
#!/usr/bin/ruby

puts "This is main Ruby Program"

BEGIN {
   puts "Initializing Ruby Program"
}
```

This will produce the following result:

```
Initializing Ruby Program
This is main Ruby Program
```

Ruby END Statement

Syntax

```
END {
   code
}
```

Declares *code* to be called at the end of the program.

Example

```
#!/usr/bin/ruby

puts "This is main Ruby Program"

END {
   puts "Terminating Ruby Program"
}
BEGIN {
   puts "Initializing Ruby Program"
}
```

This will produce the following result:

```
Initializing Ruby Program
This is main Ruby Program
Terminating Ruby Program
```

Ruby Comments

A comment hides a line, part of a line, or several lines from the Ruby interpreter. You can use the hash character (#) at the beginning of a line:

```
# I am a comment. Just ignore me.
```

Or, a comment may be on the same line after a statement or expression:

```
name = "Madisetti" # This is again comment
```

You can comment multiple lines as follows:

```
# This is a comment.
# This is a comment, too.
# This is a comment, too.
# I said that already.
```

Here is another form. This block comment conceals several lines from the interpreter with =begin/=end:

```
=begin
This is a comment.
This is a comment, too.
This is a comment, too.
I said that already.
=end
```

4. CLASSES AND OBJECTS

Ruby is a perfect Object Oriented Programming Language. The features of the object-oriented programming language include:

- Data Encapsulation
- Data Abstraction
- Polymorphism
- Inheritance

These features have been discussed in the chapter **Object Oriented Ruby**.

An object-oriented program involves classes and objects. A class is the blueprint from which individual objects are created. In object-oriented terms, we say that your *bicycle* is an instance of the *class of objects* known as bicycles.

Take the example of any vehicle. It comprises wheels, horsepower, and fuel or gas tank capacity. These characteristics form the data members of the class Vehicle. You can differentiate one vehicle from the other with the help of these characteristics.

A vehicle can also have certain functions, such as halting, driving, and speeding. Even these functions form the data members of the class Vehicle. You can, therefore, define a class as a combination of characteristics and functions.

A class Vehicle can be defined as:

```
Class Vehicle
{
   Number no_of_wheels
   Number horsepower
   Characters type_of_tank
   Number Capacity
   Function speeding
   {
   }
   Function driving
   {
   }
   Function halting
```

```
    {
    }
}
```

By assigning different values to these data members, you can form several instances of the class Vehicle. For example, an airplane has three wheels, horsepower of 1,000, fuel as the type of tank, and a capacity of 100 liters. In the same way, a car has four wheels, horsepower of 200, gas as the type of tank, and a capacity of 25 liters.

Defining a Class in Ruby

To implement object-oriented programming by using Ruby, you need to first learn how to create objects and classes in Ruby.

A class in Ruby always starts with the keyword *class* followed by the name of the class. The name should always be in initial capitals. The class *Customer* can be displayed as:

```
class Customer
end
```

You terminate a class by using the keyword *end*. All the data members in the *class* are between the class definition and the *end* keyword.

Variables in a Ruby Class

Ruby provides four types of variables:

- **Local Variables:** Local variables are the variables that are defined in a method. Local variables are not available outside the method. You will see more details about method in subsequent chapter. Local variables begin with a lowercase letter or _.
- **Instance Variables:** Instance variables are available across methods for any particular instance or object. That means that instance variables change from object to object. Instance variables are preceded by the at sign (@) followed by the variable name.
- **Class Variables:** Class variables are available across different objects. A class variable belongs to the class and is a characteristic of a class. They are preceded by the sign @@ and are followed by the variable name.
- **Global Variables:** Class variables are not available across classes. If you want to have a single variable, which is available across classes, you need to define a global variable. The global variables are always preceded by the dollar sign ($).

Example

Using the class variable @@no_of_customers, you can determine the number of objects that are being created. This enables in deriving the number of customers.

```
class Customer
   @@no_of_customers=0
end
```

Creating Objects in Ruby Using new Method

Objects are instances of the class. You will now learn how to create objects of a class in Ruby. You can create objects in Ruby by using the method *new* of the class.

The method *new* is a unique type of method, which is predefined in the Ruby library. The new method belongs to the *class* methods.

Here is the example to create two objects cust1 and cust2 of the class Customer:

```
cust1 = Customer. new
cust2 = Customer. new
```

Here, cust1 and cust2 are the names of two objects. You write the object name followed by the equal to sign (=) after which the class name will follow. Then, the dot operator and the keyword *new* will follow.

Custom Method to Create Ruby Objects

You can pass parameters to method *new* and those parameters can be used to initialize class variables.

When you plan to declare the *new* method with parameters, you need to declare the method *initialize* at the time of the class creation.

The *initialize* method is a special type of method, which will be executed when the *new* method of the class is called with parameters.

Here is the example to create initialize method:

```
class Customer
```

```
    @@no_of_customers=0
    def initialize(id, name, addr)
       @cust_id=id
       @cust_name=name
       @cust_addr=addr
    end
end
```

In this example, you declare the *initialize* method with **id, name**, and **addr** as local variables. Here, *def* and *end* are used to define a Ruby method *initialize*. You will learn more about methods in subsequent chapters.

In the *initialize* method, you pass on the values of these local variables to the instance variables @cust_id, @cust_name, and @cust_addr. Here local variables hold the values that are passed along with the new method.

Now, you can create objects as follows:

```
cust1=Customer.new("1", "John", "Wisdom Apartments, Ludhiya")
cust2=Customer.new("2", "Poul", "New Empire road, Khandala")
```

Member Functions in Ruby Class

In Ruby, functions are called methods. Each method in a *class* starts with the keyword *def* followed by the method name.

The method name always preferred in **lowercase letters**. You end a method in Ruby by using the keyword *end*.

Here is the example to define a Ruby method:

```
class Sample
   def function
      statement 1
      statement 2
   end
end
```

Here, *statement 1* and *statement 2* are part of the body of the method *function* inside the class Sample. These statements could be any valid Ruby statement. For example, we can put a method *puts* to print *Hello Ruby* as follows:

```
class Sample
```

```
   def hello
      puts "Hello Ruby!"
   end
end
```

Now in the following example, create one object of Sample class and call *hello* method and see the result:

```
#!/usr/bin/ruby

class Sample
   def hello
      puts "Hello Ruby!"
   end
end

# Now using above class to create objects
object = Sample. new
object.hello
```

This will produce the following result:

```
Hello Ruby!
```

Simple Case Study

Here is a case study if you want to do more practice with class and objects.

Ruby Class Case Study

For your case study, you will create a Ruby Class called Customer and you will declare two methods:

- *display_details*: This method will display the details of the customer.
- *total_no_of_customers*: This method will display the total number of customers created in the system.

```
#!/usr/bin/ruby

class Customer
```

```
   @@no_of_customers=0
   def initialize(id, name, addr)
      @cust_id=id
      @cust_name=name
      @cust_addr=addr
   end
   def display_details()
      puts "Customer id #@cust_id"
      puts "Customer name #@cust_name"
      puts "Customer address #@cust_addr"
    end
    def total_no_of_customers()
       @@no_of_customers += 1
       puts "Total number of customers: #@@no_of_customers"
    end
end
```

The *display_details* method contains three *puts* statements, displaying the Customer ID, the Customer name, and the Customer address. The puts statement will display the text Customer id followed by the value of the variable @cust_id in a single line as follows:

```
puts "Customer id #@cust_id"
```

When you want to display the text and the value of the instance variable in a single line, you need to precede the variable name with the hash symbol (#) in the puts statement. The text and the instance variable along with the hash symbol (#) should be enclosed in double quotation marks.

The second method, total_no_of_customers, is a method that contains the class variable @@no_of_customers. The expression @@no_of_ customers+=1 adds 1 to the variable no_of_customers each time the method total_no_of_customers is called. In this way, you will always have the total number of customers in the class variable.

Now, create two customers as follows:

```
cust1=Customer.new("1", "John", "Wisdom Apartments, Ludhiya")
cust2=Customer.new("2", "Poul", "New Empire road, Khandala")
```

Here, we create two objects of the Customer class as cust1 and cust2 and pass the necessary parameters with the new method. The initialize method is invoked, and the necessary properties of the object are initialized.

Once the objects are created, you need to call the methods of the class by using the two objects. If you want to call a method or any data member, you write the following:

```
cust1.display_details()
cust1.total_no_of_customers()
```

The object name should always be followed by a dot, which is in turn followed by the method name or any data member. We have seen how to call the two methods by using the cust1 object. Using the cust2 object, you can call both methods as shown below:

```
cust2.display_details()
cust2.total_no_of_customers()
```

Save and Execute the Code

Now, put all this source code in the main.rb file as follows:

```
#!/usr/bin/ruby


class Customer
   @@no_of_customers=0
   def initialize(id, name, addr)
      @cust_id=id
      @cust_name=name
      @cust_addr=addr
   end
   def display_details()
      puts "Customer id #@cust_id"
      puts "Customer name #@cust_name"
      puts "Customer address #@cust_addr"
   end
   def total_no_of_customers()
      @@no_of_customers += 1
      puts "Total number of customers: #@@no_of_customers"
```

```
    end
end

# Create Objects
cust1=Customer.new("1", "John", "Wisdom Apartments, Ludhiya")
cust2=Customer.new("2", "Poul", "New Empire road, Khandala")

# Call Methods
cust1.display_details()
cust1.total_no_of_customers()
cust2.display_details()
cust2.total_no_of_customers()
```

Now, run this program as follows:

```
$ ruby main.rb
```

This will produce the following result:

```
Customer id 1
Customer name John
Customer address Wisdom Apartments, Ludhiya
Total number of customers: 1
Customer id 2
Customer name Poul
Customer address New Empire road, Khandala
Total number of customers: 2
```

5. VARIABLES, CONSTANTS AND LITERALS

Variables are the memory locations, which hold any data to be used by any program.

There are five types of variables supported by Ruby. You already have gone through a small description of these variables in the previous chapter as well. These five types of variables are explained in this chapter.

Ruby Global Variables

Global variables begin with $. Uninitialized global variables have the value *nil* and produce warnings with the -w option.

Assignment to global variables alters the global status. It is not recommended to use global variables. They make programs cryptic.

Here is an example showing the usage of global variable.

```
#!/usr/bin/ruby

$global_variable = 10
class Class1
  def print_global
     puts "Global variable in Class1 is #$global_variable"
  end
end
class Class2
  def print_global
     puts "Global variable in Class2 is #$global_variable"
  end
end

class1obj = Class1.new
class1obj.print_global
class2obj = Class2.new
class2obj.print_global
```

Here $global_variable is a global variable. This will produce the following result:

NOTE: In Ruby, you CAN access value of any variable or constant by putting a hash (#) character just before that variable or constant.

```
Global variable in Class1 is 10
Global variable in Class2 is 10
```

Ruby Instance Variables

Instance variables begin with @. Uninitialized instance variables have the value *nil* and produce warnings with the -w option.

Here is an example showing the usage of Instance Variables.

```
#!/usr/bin/ruby

class Customer
   def initialize(id, name, addr)
      @cust_id=id
      @cust_name=name
      @cust_addr=addr
   end
   def display_details()
      puts "Customer id #@cust_id"
      puts "Customer name #@cust_name"
      puts "Customer address #@cust_addr"
    end
end

# Create Objects
cust1=Customer.new("1", "John", "Wisdom Apartments, Ludhiya")
cust2=Customer.new("2", "Poul", "New Empire road, Khandala")

# Call Methods
cust1.display_details()
cust2.display_details()
```

Here, @cust_id, @cust_name and @cust_addr are instance variables. This will produce the following result:

```
Customer id 1
Customer name John
Customer address Wisdom Apartments, Ludhiya
Customer id 2
Customer name Poul
Customer address New Empire road, Khandala
```

Ruby Class Variables

Class variables begin with @@ and must be initialized before they can be used in method definitions.

Referencing an uninitialized class variable produces an error. Class variables are shared among descendants of the class or module in which the class variables are defined.

Overriding class variables produce warnings with the -w option.

Here is an example showing the usage of class variable:

```
#!/usr/bin/ruby


class Customer
   @@no_of_customers=0
   def initialize(id, name, addr)
      @cust_id=id
      @cust_name=name
      @cust_addr=addr
   end
   def display_details()
      puts "Customer id #@cust_id"
      puts "Customer name #@cust_name"
      puts "Customer address #@cust_addr"
    end
    def total_no_of_customers()
       @@no_of_customers += 1
```

```
        puts "Total number of customers: #@@no_of_customers"
    end
end

# Create Objects
cust1=Customer.new("1", "John", "Wisdom Apartments, Ludhiya")
cust2=Customer.new("2", "Poul", "New Empire road, Khandala")

# Call Methods
cust1.total_no_of_customers()
cust2.total_no_of_customers()
```

Here @@no_of_customers is a class variable. This will produce the following result:

```
Total number of customers: 1
Total number of customers: 2
```

Ruby Local Variables

Local variables begin with a lowercase letter or _. The scope of a local variable ranges from class, module, def, or do to the corresponding end or from a block's opening brace to its close brace {}.

When an uninitialized local variable is referenced, it is interpreted as a call to a method that has no arguments.

Assignment to uninitialized local variables also serves as variable declaration. The variables start to exist until the end of the current scope is reached. The lifetime of local variables is determined when Ruby parses the program.

In the above example, local variables are id, name and addr.

Ruby Constants

Constants begin with an uppercase letter. Constants defined within a class or module can be accessed from within that class or module, and those defined outside a class or module can be accessed globally.

Constants may not be defined within methods. Referencing an uninitialized constant produces an error. Making an assignment to a constant that is already initialized produces a warning.

```
#!/usr/bin/ruby

class Example
   VAR1 = 100
   VAR2 = 200
   def show
       puts "Value of first Constant is #{VAR1}"
       puts "Value of second Constant is #{VAR2}"
   end
end

# Create Objects
object=Example.new()
object.show
```

Here VAR1 and VAR2 are constants. This will produce the following result:

```
Value of first Constant is 100
Value of second Constant is 200
```

Ruby Pseudo-Variables

They are special variables that have the appearance of local variables but behave like constants. You cannot assign any value to these variables.

- **self:** The receiver object of the current method.
- **true:** Value representing true.
- **false:** Value representing false.
- **nil:** Value representing undefined.
- **__FILE__:** The name of the current source file.
- **__LINE__:** The current line number in the source file.

Ruby Basic Literals

The rules Ruby uses for literals are simple and intuitive. This section explains all basic Ruby Literals.

Integer Numbers

Ruby supports integer numbers. An integer number can range from -2^{30} to 2^{30-1} or -2^{62} to 2^{62-1}. Integers within this range are objects of class *Fixnum* and integers outside this range are stored in objects of class *Bignum*.

You write integers using an optional leading sign, an optional base indicator (0 for octal, 0x for hex, or 0b for binary), followed by a string of digits in the appropriate base. Underscore characters are ignored in the digit string.

You can also get the integer value, corresponding to an ASCII character or escape the sequence by preceding it with a question mark.

Example

```
123                  # Fixnum decimal
1_234                # Fixnum decimal with underline
-500                 # Negative Fixnum
0377                 # octal
0xff                 # hexadecimal
0b1011               # binary
?a                   # character code for 'a'
?\n                  # code for a newline (0x0a)
12345678901234567890 # Bignum
```

NOTE: Class and Objects are explained in a separate chapter of this book.

Floating Numbers

Ruby supports integer numbers. They are also numbers but with decimals. Floating-point numbers are objects of class *Float* and can be any of the following:

Example

```
123.4                # floating point value
1.0e6                # scientific notation
4E20                 # dot not required
4e+20                # sign before exponential
```

String Literals

Ruby strings are simply sequences of 8-bit bytes and they are objects of class String. Double-quoted strings allow substitution and backslash notation but single-quoted strings don't allow substitution and allow backslash notation only for \\ and \'

Example

```
#!/usr/bin/ruby -w


puts 'escape using "\\"';

puts 'That\'s right';
```

This will produce the following result:

```
escape using "\"

That's right
```

You can substitute the value of any Ruby expression into a string using the sequence **#{ expr }**. Here, expr could be any ruby expression.

```
#!/usr/bin/ruby -w


puts "Multiplication Value : #{24*60*60}";
```

This will produce the following result:

```
Multiplication Value : 86400
```

Backslash Notations

Following is the list of Backslash notations supported by Ruby:

Notation	Character represented
\n	Newline (0x0a)
\r	Carriage return (0x0d)
\f	Formfeed (0x0c)
\b	Backspace (0x08)
\a	Bell (0x07)

\e	Escape (0x1b)
\s	Space (0x20)
\nnn	Octal notation (n being 0-7)
\xnn	Hexadecimal notation (n being 0-9, a-f, or A-F)
\cx, \C-x	Control-x
\M-x	Meta-x (c | 0x80)
\M-\C-x	Meta-Control-x
\x	Character x

Ruby Arrays

Literals of Ruby Array are created by placing a comma-separated series of object references between the square brackets. A trailing comma is ignored.

Example

```
#!/usr/bin/ruby


ary = [  "fred", 10, 3.14, "This is a string", "last element", ]
ary.each do |i|
   puts i
end
```

This will produce the following result:

```
fred
10
3.14
This is a string
last element
```

Ruby Hashes

A literal Ruby Hash is created by placing a list of key/value pairs between braces, with either a comma or the sequence => between the key and the value. A trailing comma is ignored.

Example

```
#!/usr/bin/ruby

hsh = colors = { "red" => 0xf00, "green" => 0x0f0, "blue" => 0x00f }
hsh.each do |key, value|
   print key, " is ", value, "\n"
end
```

This will produce the following result:

```
green is 240
red is 3840
blue is 15
```

Ruby Ranges

A Range represents an interval.a set of values with a start and an end. Ranges may be constructed using the s..e and s...e literals, or with Range.new.

Ranges constructed using .. run from the start to the end inclusively. Those created using ... exclude the end value. When used as an iterator, ranges return each value in the sequence.

A range (1..5) means it includes 1, 2, 3, 4, 5 values and a range (1...5) means it includes 1, 2, 3, 4 values.

Example

```
#!/usr/bin/ruby

(10..15).each do |n|
   print n, ' '
```

```
end
```

This will produce the following result:

```
10 11 12 13 14 15
```

6. OPERATORS

Ruby supports a rich set of operators, as you'd expect from a modern language. Most operators are actually method calls. For example, a + b is interpreted as a.+(b), where the + method in the object referred to by variable *a* is called with *b* as its argument.

For each operator (+ - * / % ** & | ^ << >> && ||), there is a corresponding form of abbreviated assignment operator (+= -= etc.).

Ruby Arithmetic Operators

Assume variable *a* holds 10 and variable *b* holds 20, then:

Operator	Description	Example
+	Addition - Adds values on either side of the operator.	a + b will give 30
-	Subtraction - Subtracts right hand operand from left hand operand.	a - b will give -10
*	Multiplication - Multiplies values on either side of the operator.	a * b will give 200
/	Division - Divides left hand operand by right hand operand.	b / a will give 2
%	Modulus - Divides left hand operand by right hand operand and returns remainder.	b % a will give 0
**	Exponent - Performs exponential (power) calculation on operators.	a**b will give 10 to the power 20

Ruby Comparison Operators

Assume variable *a* holds 10 and variable *b* holds 20, then:

Operator	Description	Example
==	Checks if the value of two operands are equal or not, if yes then condition becomes true.	(a == b) is not true.
!=	Checks if the value of two operands are equal or not, if values are not equal then condition becomes true.	(a != b) is true.
>	Checks if the value of left operand is greater than the value of right operand, if yes then condition becomes true.	(a > b) is not true.
<	Checks if the value of left operand is less than the value of right operand, if yes then condition becomes true.	(a < b) is true.
>=	Checks if the value of left operand is greater than or equal to the value of right operand, if yes then condition becomes true.	(a >= b) is not true.
<=	Checks if the value of left operand is less than or equal to the value of right operand, if yes then condition becomes true.	(a <= b) is true.
<=>	Combined comparison operator. Returns 0 if first operand equals second, 1 if first operand is greater than the second and -1 if first operand is less than the second.	(a <=> b) returns -1.
===	Used to test equality within a when clause of a *case* statement.	(1...10) === 5 returns true.
.eql?	True if the receiver and argument have both the same type and equal values.	1 == 1.0 returns true, but 1.eql?(1.0) is false.

equal?	True if the receiver and argument have the same object id.	if aObj is duplicate of bObj then aObj == bObj is true, a.equal?bObj is false but a.equal?aObj is true.

Ruby Assignment Operators

Assume variable *a* holds 10 and variable *b* holds 20, then:

Operator	Description	Example
=	Simple assignment operator, assigns values from right side operands to left side operand.	c = a + b will assign the value of a + b into c
+=	Add AND assignment operator, adds right operand to the left operand and assign the result to left operand.	c += a is equivalent to c = c + a
-=	Subtract AND assignment operator, subtracts right operand from the left operand and assign the result to left operand.	c -= a is equivalent to c = c - a
*=	Multiply AND assignment operator, multiplies right operand with the left operand and assign the result to left operand.	c *= a is equivalent to c = c * a
/=	Divide AND assignment operator, divides left operand with the right operand and assign the result to left operand.	c /= a is equivalent to c = c / a
%=	Modulus AND assignment operator, takes modulus using two operands and assign the result to left operand.	c %= a is equivalent to c = c % a

**=	Exponent AND assignment operator, performs exponential (power) calculation on operators and assign value to the left operand.	c **= a is equivalent to c = c ** a

Ruby Parallel Assignment

Ruby also supports the parallel assignment of variables. This enables multiple variables to be initialized with a single line of Ruby code. For example:

```
a = 10
b = 20
c = 30
```

This may be more quickly declared using parallel assignment:

```
a, b, c = 10, 20, 30
```

Parallel assignment is also useful for swapping the values held in two variables:

```
a, b = b, c
```

Ruby Bitwise Operators

Bitwise operator works on bits and performs bit by bit operation.

Assume if a = 60; and b = 13; now in binary format they will be as follows:

a = 0011 1100

b = 0000 1101

----

a&b = 0000 1100

a|b = 0011 1101

a^b = 0011 0001

~a = 1100 0011

The following Bitwise operators are supported by Ruby language.

Operator	Description	Example
&	Binary AND Operator copies a bit to the result if it exists in both operands.	(a & b) will give 12, which is 0000 1100
|	Binary OR Operator copies a bit if it exists in either operand.	(a | b) will give 61, which is 0011 1101
^	Binary XOR Operator copies the bit if it is set in one operand but not both.	(a ^ b) will give 49, which is 0011 0001
~	Binary Ones Complement Operator is unary and has the effect of 'flipping' bits.	(~a) will give -61, which is 1100 0011 in 2's complement form due to a signed binary number.
<<	Binary Left Shift Operator. The left operands value is moved left by the number of bits specified by the right operand.	a << 2 will give 240, which is 1111 0000
>>	Binary Right Shift Operator. The left operands value is moved right by the number of bits specified by the right operand.	a >> 2 will give 15, which is 0000 1111

Ruby Logical Operators

The following logical operators are supported by Ruby language

Assume variable *a* holds 10 and variable *b* holds 20, then:

Operator	Description	Example
and	Called Logical AND operator. If both the operands are true, then the condition	(a and b) is true.

	becomes true.	
or	Called Logical OR Operator. If any of the two operands are non zero, then the condition becomes true.	(a or b) is true.
&&	Called Logical AND operator. If both the operands are non zero, then the condition becomes true.	(a && b) is true.
||	Called Logical OR Operator. If any of the two operands are non zero, then the condition becomes true.	(a || b) is true.
!	Called Logical NOT Operator. Use to reverses the logical state of its operand. If a condition is true, then Logical NOT operator will make false.	!(a && b) is false.
not	Called Logical NOT Operator. Use to reverses the logical state of its operand. If a condition is true, then Logical NOT operator will make false.	not(a && b) is false.

Ruby Ternary Operator

There is one more operator called Ternary Operator. It first evaluates an expression for a true or false value and then executes one of the two given statements depending upon the result of the evaluation. The conditional operator has this syntax:

Operator	Description	Example
? :	Conditional Expression	If Condition is true ? Then value X : Otherwise value Y

Ruby Range Operators

Sequence ranges in Ruby are used to create a range of successive values - consisting of a start value, an end value, and a range of values in between.

In Ruby, these sequences are created using the ".." and "..." range operators. The two-dot form creates an inclusive range, while the three-dot form creates a range that excludes the specified high value.

Operator	Description	Example
..	Creates a range from start point to end point inclusive.	1..10 Creates a range from 1 to 10 inclusive.
...	Creates a range from start point to end point exclusive.	1...10 Creates a range from 1 to 9.

Ruby defined? Operators

defined? is a special operator that takes the form of a method call to determine whether or not the passed expression is defined. It returns a description string of the expression, or *nil* if the expression isn't defined.

There are various usage of defined? Operator.

Usage 1

```
defined? variable # True if variable is initialized
```

For Example

```
foo = 42
defined? foo     # => "local-variable"
defined? $_      # => "global-variable"
defined? bar     # => nil (undefined)
```

Usage 2

```
defined? method_call # True if a method is defined
```

For Example

```
defined? puts        # => "method"
```

```
defined? puts(bar)    # => nil (bar is not defined here)
defined? unpack       # => nil (not defined here)
```

Usage 3

```
# True if a method exists that can be called with super user
defined? super
```

For Example

```
defined? super      # => "super" (if it can be called)
defined? super      # => nil (if it cannot be)
```

Usage 4

```
defined? yield   # True if a code block has been passed
```

For Example

```
defined? yield    # => "yield" (if there is a block passed)
defined? yield    # => nil (if there is no block)
```

Ruby Dot "." and Double Colon "::" Operators

You call a module method by preceding its name with the module's name and a period, and you reference a constant using the module name and two colons.

The **::** is a unary operator that allows: constants, instance methods and class methods defined within a class or module, to be accessed from anywhere outside the class or module.

Remember in Ruby, classes and methods may be considered constants too.

You need to just prefix the **::** Const_name with an expression that returns the appropriate class or module object.

If no prefix expression is used, the main Object class is used by default.

Here are two examples:

```
MR_COUNT = 0        # constant defined on main Object class
```

```
module Foo
  MR_COUNT = 0
  ::MR_COUNT = 1    # set global count to 1
  MR_COUNT = 2      # set local count to 2
end
puts MR_COUNT       # this is the global constant
puts Foo::MR_COUNT  # this is the local "Foo" constant
```

Second Example

```
CONST = ' out there'
class Inside_one
   CONST = proc {' in there'}
   def where_is_my_CONST
      ::CONST + ' inside one'
   end
end
class Inside_two
   CONST = ' inside two'
   def where_is_my_CONST
      CONST
   end
end
puts Inside_one.new.where_is_my_CONST
puts Inside_two.new.where_is_my_CONST
puts Object::CONST + Inside_two::CONST
puts Inside_two::CONST + CONST
puts Inside_one::CONST
puts Inside_one::CONST.call + Inside_two::CONST
```

Ruby Operators Precedence

The following table lists all operators from highest precedence to lowest.

Method	Operator	Description

<table>
<tr><td>Yes</td><td>::</td><td>Constant resolution operator</td></tr>
<tr><td>Yes</td><td>[ ] [ ]=</td><td>Element reference, element set</td></tr>
<tr><td>Yes</td><td>**</td><td>Exponentiation (raise to the power)</td></tr>
<tr><td>Yes</td><td>! ~ + -</td><td>Not, complement, unary plus and minus (method names for the last two are +@ and -@)</td></tr>
<tr><td>Yes</td><td>* / %</td><td>Multiply, divide, and modulo</td></tr>
<tr><td>Yes</td><td>+ -</td><td>Addition and subtraction</td></tr>
<tr><td>Yes</td><td>>> <<</td><td>Right and left bitwise shift</td></tr>
<tr><td>Yes</td><td>&</td><td>Bitwise 'AND'</td></tr>
<tr><td>Yes</td><td>^ |</td><td>Bitwise exclusive `OR' and regular `OR'</td></tr>
<tr><td>Yes</td><td><= < > >=</td><td>Comparison operators</td></tr>
<tr><td>Yes</td><td><=> == === != =~ !~</td><td>Equality and pattern match operators (!= and !~ may not be defined as methods)</td></tr>
<tr><td></td><td>&&</td><td>Logical 'AND'</td></tr>
<tr><td></td><td>||</td><td>Logical 'OR'</td></tr>
<tr><td></td><td>.. ...</td><td>Range (inclusive and exclusive)</td></tr>
<tr><td></td><td>? :</td><td>Ternary if-then-else</td></tr>
<tr><td></td><td>= %= { /= -= += |= &= >>= <<= *= &&= ||= **=</td><td>Assignment</td></tr>
</table>

	defined?	Check if specified symbol defined
	not	Logical negation
	or and	Logical composition

NOTE: Operators with a *Yes* in the method column are actually methods, and as such may be overridden.

7. COMMENTS

Comments are lines of annotation within Ruby code that are ignored at runtime. A single line comment starts with # character and they extend from # to the end of the line as follows:

```
#!/usr/bin/ruby -w

# This is a single line comment.

puts "Hello, Ruby!"
```

When executed, the above program produces the following result:

```
Hello, Ruby!
```

Ruby Multiline Comments

You can comment multiple lines using **=begin** and **=end** syntax as follows:

```
#!/usr/bin/ruby -w

puts "Hello, Ruby!"

=begin
This is a multiline comment and con spwan as many lines as you
like. But =begin and =end should come in the first line only.
=end
```

When executed, the above program produces the following result:

```
Hello, Ruby!
```

Make sure trailing comments are far enough from the code and that they are easily distinguished. If more than one trailing comment exists in a block, align them. For example:

```
@counter      # keeps track times page has been hit
@siteCounter  # keeps track of times all pages have been hit
```

8. IF...ELSE, CASE, UNLESS

Ruby offers conditional structures that are pretty common to modern languages. Here, we will explain all the conditional statements and modifiers available in Ruby.

Ruby if...else Statement

Syntax

```
if conditional [then]
      code...
[elsif conditional [then]
      code...]...
[else
      code...]
end
```

if expressions are used for conditional execution. The values *false* and *nil* are false, and everything else are true. Notice, Ruby uses elsif, not else if nor elif.

Executes *code* if the *conditional* is true. If the *conditional* is not true, *code* specified in the else clause is executed.

An if expression's *conditional* is separated from code by the reserved word *then*, a newline, or a semicolon.

Example

```
#!/usr/bin/ruby


x=1
if x > 2
   puts "x is greater than 2"
elsif x <= 2 and x!=0
   puts "x is 1"
else
   puts "I can't guess the number"
```

```
end
x is 1
```

Ruby if modifier

Syntax

```
code if condition
```

Executes *code* if the *conditional* is true.

Example

```
#!/usr/bin/ruby


$debug=1
print "debug\n" if $debug
```

This will produce the following result:

```
debug
```

Ruby unless Statement

Syntax

```
unless conditional [then]
   code
[else
   code ]
end
```

Executes *code* if *conditional* is false. If the *conditional* is true, code specified in the else clause is executed.

Example

```
#!/usr/bin/ruby

x=1
unless x>2
   puts "x is less than 2"
 else
  puts "x is greater than 2"
end
```

This will produce the following result:

```
x is less than 2
```

Ruby unless modifier

Syntax

```
code unless conditional
```

Executes *code* if *conditional* is false.

Example

```
#!/usr/bin/ruby

$var =  1
print "1 -- Value is set\n" if $var
print "2 -- Value is set\n" unless $var

$var = false
print "3 -- Value is set\n" unless $var
```

This will produce the following result:

```
1 -- Value is set
3 -- Value is set
```

Ruby case Statement

Syntax

```
case expression
[when expression [, expression ...] [then]
   code ]...
[else
   code ]
end
```

Compares the *expression* specified by case and that specified by when using the === operator and executes the *code* of the when clause that matches.

The *expression* specified by the when clause is evaluated as the left operand. If no when clauses match, *case* executes the code of the *else* clause.

A *when* statement's expression is separated from code by the reserved word then, a newline, or a semicolon. Thus:

```
case expr0
when expr1, expr2
   stmt1
when expr3, expr4
   stmt2
else
   stmt3
end
```

is basically similar to the following:

```
_tmp = expr0
if expr1 === _tmp || expr2 === _tmp
   stmt1
elsif expr3 === _tmp || expr4 === _tmp
   stmt2
else
   stmt3
end
```

Example

```
#!/usr/bin/ruby

$age =  5
case $age
when 0 .. 2
    puts "baby"
when 3 .. 6
    puts "little child"
when 7 .. 12
    puts "child"
when 13 .. 18
    puts "youth"
else
    puts "adult"
end
```

This will produce the following result:

```
little child
```

9. LOOPS

Loops in Ruby are used to execute the same block of code a specified number of times. This chapter details all the loop statements supported by Ruby.

Ruby while Statement

Syntax

```
while conditional [do]
   code
end
```

Executes *code* while *conditional* is true. A *while* loop's *conditional* is separated from *code* by the reserved word do, a newline, backslash \, or a semicolon ;.

Example

```
#!/usr/bin/ruby


$i = 0
$num = 5


while $i < $num  do
   puts("Inside the loop i = #$i" )
   $i +=1
end
```

This will produce the following result:

```
Inside the loop i = 0
Inside the loop i = 1
Inside the loop i = 2
Inside the loop i = 3
Inside the loop i = 4
```

Ruby while modifier

Syntax

```
code while condition

OR

begin
  code
end while conditional
```

Executes *code* while *conditional* is true.

If a *while* modifier follows a *begin* statement with no *rescue* or ensure clauses, *code* is executed once before conditional is evaluated.

Example

```
#!/usr/bin/ruby

$i = 0
$num = 5
begin
   puts("Inside the loop i = #$i" )
   $i +=1
end while $i < $num
```

This will produce the following result:

```
Inside the loop i = 0
Inside the loop i = 1
Inside the loop i = 2
Inside the loop i = 3
Inside the loop i = 4
```

Ruby until Statement

```
until conditional [do]
   code
end
```

Executes *code* while *conditional* is false. An *until* statement's conditional is separated from *code* by the reserved word *do*, a newline, or a semicolon.

Example

```
#!/usr/bin/ruby


$i = 0
$num = 5


until $i > $num  do
   puts("Inside the loop i = #$i" )
   $i +=1;
end
```

This will produce the following result:

```
Inside the loop i = 0
Inside the loop i = 1
Inside the loop i = 2
Inside the loop i = 3
Inside the loop i = 4
Inside the loop i = 5
```

Ruby until modifier

Syntax

```
code until conditional


OR

```

```
begin
   code
end until conditional
```

Executes *code* while *conditional* is false.

If an *until* modifier follows a *begin* statement with no *rescue* or ensure clauses, *code* is executed once before *conditional* is evaluated.

Example

```
#!/usr/bin/ruby


$i = 0
$num = 5
begin
   puts("Inside the loop i = #$i" )
   $i +=1;
end until $i > $num
```

This will produce the following result:

```
Inside the loop i = 0
Inside the loop i = 1
Inside the loop i = 2
Inside the loop i = 3
Inside the loop i = 4
Inside the loop i = 5
```

Ruby for Statement

Syntax

```
for variable [, variable ...] in expression [do]
   code
end
```

Executes *code* once for each element in *expression*.

Example

```
#!/usr/bin/ruby

for i in 0..5
   puts "Value of local variable is #{i}"
end
```

Here, we have defined the range 0..5. The statement for *i* in 0..5 will allow *i* to take values in the range from 0 to 5 (including 5). This will produce the following result:

```
Value of local variable is 0
Value of local variable is 1
Value of local variable is 2
Value of local variable is 3
Value of local variable is 4
Value of local variable is 5
```

A *for...in* loop is almost exactly equivalent to the following:

```
(expression).each do |variable[, variable...]| code end
```

except that a *for* loop doesn't create a new scope for the local variables. A *for* loop's *expression* is separated from *code* by the reserved word do, a newline, or a semicolon.

Example

```
#!/usr/bin/ruby

(0..5).each do |i|
   puts "Value of local variable is #{i}"
end
```

This will produce the following result:

```
Value of local variable is 0
Value of local variable is 1
Value of local variable is 2
Value of local variable is 3
Value of local variable is 4
```

```
Value of local variable is 5
```

Ruby break Statement

Syntax

```
break
```

Terminates the most internal loop. Terminates a method with an associated block if called within the block (with the method returning nil).

Example

```
#!/usr/bin/ruby


for i in 0..5
   if i > 2 then
      break
   end
   puts "Value of local variable is #{i}"
end
```

This will produce the following result:

```
Value of local variable is 0
Value of local variable is 1
Value of local variable is 2
```

Ruby next Statement

Syntax

```
next
```

Jumps to the next iteration of the most internal loop. Terminates execution of a block if called within a block (with *yield* or call returning nil).

Example

```
#!/usr/bin/ruby

for i in 0..5
   if i < 2 then
      next
   end
   puts "Value of local variable is #{i}"
end
```

This will produce the following result:

```
Value of local variable is 2
Value of local variable is 3
Value of local variable is 4
Value of local variable is 5
```

Ruby redo Statement

Syntax

```
redo
```

Restarts this iteration of the most internal loop, without checking loop condition. Restarts *yield* or *call* if called within a block.

Example

```
#!/usr/bin/ruby

for i in 0..5
   if i < 2 then
      puts "Value of local variable is #{i}"
      redo
   end
end
```

This will produce the following result and will go in an infinite loop:

```
Value of local variable is 0
Value of local variable is 0
............................
```

Ruby retry Statement

Syntax

```
retry
```

If *retry* appears in rescue clause of begin expression, restart from the beginning of the begin body.

```
begin
   do_something # exception raised
rescue
   # handles error
   retry  # restart from beginning
end
```

If retry appears in the iterator, the block, or the body of the *for* expression, restarts the invocation of the iterator call. Arguments to the iterator is re-evaluated.

```
for i in 1..5
   retry if some_condition # restart from i == 1
end
```

Example

```
#!/usr/bin/ruby


for i in 1..5
   retry if  i > 2
   puts "Value of local variable is #{i}"
end
```

This will produce the following result and will go in an infinite loop:

```
Value of local variable is 1
Value of local variable is 2
Value of local variable is 1
Value of local variable is 2
Value of local variable is 1
Value of local variable is 2
............................
```

10. METHODS

Ruby methods are very similar to functions in any other programming language. Ruby methods are used to bundle one or more repeatable statements into a single unit.

Method names should begin with a lowercase letter. If you begin a method name with an uppercase letter, Ruby might think that it is a constant and hence can parse the call incorrectly.

Methods should be defined before calling them, otherwise Ruby will raise an exception for undefined method invoking.

Syntax

```
def method_name [( [arg [= default]]...[, * arg [, &expr ]])]
   expr..
end
```

So, you can define a simple method as follows:

```
def method_name
   expr..
end
```

You can represent a method that accepts parameters like this:

```
def method_name (var1, var2)
   expr..
end
```

You can set default values for the parameters, which will be used if method is called without passing the required parameters:

```
def method_name (var1=value1, var2=value2)
   expr..
end
```

Whenever you call the simple method, you write only the method name as follows:

```
method_name
```

However, when you call a method with parameters, you write the method name along with the parameters, such as:

```
method_name 25, 30
```

The most important drawback to using methods with parameters is that you need to remember the number of parameters whenever you call such methods. For example, if a method accepts three parameters and you pass only two, then Ruby displays an error.

Example

```
#!/usr/bin/ruby


def test(a1="Ruby", a2="Perl")
   puts "The programming language is #{a1}"
   puts "The programming language is #{a2}"
end
test "C", "C++"
test
```

This will produce the following result:

```
The programming language is C
The programming language is C++
The programming language is Ruby
The programming language is Perl
```

Return Values from Methods

Every method in Ruby returns a value by default. This returned value will be the value of the last statement. For example:

```
def test
   i = 100
   j = 10
   k = 0
```

```
end
```

This method, when called, will return the last declared variable *k*.

Ruby return Statement

The *return* statement in ruby is used to return one or more values from a Ruby Method.

Syntax

```
return [expr[`,' expr...]]
```

If more than two expressions are given, the array containing these values will be the return value. If no expression given, nil will be the return value.

Example

```
return

OR

return 12

OR

return 1,2,3
```

Have a look at this example:

```
#!/usr/bin/ruby

def test
   i = 100
   j = 200
   k = 300
return i, j, k
end
var = test
```

```
puts var
```

This will produce the following result:

```
100
200
300
```

Variable Number of Parameters

Suppose you declare a method that takes two parameters, whenever you call this method, you need to pass two parameters along with it.

However, Ruby allows you to declare methods that work with a variable number of parameters. Let us examine a sample of this:

```
#!/usr/bin/ruby

def sample (*test)
   puts "The number of parameters is #{test.length}"
   for i in 0...test.length
      puts "The parameters are #{test[i]}"
   end
end
sample "Zara", "6", "F"
sample "Mac", "36", "M", "MCA"
```

In this code, you have declared a method sample that accepts one parameter test. However, this parameter is a variable parameter. This means that this parameter can take in any number of variables. So, the above code will produce the following result:

```
The number of parameters is 3
The parameters are Zara
The parameters are 6
The parameters are F
The number of parameters is 4
The parameters are Mac
The parameters are 36
```

```
The parameters are M

The parameters are MCA
```

Class Methods

When a method is defined outside of the class definition, the method is marked as *private* by default. On the other hand, the methods defined in the class definition are marked as public by default. The default visibility and the *private* mark of the methods can be changed by *public* or *private* of the Module.

Whenever you want to access a method of a class, you first need to instantiate the class. Then, using the object, you can access any member of the class.

Ruby gives you a way to access a method without instantiating a class. Let us see how a class method is declared and accessed:

```
class Accounts
   def reading_charge
   end
   def Accounts.return_date
   end
end
```

See how the method return_date is declared. It is declared with the class name followed by a period, which is followed by the name of the method. You can access this class method directly as follows:

```
Accounts.return_date
```

To access this method, you need not create objects of the class Accounts.

Ruby alias Statement

This gives alias to methods or global variables. Aliases cannot be defined within the method body. The alias of the method keeps the current definition of the method, even when methods are overridden.

Making aliases for the numbered global variables ($1, $2,...) is prohibited. Overriding the built-in global variables may cause serious problems.

Syntax

```
alias method-name method-name
```

```
alias global-variable-name global-variable-name
```

Example

```
alias foo bar

alias $MATCH $&
```

Here, we have defined foo alias for bar, and $MATCH is an alias for $&

Ruby undef Statement

This cancels the method definition. An *undef* cannot appear in the method body.

By using *undef* and *alias*, the interface of the class can be modified independently from the superclass, but notice it may be broke programs by the internal method call to self.

Syntax

```
undef method-name
```

Example

To undefine a method called *bar*, do the following:

```
undef bar
```

11. BLOCKS

You have seen how Ruby defines methods where you can put number of statements and then you call that method. Similarly, Ruby has a concept of Block.

- A block consists of chunks of code.
- You assign a name to a block.
- The code in the block is always enclosed within braces ({}).
- A block is always invoked from a function with the same name as that of the block. This means that if you have a block with the name *test*, then you use the function *test* to invoke this block.
- You invoke a block by using the *yield* statement.

Syntax

```
block_name{
   statement1
   statement2
   ..........
}
```

Here, you will learn to invoke a block by using a simple *yield* statement. You will also learn to use a *yield* statement with parameters for invoking a block. You will check the sample code with both types of *yield* statements.

The yield Statement

Let's look at an example of the yield statement:

```
#!/usr/bin/ruby


def test
   puts "You are in the method"
   yield
   puts "You are again back to the method"
   yield
```

```
end
test {puts "You are in the block"}
```

This will produce the following result:

```
You are in the method
You are in the block
You are again back to the method
You are in the block
```

You also can pass parameters with the yield statement. Here is an example:

```
#!/usr/bin/ruby

def test
   yield 5
   puts "You are in the method test"
   yield 100
end
test {|i| puts "You are in the block #{i}"}
```

This will produce the following result:

```
You are in the block 5
You are in the method test
You are in the block 100
```

Here, the *yield* statement is written followed by parameters. You can even pass more than one parameter. In the block, you place a variable between two vertical lines (||) to accept the parameters. Therefore, in the preceding code, the yield 5 statement passes the value 5 as a parameter to the test block.

Now, look at the following statement:

```
test {|i| puts "You are in the block #{i}"}
```

Here, the value 5 is received in the variable *i*. Now, observe the following *puts* statement:

```
puts "You are in the block #{i}"
```

The output of this *puts* statement is:

```
You are in the block 5
```

If you want to pass more than one parameters, then the *yield* statement becomes:

```
yield a, b
```

and the block is:

```
test {|a, b| statement}
```

The parameters will be separated by commas.

Blocks and Methods

You have seen how a block and a method can be associated with each other. You normally invoke a block by using the yield statement from a method that has the same name as that of the block. Therefore, you write:

```
#!/usr/bin/ruby


def test
  yield
end
test{ puts "Hello world"}
```

This example is the simplest way to implement a block. You call the test block by using the *yield* statement.

But if the last argument of a method is preceded by &, then you can pass a block to this method and this block will be assigned to the last parameter. In case both * and & are present in the argument list, & should come later.

```
#!/usr/bin/ruby


def test(&block)
   block.call
end
test { puts "Hello World!"}
```

This will produce the following result:

```
Hello World!
```

BEGIN and END Blocks

Every Ruby source file can declare blocks of code to be run as the file is being loaded (the BEGIN blocks) and after the program has finished executing (the END blocks).

```
#!/usr/bin/ruby


BEGIN {
  # BEGIN block code
  puts "BEGIN code block"
}


END {
  # END block code
  puts "END code block"
}
  # MAIN block code
puts "MAIN code block"
```

A program may include multiple BEGIN and END blocks. BEGIN blocks are executed in the order they are encountered. END blocks are executed in reverse order. When executed, the above program produces the following result:

```
BEGIN code block
MAIN code block
END code block
```

12. MODULES AND MIXINS

Modules are a way of grouping together methods, classes, and constants. Modules give you two major benefits.

- Modules provide a *namespace* and prevent name clashes.
- Modules implement the *mixin* facility.

Modules define a namespace, a sandbox in which your methods and constants can play without having to worry about being stepped on by other methods and constants.

Syntax

```
module Identifier
   statement1
   statement2
   ...........
end
```

Module constants are named just like class constants, with an initial uppercase letter. The method definitions look similar, too: Module methods are defined just like class methods.

As with class methods, you call a module method by preceding its name with the module's name and a period, and you reference a constant using the module name and two colons.

Example

```
#!/usr/bin/ruby

# Module defined in trig.rb file

module Trig
   PI = 3.141592654
   def Trig.sin(x)
   # ..
   end
```

```
    def Trig.cos(x)
    # ..
    end
end
```

We can define one more module with the same function name but different functionality:

```
#!/usr/bin/ruby

# Module defined in moral.rb file

module Moral
   VERY_BAD = 0
   BAD = 1
   def Moral.sin(badness)
   # ...
   end
end
```

Like class methods, whenever you define a method in a module, you specify the module name followed by a dot and then the method name.

Ruby require Statement

The require statement is similar to the include statement of C and C++ and the import statement of Java. If a third program wants to use any defined module, it can simply load the module files using the Ruby *require* statement:

Syntax

```
require filename
```

Here, it is not required to give **.rb** extension along with a file name.

Example:

```
$LOAD_PATH << '.'

require 'trig.rb'
```

```
require 'moral'


y = Trig.sin(Trig::PI/4)
wrongdoing = Moral.sin(Moral::VERY_BAD)
```

Here we are using **$LOAD_PATH << '.'** to make Ruby aware that included files must be searched in the current directory. If you do not want to use $LOAD_PATH then you can use **require_relative** to include files from a relative directory.

IMPORTANT: Here, both the files contain the same function name. So, this will result in code ambiguity while including in calling program but modules avoid this code ambiguity and we are able to call appropriate function using module name.

Ruby include Statement

You can embed a module in a class. To embed a module in a class, you use the *include* statement in the class:

Syntax

```
include modulename
```

If a module is defined in a separate file, then it is required to include that file using *require* statement before embedding module in a class.

Example

Consider the following module written in *support.rb* file.

```
module Week
   FIRST_DAY = "Sunday"
   def Week.weeks_in_month
      puts "You have four weeks in a month"
   end
   def Week.weeks_in_year
      puts "You have 52 weeks in a year"
   end
end
```

Now, you can include this module in a class as follows:

```
#!/usr/bin/ruby
$LOAD_PATH << '.'
require "support"

class Decade
include Week
   no_of_yrs=10
   def no_of_months
      puts Week::FIRST_DAY
      number=10*12
      puts number
   end
end
d1=Decade.new
puts Week::FIRST_DAY
Week.weeks_in_month
Week.weeks_in_year
d1.no_of_months
```

This will produce the following result:

```
Sunday
You have four weeks in a month
You have 52 weeks in a year
Sunday
120
```

Mixins in Ruby

Before going through this section, we assume you have the knowledge of Object Oriented Concepts.

When a class can inherit features from more than one parent class, the class is supposed to show multiple inheritance.

Ruby does not support multiple inheritance directly but Ruby Modules have another wonderful use. At a stroke, they pretty much eliminate the need for multiple inheritance, providing a facility called a *mixin*.

Mixins give you a wonderfully controlled way of adding functionality to classes. However, their true power comes out when the code in the mixin starts to interact with code in the class that uses it.

Let us examine the following sample code to gain an understand of mixin:

```
module A
   def a1
   end
   def a2
   end
end
module B
   def b1
   end
   def b2
   end
end

class Sample
include A
include B
   def s1
   end
end

samp=Sample.new
samp.a1
samp.a2
samp.b1
samp.b2
samp.s1
```

Module A consists of the methods a1 and a2. Module B consists of the methods b1 and b2. The class Sample includes both modules A and B. The class Sample can access all four methods, namely, a1, a2, b1, and b2. Therefore, you can see that the class Sample inherits from both the modules. Thus, you can say the class Sample shows multiple inheritance or a *mixin*.

13. STRINGS

A String object in Ruby holds and manipulates an arbitrary sequence of one or more bytes, typically representing characters that represent human language.

The simplest string literals are enclosed in single quotes (the apostrophe character). The text within the quote marks is the value of the string:

```
'This is a simple Ruby string literal'
```

If you need to place an apostrophe within a single-quoted string literal, precede it with a backslash, so that the Ruby interpreter does not think that it terminates the string:

```
'Won\'t you read O\'Reilly\'s book?'
```

The backslash also works to escape another backslash, so that the second backslash is not itself interpreted as an escape character.

Following are the string-related features of Ruby.

Expression Substitution

Expression substitution is a means of embedding the value of any Ruby expression into a string using #{ and }:

```
#!/usr/bin/ruby


x, y, z = 12, 36, 72
puts "The value of x is #{ x }."
puts "The sum of x and y is #{ x + y }."
puts "The average was #{ (x + y + z)/3 }."
```

This will produce the following result:

```
The value of x is 12.
The sum of x and y is 48.
The average was 40.
```

General Delimited Strings

With general delimited strings, you can create strings inside a pair of matching though arbitrary delimiter characters, e.g., !, (, {, <, etc., preceded by a percent character (%). Q, q, and x have special meanings. General delimited strings can be:

```
%{Ruby is fun.}  equivalent to "Ruby is fun."

%Q{ Ruby is fun. } equivalent to " Ruby is fun. "

%q[Ruby is fun.]  equivalent to a single-quoted string

%x!ls! equivalent to back tick command output `ls`
```

Escape Characters

Following table is a list of escape or non-printable characters that can be represented with the backslash notation.

NOTE: In a double-quoted string, an escape character is interpreted; in a single-quoted string, an escape character is preserved.

Backslash notation	Hexadecimal character	Description
\a	0x07	Bell or alert
\b	0x08	Backspace
\cx		Control-x
\C-x		Control-x
\e	0x1b	Escape
\f	0x0c	Formfeed
\M-\C-x		Meta-Control-x
\n	0x0a	Newline
\nnn		Octal notation, where n is in the range 0.7

\r	0x0d	Carriage return
\s	0x20	Space
\t	0x09	Tab
\v	0x0b	Vertical tab
\x		Character x
\xnn		Hexadecimal notation, where n is in the range 0.9, a.f, or A.F

Character Encoding

The default character set for Ruby is ASCII, whose characters may be represented by single bytes. If you use UTF-8, or another modern character set, characters may be represented in one to four bytes.

You can change your character set using $KCODE at the beginning of your program, like this:

```
$KCODE = 'u'
```

Following are the possible values for $KCODE.

Code	Description
a	ASCII (same as none). This is the default.
e	EUC.
n	None (same as ASCII).
u	UTF-8.

String Built-in Methods

We need to have an instance of String object to call a String method. Following is the way to create an instance of String object:

```
new [String.new(str="")]
```

This will return a new string object containing a copy of *str*. Now, using *str* object, we can all use any available instance methods. For example:

```
#!/usr/bin/ruby


myStr = String.new("THIS IS TEST")
foo = myStr.downcase


puts "#{foo}"
```

This will produce the following result:

```
this is test
```

Following are the public String methods (Assuming str is a String object):

SN	Methods with Description
1	**str % arg** Formats a string using a format specification. arg must be an array if it contains more than one substitution. For information on the format specification, see sprintf under "Kernel Module."
2	**str * integer** Returns a new string containing integer times str. In other words, str is repeated integer imes.
3	**str + other_str** Concatenates other_str to str.
4	**str << obj** Concatenates an object to str. If the object is a Fixnum in the range 0.255, it is converted to a character. Compare it with concat.
5	**str <=> other_str** Compares str with other_str, returning -1 (less than), 0 (equal), or 1

	(greater than). The comparison is case-sensitive.
6	**str == obj** Tests str and obj for equality. If obj is not a String, returns false; returns true if str <=> obj returns 0.
7	**str =~ obj** Matches str against a regular expression pattern obj. Returns the position where the match starts; otherwise, false.
8	**str.capitalize** Capitalizes a string.
9	**str.capitalize!** Same as capitalize, but changes are made in place.
10	**str.casecmp** Makes a case-insensitive comparison of strings.
11	**str.center** Centers a string.
12	**str.chomp** Removes the record separator ($/), usually \n, from the end of a string. If no record separator exists, does nothing.
13	**str.chomp!** Same as chomp, but changes are made in place.
14	**str.chop** Removes the last character in str.
15	**str.chop!** Same as chop, but changes are made in place.

16	**str.concat(other_str)** Concatenates other_str to str.
17	**str.count(str, ...)** Counts one or more sets of characters. If there is more than one set of characters, counts the intersection of those sets
18	**str.crypt(other_str)** Applies a one-way cryptographic hash to str. The argument is the salt string, which should be two characters long, each character in the range a.z, A.Z, 0.9, . or /.
19	**str.delete(other_str, ...)** Returns a copy of str with all characters in the intersection of its arguments deleted.
20	**str.delete!(other_str, ...)** Same as delete, but changes are made in place.
21	**str.downcase** Returns a copy of str with all uppercase letters replaced with lowercase.
22	**str.downcase!** Same as downcase, but changes are made in place.
23	**str.dump** Returns a version of str with all nonprinting characters replaced by \nnn notation and all special characters escaped.
24	**str.each(separator=$/) { \|substr\| block }** Splits str using argument as the record separator ($/ by default), passing each substring to the supplied block.
25	**str.each_byte { |fixnum| block }** Passes each byte from str to the block, returning each byte as a decimal

	representation of the byte.
26	**str.each_line(separator=$/) { \|substr\| block }** Splits str using argument as the record separator ($/ by default), passing each substring to the supplied block.
27	**str.empty?** Returns true if str is empty (has a zero length).
28	**str.eql?(other)** Two strings are equal if they have the same length and content.
29	**str.gsub(pattern, replacement) [or] str.gsub(pattern) { |match| block }** Returns a copy of str with all occurrences of pattern replaced with either replacement or the value of the block. The pattern will typically be a Regexp; if it is a String then no regular expression metacharacters will be interpreted (that is, /\d/ will match a digit, but '\d' will match a backslash followed by a 'd')
30	**str[fixnum] [or] str[fixnum,fixnum] [or] str[range] [or] str[regexp] [or] str[regexp, fixnum] [or] str[other_str]** References str, using the following arguments: one Fixnum, returns a character code at fixnum; two Fixnums, returns a substring starting at an offset (first fixnum) to length (second fixnum); range, returns a substring in the range; regexp returns portion of matched string; regexp with fixnum, returns matched data at fixnum; other_str returns substring matching other_str. A negative Fixnum starts at end of string with -1.
31	**str[fixnum] = fixnum [or] str[fixnum] = new_str [or] str[fixnum, fixnum] = new_str [or] str[range] = aString [or] str[regexp] =new_str [or] str[regexp, fixnum] =new_str [or] str[other_str] = new_str]** Replace (assign) all or part of a string. Synonym of slice!.
32	**str.gsub!(pattern, replacement) [or] str.gsub!(pattern) { |match| block }** Performs the substitutions of String#gsub in place, returning str, or nil if

	no substitutions were performed.
33	**str.hash** Returns a hash based on the string's length and content.
34	**str.hex** Treats leading characters from str as a string of hexadecimal digits (with an optional sign and an optional 0x) and returns the corresponding number. Zero is returned on error.
35	**str.include? other_str [or] str.include? fixnum** Returns true if str contains the given string or character.
36	**str.index(substring [, offset]) [or]** **str.index(fixnum [, offset]) [or]** **str.index(regexp [, offset])** Returns the index of the first occurrence of the given substring, character (fixnum), or pattern (regexp) in str. Returns nil if not found. If the second parameter is present, it specifies the position in the string to begin the search.
37	**str.insert(index, other_str)** Inserts other_str before the character at the given index, modifying str. Negative indices count from the end of the string, and insert after the given character. The intent is to insert a string so that it starts at the given index.
38	**str.inspect** Returns a printable version of str, with special characters escaped.
39	**str.intern [or] str.to_sym** Returns the Symbol corresponding to str, creating the symbol if it did not previously exist.
40	**str.length** Returns the length of str. Compare size.

41	**str.ljust(integer, padstr=' ')** If integer is greater than the length of str, returns a new String of length integer with str left-justified and padded with padstr; otherwise, returns str.
42	**str.lstrip** Returns a copy of str with leading whitespace removed.
43	**str.lstrip!** Removes leading whitespace from str, returning nil if no change was made.
44	**str.match(pattern)** Converts pattern to a Regexp (if it isn't already one), then invokes its match method on str.
45	**str.oct** Treats leading characters of str as a string of octal digits (with an optional sign) and returns the corresponding number. Returns 0 if the conversion fails.
46	**str.replace(other_str)** Replaces the contents and taintedness of str with the corresponding values in other_str.
47	**str.reverse** Returns a new string with the characters from str in reverse order.
48	**str.reverse!** Reverses str in place.
49	**str.rindex(substring [, fixnum]) [or]** **str.rindex(fixnum [, fixnum]) [or]** **str.rindex(regexp [, fixnum])** Returns the index of the last occurrence of the given substring, character (fixnum), or pattern (regexp) in str. Returns nil if not found. If the

	second parameter is present, it specifies the position in the string to end the search.characters beyond this point won't be considered.
50	**str.rjust(integer, padstr=' ')** If integer is greater than the length of str, returns a new String of length integer with str right-justified and padded with padstr; otherwise, returns str.
51	**str.rstrip** Returns a copy of str with trailing whitespace removed.
52	**str.rstrip!** Removes trailing whitespace from str, returning nil if no change was made.
53	**str.scan(pattern) [or]** **str.scan(pattern) { |match, ...| block }** Both forms iterate through str, matching the pattern (which may be a Regexp or a String). For each match, a result is generated and either added to the result array or passed to the block. If the pattern contains no groups, each individual result consists of the matched string, $&. If the pattern contains groups, each individual result is itself an array containing one entry per group.
54	**str.slice(fixnum) [or] str.slice(fixnum, fixnum) [or]** **str.slice(range) [or] str.slice(regexp) [or]** **str.slice(regexp, fixnum) [or] str.slice(other_str)** **See str[fixnum], etc.** **str.slice!(fixnum) [or] str.slice!(fixnum, fixnum) [or]** **str.slice!(range) [or] str.slice!(regexp) [or]** **str.slice!(other_str)** Deletes the specified portion from str, and returns the portion deleted. The forms that take a Fixnum will raise an IndexError if the value is out of range; the Range form will raise a RangeError, and the Regexp and String forms will silently ignore the assignment.

55	**str.split(pattern=$;, [limit])** Divides str into substrings based on a delimiter, returning an array of these substrings. If *pattern* is a String, then its contents are used as the delimiter when splitting str. If pattern is a single space, str is split on whitespace, with leading whitespace and runs of contiguous whitespace characters ignored. If *pattern* is a Regexp, str is divided where the pattern matches. Whenever the pattern matches a zero-length string, str is split into individual characters. If *pattern* is omitted, the value of $; is used. If $; is nil (which is the default), str is split on whitespace as if ` ` were specified. If the *limit* parameter is omitted, trailing null fields are suppressed. If limit is a positive number, at most that number of fields will be returned (if limit is 1, the entire string is returned as the only entry in an array). If negative, there is no limit to the number of fields returned, and trailing null fields are not suppressed.
56	**str.squeeze([other_str]*)** Builds a set of characters from the other_str parameter(s) using the procedure described for String#count. Returns a new string where runs of the same character that occur in this set are replaced by a single character. If no arguments are given, all runs of identical characters are replaced by a single character.
57	**str.squeeze!([other_str]*)** Squeezes str in place, returning either str, or nil if no changes were made.
58	**str.strip** Returns a copy of str with leading and trailing whitespace removed.
59	**str.strip!** Removes leading and trailing whitespace from str. Returns nil if str was not altered.
60	**str.sub(pattern, replacement) [or]**

	str.sub(pattern) { |match| block } Returns a copy of str with the first occurrence of pattern replaced with either replacement or the value of the block. The pattern will typically be a Regexp; if it is a String then no regular expression metacharacters will be interpreted.
61	**str.sub!(pattern, replacement) [or]** **str.sub!(pattern) { |match| block }** Performs the substitutions of String#sub in place, returning str, or nil if no substitutions were performed.
62	**str.succ [or] str.next** Returns the successor to str.
63	**str.succ! [or] str.next!** Equivalent to String#succ, but modifies the receiver in place.
64	**str.sum(n=16)** Returns a basic n-bit checksum of the characters in str, where n is the optional Fixnum parameter, defaulting to 16. The result is simply the sum of the binary value of each character in str modulo 2n - 1. This is not a particularly good checksum.
65	**str.swapcase** Returns a copy of str with uppercase alphabetic characters converted to lowercase and lowercase characters converted to uppercase.
66	**str.swapcase!** Equivalent to String#swapcase, but modifies the receiver in place, returning str, or nil if no changes were made.
67	**str.to_f** >Returns the result of interpreting leading characters in str as a floating-point number. Extraneous characters past the end of a valid number are ignored. If there is not a valid number at the start of str, 0.0 is returned. This method never raises an exception.

68	**str.to_i(base=10)** Returns the result of interpreting leading characters in str as an integer base (base 2, 8, 10, or 16). Extraneous characters past the end of a valid number are ignored. If there is not a valid number at the start of str, 0 is returned. This method never raises an exception.
69	**str.to_s [or] str.to_str** Returns the receiver.
70	**str.tr(from_str, to_str)** Returns a copy of str with the characters in from_str replaced by the corresponding characters in to_str. If to_str is shorter than from_str, it is padded with its last character. Both strings may use the c1.c2 notation to denote ranges of characters, and from_str may start with a ^, which denotes all characters except those listed.
71	**str.tr!(from_str, to_str)** Translates str in place, using the same rules as String#tr. Returns str, or nil if no changes were made.
72	**str.tr_s(from_str, to_str)** Processes a copy of str as described under String#tr, then removes duplicate characters in regions that were affected by the translation.
73	**str.tr_s!(from_str, to_str)** Performs String#tr_s processing on str in place, returning str, or nil if no changes were made.
74	**str.unpack(format)** >Decodes str (which may contain binary data) according to the format string, returning an array of each value extracted. The format string consists of a sequence of single-character directives, summarized in Table 18. Each directive may be followed by a number, indicating the number of times to repeat with this directive. An asterisk (*) will use up all remaining elements. The directives sSiIlL may each be followed by an underscore (_) to use the underlying platform's native size for the specified type; otherwise, it uses a platform-independent consistent size. Spaces are ignored in the format string.

75	**str.upcase** Returns a copy of str with all lowercase letters replaced with their uppercase counterparts. The operation is locale insensitive. Only characters a to z are affected.
76	**str.upcase!** Changes the contents of str to uppercase, returning nil if no changes are made.
77	**str.upto(other_str) { |s| block }** Iterates through successive values, starting at str and ending at other_str inclusive, passing each value in turn to the block. The String#succ method is used to generate each value.

String unpack Directives

Following table lists the unpack directives for method String#unpack.

Directive	Returns	Description
A	String	With trailing nulls and spaces removed.
a	String	String.
B	String	Extracts bits from each character (most significant bit first).
b	String	Extracts bits from each character (least significant bit first).
C	Fixnum	Extracts a character as an unsigned integer.
c	Fixnum	Extracts a character as an integer.
D, d	Float	Treats sizeof(double) characters as a native double.

E	Float	Treats sizeof(double) characters as a double in littleendian byte order.
e	Float	Treats sizeof(float) characters as a float in littleendian byte order.
F, f	Float	Treats sizeof(float) characters as a native float.
G	Float	Treats sizeof(double) characters as a double in network byte order.
g	String	Treats sizeof(float) characters as a float in network byte order.
H	String	Extracts hex nibbles from each character (most significant bit first)
h	String	Extracts hex nibbles from each character (least significant bit first).
I	Integer	Treats sizeof(int) (modified by _) successive characters as an unsigned native integer.
i	Integer	Treats sizeof(int) (modified by _) successive characters as a signed native integer.
L	Integer	Treats four (modified by _) successive characters as an unsigned native long integer.
l	Integer	Treats four (modified by _) successive characters as a signed native long integer.
M	String	Quoted-printable.
m	String	Base64-encoded.
N	Integer	Treats four characters as an unsigned long in network byte order.

n	Fixnum	Treats two characters as an unsigned short in network byte order.
P	String	Treats sizeof(char *) characters as a pointer, and return \emph{len} characters from the referenced location.
p	String	Treats sizeof(char *) characters as a pointer to a null-terminated string.
Q	Integer	Treats eight characters as an unsigned quad word (64 bits).
q	Integer	Treats eight characters as a signed quad word (64 bits).
S	Fixnum	Treats two (different if _ used) successive characters as an unsigned short in native byte order.
s	Fixnum	Treats two (different if _ used) successive characters as a signed short in native byte order.
U	Integer	UTF-8 characters as unsigned integers.
u	String	UU-encoded.
V	Fixnum	Treats four characters as an unsigned long in little-endian byte order.
v	Fixnum	Treats two characters as an unsigned short in little-endian byte order.
w	Integer	BER-compressed integer.
X		Skips backward one character.
x		Skips forward one character.

Z	String	With trailing nulls removed up to first null with *.
@		Skips to the offset given by the length argument.

Example

Try the following example to unpack various data.

```
"abc \0\0abc \0\0".unpack('A6Z6')   #=> ["abc", "abc "]
"abc \0\0".unpack('a3a3')           #=> ["abc", " \000\000"]
"abc \0abc \0".unpack('Z*Z*')       #=> ["abc ", "abc "]
"aa".unpack('b8B8')                 #=> ["10000110", "01100001"]
"aaa".unpack('h2H2c')               #=> ["16", "61", 97]
"\xfe\xff\xfe\xff".unpack('sS')     #=> [-2, 65534]
"now=20is".unpack('M*')             #=> ["now is"]
"whole".unpack('xax2aX2aX1aX2a')    #=> ["h", "e", "l", "l", "o"]
```

14. ARRAYS

Ruby arrays are ordered, integer-indexed collections of any object. Each element in an array is associated with and referred to by an index.

Array indexing starts at 0, as in C or Java. A negative index is assumed relative to the end of the array --- that is, an index of -1 indicates the last element of the array, -2 is the next to last element in the array, and so on.

Ruby arrays can hold objects such as String, Integer, Fixnum, Hash, Symbol, even other Array objects. Ruby arrays are not as rigid as arrays in other languages. Ruby arrays grow automatically while adding elements to them.

Creating Arrays

There are many ways to create or initialize an array. One way is with the *new* class method:

```
names = Array.new
```

You can set the size of an array at the time of creating array:

```
names = Array.new(20)
```

The array *names* now has a size or length of 20 elements. You can return the size of an array with either the size or length methods:

```
#!/usr/bin/ruby


names = Array.new(20)
puts names.size  # This returns 20
puts names.length # This also returns 20
```

This will produce the following result:

```
20
20
```

You can assign a value to each element in the array as follows:

```
#!/usr/bin/ruby


names = Array.new(4, "mac")


puts "#{names}"
```

This will produce the following result:

```
macmacmacmac
```

You can also use a block with new, populating each element with what the block evaluates to:

```
#!/usr/bin/ruby


nums = Array.new(10) { |e| e = e * 2 }


puts "#{nums}"
```

This will produce the following result:

```
024681012141618
```

There is another method of Array, []. It works like this:

```
nums = Array.[](1, 2, 3, 4,5)
```

One more form of array creation is as follows:

```
nums = Array[1, 2, 3, 4,5]
```

The *Kernel* module available in core Ruby has an Array method, which only accepts a single argument. Here, the method takes a range as an argument to create an array of digits:

```
#!/usr/bin/ruby


digits = Array(0..9)
puts "#{digits}"
```

This will produce the following result:

```
0123456789
```

Array Built-in Methods

We need to have an instance of Array object to call an Array method. As we have seen, following is the way to create an instance of Array object:

```
Array.[](...) [or] Array[...] [or] [...]
```

This will return a new array populated with the given objects. Now, using the created object, we can call any available instance methods. For example:

```
#!/usr/bin/ruby

digits = Array(0..9)

num = digits.at(6)

puts "#{num}"
```

This will produce the following result:

```
6
```

Following are the public array methods (assuming *array* is an array object):

SN	Methods with Description
1	**array & other_array** Returns a new array containing elements common to the two arrays, with no duplicates.
2	**array * int [or] array * str** Returns a new array built by concatenating the int copies of self. With a String argument, equivalent to self.join(str).
3	**array + other_array** Returns a new array built by concatenating the two arrays together to

	produce a third array.
4	**array - other_array** Returns a new array that is a copy of the original array, removing any items that also appear in other_array.
5	**str <=> other_str** Compares str with other_str, returning -1 (less than), 0 (equal), or 1 (greater than). The comparison is casesensitive.
6	**array | other_array** Returns a new array by joining array with other_array, removing duplicates.
7	**array << obj** Pushes the given object onto the end of array. This expression returns the array itself, so several appends may be chained together.
8	**array <=> other_array** Returns an integer (-1, 0, or +1) if this array is less than, equal to, or greater than other_array.
9	**array == other_array** Two arrays are equal if they contain the same number of elements and if each element is equal to (according to Object.==) the corresponding element in the other array.
10	**array[index] [or] array[start, length] [or]** **array[range] [or] array.slice(index) [or]** **array.slice(start, length) [or] array.slice(range)** Returns the element at *index*, or returns a subarray starting at *start* and continuing for *length* elements, or returns a subarray specified by *range*. Negative indices count backward from the end of the array (-1 is the last element). Returns *nil* if the index (or starting index) is out of range.
11	**array[index] = obj [or]**

	array[start, length] = obj or an_array or nil [or] **array[range] = obj or an_array or nil** Sets the element at *index*, or replaces a subarray starting at *start* and continuing for *length* elements, or replaces a subarray specified by *range*. If indices are greater than the current capacity of the array, the array grows automatically. Negative indices will count backward from the end of the array. Inserts elements if *length* is zero. If *nil* is used in the second and third form, deletes elements from *self*.
12	**array.abbrev(pattern = nil)** Calculates the set of unambiguous abbreviations for the strings in *self*. If passed a pattern or a string, only the strings matching the pattern or starting with the string are considered.
13	**array.assoc(obj)** Searches through an array whose elements are also arrays comparing obj with the first element of each contained array using obj.==. Returns the first contained array that matches or *nil* if no match is found.
14	**array.at(index)** Returns the element at index. A negative index counts from the end of self. Returns nil if the index is out of range.
15	**array.clear** Removes all elements from array.
16	**array.collect { |item| block } [or]** **array.map { |item| block }** Invokes block once for each element of *self*. Creates a new array containing the values returned by the block.
17	**array.collect! { |item| block } [or]** **array.map! { |item| block }** Invokes *block* once for each element of *self*, replacing the element with the value returned by *block*.

18	**array.compact** Returns a copy of *self* with all *nil* elements removed.
19	**array.compact!** Removes *nil* elements from array. Returns *nil* if no changes were made.
20	**array.concat(other_array)** Appends the elements in other_array to *self*.
21	**array.delete(obj) [or]** **array.delete(obj) { block }** Deletes items from *self* that are equal to *obj*. If the item is not found, returns *nil*. If the optional code *block* is given, returns the result of *block* if the item is not found.
22	**array.delete_at(index)** Deletes the element at the specified *index*, returning that element, or *nil* if the index is out of range.
23	**array.delete_if { |item| block }** Deletes every element of *self* for which *block* evaluates to true.
24	**array.each { |item| block }** Calls *block* once for each element in *self*, passing that element as a parameter.
25	**array.each_index { |index| block }** Same as Array#each, but passes the *index* of the element instead of the element itself.
26	**array.empty?** Returns true if the self array contains no elements.
27	**array.eql?(other)** Returns true if *array* and *other* are the same object, or are both arrays

	with the same content.
28	**array.fetch(index) [or]** **array.fetch(index, default) [or]** **array.fetch(index) { |index| block }** Tries to return the element at position *index*. If *index* lies outside the array, the first form throws an *IndexError* exception, the second form returns *default*, and the third form returns the value of invoking *block*, passing in *index*. Negative values of *index* count from the end of the array.
29	**array.fill(obj) [or]** **array.fill(obj, start [, length]) [or]** **array.fill(obj, range) [or]** **array.fill { |index| block } [or]** **array.fill(start [, length]) { |index| block } [or]** **array.fill(range) { |index| block }** The first three forms set the selected elements of *self* to *obj*. A start of *nil* is equivalent to zero. A length of *nil* is equivalent to *self.length*. The last three forms *fill* the array with the value of the block. The *block* is passed with the absolute index of each element to be filled.
30	**array.first [or]** **array.first(n)** Returns the first element, or the first *n* elements, of the array. If the array is empty, the first form returns *nil*, and the second form returns an empty array.
31	**array.flatten** Returns a new array that is a one-dimensional flattening of this array (recursively).
32	**array.flatten!** Flattens *array* in place. Returns *nil* if no modifications were made. (array contains no subarrays.)

33	**array.frozen?** Returns true if *array* is frozen (or temporarily frozen while being sorted).
34	**array.hash** Computes a hash-code for array. Two arrays with the same content will have the same hash code.
35	**array.include?(obj)** Returns true if *obj* is present in *self*, false otherwise.
36	**array.index(obj)** Returns the *index* of the first object in *self* that is == to obj. Returns *nil* if no match is found.
37	**array.indexes(i1, i2, ... iN) [or]** **array.indices(i1, i2, ... iN)** This methods is deprecated in latest version of Ruby so please use Array#values_at.
38	**array.indices(i1, i2, ... iN) [or]** **array.indexes(i1, i2, ... iN)** This methods is deprecated in latest version of Ruby so please use Array#values_at.
39	**array.insert(index, obj...)** Inserts the given values before the element with the given *index* (which may be negative).
40	**array.inspect** Creates a printable version of array.
41	**array.join(sep=$,)** Returns a string created by converting each element of the array to a string, separated by *sep*.

42	**array.last [or] array.last(n)** Returns the last element(s) of *self*. If array is *empty*, the first form returns *nil*.
43	**array.length** Returns the number of elements in *self*. May be zero.
44	**array.map { |item| block } [or]** **array.collect { |item| block }** Invokes *block* once for each element of *self*. Creates a *new* array containing the values returned by the block.
45	**array.map! { |item| block } [or]** **array.collect! { |item| block }** Invokes *block* once for each element of *array*, replacing the element with the value returned by block.
46	**array.nitems** Returns the number of non-nil elements in *self*. May be zero.
47	**array.pack(aTemplateString)** Packs the contents of array into a binary sequence according to the directives in a TemplateString. Directives A, a, and Z may be followed by a count, which gives the width of the resulting field. The remaining directives also may take a count, indicating the number of array elements to convert. If the count is an asterisk (*), all remaining array elements will be converted. Any of the directives is still may be followed by an underscore (_) to use the underlying platform's native size for the specified type; otherwise, they use a platform independent size. Spaces are ignored in the template string.
48	**array.pop** Removes the last element from *array* and returns it, or *nil* if *array* is empty.
49	**array.push(obj, ...)** Pushes (appends) the given obj onto the end of this array. This

	expression returns the array itself, so several appends may be chained together.
50	**array.rassoc(key)** Searches through the array whose elements are also arrays. Compares *key* with the second element of each contained array using ==. Returns the first contained array that matches.
51	**array.reject { |item| block }** Returns a new array containing the items *array* for which the block is not *true*.
52	**array.reject! { |item| block }** Deletes elements from *array* for which the block evaluates to *true*, but returns *nil* if no changes were made. Equivalent to Array#delete_if.
53	**array.replace(other_array)** Replaces the contents of *array* with the contents of *other_array*, truncating or expanding if necessary.
54	**array.reverse** Returns a new array containing array's elements in reverse order.
55	**array.reverse!** Reverses *array* in place.
56	**array.reverse_each {|item| block }** Same as Array#each, but traverses *array* in reverse order.
57	**array.rindex(obj)** Returns the index of the last object in array == to obj. Returns *nil* if no match is found.
58	**array.select {|item| block }** Invokes the block passing in successive elements from array, returning an array containing those elements for which the block returns a *true*

	value.
59	**array.shift** Returns the first element of *self* and removes it (shifting all other elements down by one). Returns *nil* if the array is empty.
60	**array.size** Returns the length of *array* (number of elements). Alias for length.
61	**array.slice(index) [or] array.slice(start, length) [or]** **array.slice(range) [or] array[index] [or]** **array[start, length] [or] array[range]** Returns the element at *index*, or returns a subarray starting at *start* and continuing for *length* elements, or returns a subarray specified by *range*. Negative indices count backward from the end of the array (-1 is the last element). Returns *nil* if the *index* (or starting index) are out of range.
62	**array.slice!(index) [or] array.slice!(start, length) [or]** **array.slice!(range)** Deletes the element(s) given by an *index* (optionally with a length) or by a *range*. Returns the deleted object, subarray, or *nil* if *index* is out of range.
63	**array.sort [or] array.sort { | a,b | block }** Returns a new array created by sorting self.
64	**array.sort! [or] array.sort! { | a,b | block }** Sorts self.
65	**array.to_a** Returns *self*. If called on a subclass of *Array*, converts the receiver to an Array object.
66	**array.to_ary** Returns self.

67	**array.to_s** Returns self.join.
68	**array.transpose** Assumes that self is an array of arrays and transposes the rows and columns.
69	**array.uniq** Returns a new array by removing duplicate values in *array*.
70	**array.uniq!** Removes duplicate elements from *self*. Returns *nil* if no changes are made (that is, no duplicates are found).
71	**array.unshift(obj, ...)** Prepends objects to the front of array, other elements up one.
72	**array.values_at(selector,...)** Returns an array containing the elements in self corresponding to the given *selector* (one or more). The selectors may be either integer indices or ranges.
73	**array.zip(arg, ...) [or]** **array.zip(arg, ...){ | arr | block }** Converts any arguments to arrays, then merges elements of *array* with corresponding elements from each argument.

Array pack Directives

Following table lists the pack directives for use with Array#pack.

Directive	Description
@	Moves to absolute position.

A	ASCII string (space padded, count is width).
a	ASCII string (null padded, count is width).
B	Bit string (descending bit order).
b	Bit string (ascending bit order).
C	Unsigned char.
c	Char.
D, d	Double-precision float, native format.
E	Double-precision float, little-endian byte order.
e	Single-precision float, little-endian byte order.
F, f	Single-precision float, native format.
G	Double-precision float, network (big-endian) byte order.
g	Single-precision float, network (big-endian) byte order.
H	Hex string (high nibble first).
h	Hex string (low nibble first).
I	Unsigned integer.
i	Integer.
L	Unsigned long.
l	Long.
M	Quoted printable, MIME encoding (see RFC 2045).

m	Base64-encoded string.
N	Long, network (big-endian) byte order.
n	Short, network (big-endian) byte order.
P	Pointer to a structure (fixed-length string).
p	Pointer to a null-terminated string.
Q, q	64-bit number.
S	Unsigned short.
s	Short.
U	UTF-8.
u	UU-encoded string.
V	Long, little-endian byte order.
v	Short, little-endian byte order.
w	BER-compressed integer \fnm.
X	Back up a byte.
x	Null byte.
Z	Same as a, except that null is added with *.

Example

Try the following example to pack various data.

```
a = [ "a", "b", "c" ]
n = [ 65, 66, 67 ]
```

```
puts a.pack("A3A3A3")   #=> "a  b  c  "
puts a.pack("a3a3a3")   #=> "a\000\000b\000\000c\000\000"
puts n.pack("ccc")      #=> "ABC"
```

This will produce the following result:

```
a  b  c
abc
ABC
```

15. HASHES

A Hash is a collection of key-value pairs like this: "employee" => "salary". It is similar to an Array, except that indexing is done via arbitrary keys of any object type, not an integer index.

The order in which you traverse a hash by either key or value may seem arbitrary and will generally not be in the insertion order. If you attempt to access a hash with a key that does not exist, the method will return *nil*.

Creating Hashes

As with arrays, there is a variety of ways to create hashes. You can create an empty hash with the *new* class method:

```
months = Hash.new
```

You can also use *new* to create a hash with a default value, which is otherwise just *nil*:

```
months = Hash.new( "month" )

or

months = Hash.new "month"
```

When you access any key in a hash that has a default value, if the key or value doesn't exist, accessing the hash will return the default value:

```
#!/usr/bin/ruby

months = Hash.new( "month" )

puts "#{months[0]}"
puts "#{months[72]}"
```

This will produce the following result:

```
month
month
```

```
#!/usr/bin/ruby

H = Hash["a" => 100, "b" => 200]

puts "#{H['a']}"
puts "#{H['b']}"
```

This will produce the following result:

```
100
200
```

You can use any Ruby object as a key or value, even an array, so the following example is a valid one:

```
[1,"jan"] => "January"
```

Hash Built-in Methods

We need to have an instance of Hash object to call a Hash method. As we have seen, following is the way to create an instance of Hash object:

```
Hash[[key =>|, value]* ] or

Hash.new [or] Hash.new(obj) [or]

Hash.new { |hash, key| block }
```

This will return a new hash populated with the given objects. Now using the created object, we can call any available instance methods. For example:

```
#!/usr/bin/ruby

$, = ", "
months = Hash.new( "month" )

months = {"1" => "January", "2" => "February"}

keys = months.keys
```

```
puts "#{keys}"
```

This will produce the following result:

```
["1", "2"]
```

Following are the public hash methods (assuming *hash* is an array object):

SN	Methods with Description
1	**hash == other_hash** Tests whether two hashes are equal, based on whether they have the same number of key-value pairs, and whether the key-value pairs match the corresponding pair in each hash.
2	**hash.[key]** Using a key, references a value from hash. If the key is not found, returns a default value.
3	**hash.[key]=value** Associates the value given by *value* with the key given by *key*.
4	**hash.clear** Removes all key-value pairs from hash.
5	**hash.default(key = nil)** Returns the default value for *hash*, nil if not set by default=. ([] returns a default value if the key does not exist in *hash*.)
6	**hash.default = obj** Sets a default value for *hash*.
7	**hash.default_proc** Returns a block if *hash* was created by a block.
8	**hash.delete(key) [or]** **array.delete(key) { |key| block }** Deletes a key-value pair from *hash* by *key*. If block is used, returns the

	result of a block if pair is not found. Compare *delete_if*.
9	**hash.delete_if { |key,value| block }** Deletes a key-value pair from *hash* for every pair the block evaluates to *true*.
10	**hash.each { |key,value| block }** Iterates over *hash*, calling the block once for each key, passing the key-value as a two-element array.
11	**hash.each_key { |key| block }** Iterates over *hash*, calling the block once for each key, passing *key* as a parameter.
12	**hash.each_key { |key_value_array| block }** Iterates over *hash*, calling the block once for each *key*, passing the *key* and *value* as parameters.
13	**hash.each_key { |value| block }** Iterates over *hash*, calling the block once for each *key*, passing *value* as a parameter.
14	**hash.empty?** Tests whether hash is empty (contains no key-value pairs), returning *true* or *false*.
15	**hash.fetch(key [, default]) [or]** **hash.fetch(key) { | key | block }** Returns a value from *hash* for the given *key*. If the *key* can't be found, and there are no other arguments, it raises an *IndexError* exception; if *default* is given, it is returned; if the optional block is specified, its result is returned.
16	**hash.has_key?(key) [or] hash.include?(key) [or]** **hash.key?(key) [or] hash.member?(key)** Tests whether a given *key* is present in hash, returning *true* or *false*.
17	**hash.has_value?(value)** Tests whether hash contains the given *value*.

18	**hash.index(value)** Returns the *key* for the given *value* in hash, *nil* if no matching value is found.
19	**hash.indexes(keys)** Returns a new array consisting of values for the given key(s). Will insert the default value for keys that are not found. This method is deprecated. Use select.
20	**hash.indices(keys)** Returns a new array consisting of values for the given key(s). Will insert the default value for keys that are not found. This method is deprecated. Use select.
21	**hash.inspect** Returns a pretty print string version of hash.
22	**hash.invert** Creates a new *hash*, inverting *keys* and *values* from *hash*; that is, in the new hash, the keys from *hash* become values and values become keys.
23	**hash.keys** Creates a new array with keys from *hash*.
24	**hash.length** Returns the size or length of *hash* as an integer.
25	**hash.merge(other_hash) [or]** **hash.merge(other_hash) { |key, oldval, newval| block }** Returns a new hash containing the contents of *hash* and *other_hash*, overwriting pairs in hash with duplicate keys with those from *other_hash*.
26	**hash.merge!(other_hash) [or]** **hash.merge!(other_hash) { |key, oldval, newval| block }** Same as merge, but changes are done in place.
27	**hash.rehash** Rebuilds *hash* based on the current values for each *key*. If values have

	changed since they were inserted, this method reindexes *hash*.
28	**hash.reject { |key, value| block }** Creates a new *hash* for every pair the *block* evaluates to *true.*
29	**hash.reject! { |key, value| block }** Same as *reject*, but changes are made in place.
30	**hash.replace(other_hash)** Replaces the contents of *hash* with the contents of *other_hash*.
31	**hash.select { |key, value| block }** Returns a new array consisting of key-value pairs from *hash* for which the *block*returns *true*.
32	**hash.shift** Removes a key-value pair from *hash*, returning it as a two-element array.
33	**hash.size** Returns the *size* or length of *hash* as an integer.
34	**hash.sort** Converts *hash* to a two-dimensional array containing arrays of key-value pairs, then sorts it as an array.
35	**hash.store(key, value)** Stores a key-value pair in *hash*.
36	**hash.to_a** Creates a two-dimensional array from hash. Each key/value pair is converted to an array, and all these arrays are stored in a containing array.
37	**hash.to_hash** Returns *hash* (self).
38	**hash.to_s** Converts *hash* to an array, then converts that array to a string.

39	**hash.update(other_hash) [or]** **hash.update(other_hash) {|key, oldval, newval| block}** Returns a new hash containing the contents of *hash* and *other_hash*, overwriting pairs in *hash* with duplicate keys with those from *other_hash*.
40	**hash.value?(value)** Tests whether *hash* contains the given *value*.
41	**hash.values** Returns a new array containing all the values of *hash*.
42	**hash.values_at(obj, ...)** Returns a new array containing the values from *hash* that are associated with the given key or keys.

16. DATE AND TIME

The **Time** class represents dates and times in Ruby. It is a thin layer over the system date and time functionality provided by the operating system. This class may be unable on your system to represent dates before 1970 or after 2038.

This chapter makes you familiar with all the most wanted concepts of date and time.

Getting Current Date and Time

Following is the simple example to get current date and time:

```
#!/usr/bin/ruby -w

time1 = Time.new

puts "Current Time : " + time1.inspect

# Time.now is a synonym:
time2 = Time.now
puts "Current Time : " + time2.inspect
```

This will produce the following result:

```
Current Time : Mon Jun 02 12:02:39 -0700 2008
Current Time : Mon Jun 02 12:02:39 -0700 2008
```

Getting Components of a Date & Time

We can use *Time* object to get various components of date and time. Following is the example showing the same:

```
#!/usr/bin/ruby -w

time = Time.new

# Components of a Time
```

```
puts "Current Time : " + time.inspect
puts time.year    # => Year of the date
puts time.month   # => Month of the date (1 to 12)
puts time.day     # => Day of the date (1 to 31 )
puts time.wday    # => 0: Day of week: 0 is Sunday
puts time.yday    # => 365: Day of year
puts time.hour    # => 23: 24-hour clock
puts time.min     # => 59
puts time.sec     # => 59
puts time.usec    # => 999999: microseconds
puts time.zone    # => "UTC": timezone name
```

This will produce the following result:

```
Current Time : Mon Jun 02 12:03:08 -0700 2008
2008
6
2
1
154
12
3
8
247476
UTC
```

Time.utc, Time.gm and Time.local Functions

These two functions can be used to format date in a standard format as follows:

```
# July 8, 2008
Time.local(2008, 7, 8)
# July 8, 2008, 09:10am, local time
Time.local(2008, 7, 8, 9, 10)
# July 8, 2008, 09:10 UTC
Time.utc(2008, 7, 8, 9, 10)
```

```
# July 8, 2008, 09:10:11 GMT (same as UTC)
Time.gm(2008, 7, 8, 9, 10, 11)
```

Following is the example to get all the components in an array in the following format:

```
[sec,min,hour,day,month,year,wday,yday,isdst,zone]
```

Try the following:

```
#!/usr/bin/ruby -w


time = Time.new


values = time.to_a
p values
```

This will generate the following result:

```
[26, 10, 12, 2, 6, 2008, 1, 154, false, "MST"]
```

This array could be passed to *Time.utc* or *Time.local* functions to get different format of dates as follows:

```
#!/usr/bin/ruby -w


time = Time.new


values = time.to_a
puts Time.utc(*values)
```

This will generate the following result:

```
Mon Jun 02 12:15:36 UTC 2008
```

Following is the way to get time represented internally as seconds since the (platform-dependent) epoch:

```
# Returns number of seconds since epoch
time = Time.now.to_i
```

```
# Convert number of seconds into Time object.
Time.at(time)

# Returns second since epoch which includes microseconds
time = Time.now.to_f
```

Timezones and Daylight Savings Time

You can use a *Time* object to get all the information related to Timezones and daylight savings as follows:

```
time = Time.new

# Here is the interpretation
time.zone       # => "UTC": return the timezone
time.utc_offset # => 0: UTC is 0 seconds offset from UTC
time.zone       # => "PST" (or whatever your timezone is)
time.isdst      # => false: If UTC does not have DST.
time.utc?       # => true: if t is in UTC time zone
time.localtime  # Convert to local timezone.
time.gmtime     # Convert back to UTC.
time.getlocal   # Return a new Time object in local zone
time.getutc     # Return a new Time object in UTC
```

Formatting Times and Dates

There are various ways to format date and time. Here is one example showing a few:

```
#!/usr/bin/ruby -w
time = Time.new

puts time.to_s
puts time.ctime
puts time.localtime
puts time.strftime("%Y-%m-%d %H:%M:%S")
```

This will produce the following result:

```
Mon Jun 02 12:35:19 -0700 2008
Mon Jun  2 12:35:19 2008
Mon Jun 02 12:35:19 -0700 2008
2008-06-02 12:35:19
```

Time Formatting Directives

These directives in the following table are used with the method *Time.strftime*.

Directive	Description
%a	The abbreviated weekday name (Sun).
%A	The full weekday name (Sunday).
%b	The abbreviated month name (Jan).
%B	The full month name (January).
%c	The preferred local date and time representation.
%d	Day of the month (01 to 31).
%H	Hour of the day, 24-hour clock (00 to 23).
%I	Hour of the day, 12-hour clock (01 to 12).
%j	Day of the year (001 to 366).
%m	Month of the year (01 to 12).
%M	Minute of the hour (00 to 59).
%p	Meridian indicator (AM or PM).
%S	Second of the minute (00 to 60).

%U	Week number of the current year, starting with the first Sunday as the first day of the first week (00 to 53).
%W	Week number of the current year, starting with the first Monday as the first day of the first week (00 to 53).
%w	Day of the week (Sunday is 0, 0 to 6).
%x	Preferred representation for the date alone, no time.
%X	Preferred representation for the time alone, no date.
%y	Year without a century (00 to 99).
%Y	Year with century.
%Z	Time zone name.
%%	Literal % character.

Time Arithmetic

You can perform simple arithmetic with time as follows:

```
now = Time.now            # Current time
puts now

past = now - 10           # 10 seconds ago. Time - number => Time
puts past

future = now + 10         # 10 seconds from now Time + number => Time
puts future

diff = future - now       # => 10  Time - Time => number of seconds
puts diff
```

This will produce the following result:

```
Thu Aug 01 20:57:05 -0700 2013
Thu Aug 01 20:56:55 -0700 2013
Thu Aug 01 20:57:15 -0700 2013
10.0
```

17. RANGES

Ranges occur everywhere: January to December, 0 to 9, lines 50 through 67, and so on. Ruby supports ranges and allows us to use ranges in a variety of ways:

- Ranges as Sequences
- Ranges as Conditions
- Ranges as Intervals

Ranges as Sequences

The first and perhaps the most natural use of ranges is to express a sequence. Sequences have a start point, an end point, and a way to produce successive values in the sequence.

Ruby creates these sequences using the **".."** and **"..."** range operators. The two-dot form creates an inclusive range, while the three-dot form creates a range that excludes the specified high value.

```
(1..5)        #==> 1, 2, 3, 4, 5
(1...5)       #==> 1, 2, 3, 4
('a'..'d')    #==> 'a', 'b', 'c', 'd'
```

The sequence 1..100 is held as a Range *object* containing references to two *Fixnum* objects. If you need to, you can convert a range to a list using the *to_a* method. Try the following example:

```
#!/usr/bin/ruby

$, =", "   # Array value separator
range1 = (1..10).to_a
range2 = ('bar'..'bat').to_a

puts "#{range1}"
puts "#{range2}"
```

This will produce the following result:

```
1, 2, 3, 4, 5, 6, 7, 8, 9, 10
bar, bas, bat
```

Ranges implement methods that let you iterate over them and test their contents in a variety of ways:

```
#!/usr/bin/ruby


# Assume a range
digits = 0..9


puts digits.include?(5)
ret = digits.min
puts "Min value is #{ret}"


ret = digits.max
puts "Max value is #{ret}"


ret = digits.reject {|i| i < 5 }
puts "Rejected values are #{ret}"


digits.each do |digit|
   puts "In Loop #{digit}"
end
```

This will produce the following result:

```
true
Min value is 0
Max value is 9
Rejected values are 5, 6, 7, 8, 9
In Loop 0
In Loop 1
In Loop 2
In Loop 3
```

```
In Loop 4
In Loop 5
In Loop 6
In Loop 7
In Loop 8
In Loop 9
```

Ranges as Conditions

Ranges may also be used as conditional expressions. For example, the following code fragment prints sets of lines from the standard input, where the first line in each set contains the word *start* and the last line the word *end.*:

```
while gets
   print if /start/../end/
end
```

Ranges can be used in case statements:

```
#!/usr/bin/ruby

score = 70

result = case score
   when 0..40: "Fail"
   when 41..60: "Pass"
   when 61..70: "Pass with Merit"
   when 71..100: "Pass with Distinction"
   else "Invalid Score"
end

puts result
```

This will produce the following result:

```
Pass with Merit
```

Ranges as Intervals

A final use of the versatile range is as an interval test: seeing if some value falls within the interval represented by the range. This is done using ===, the case equality operator.

```
#!/usr/bin/ruby


if ((1..10) === 5)
  puts "5 lies in (1..10)"
end


if (('a'..'j') === 'c')
  puts "c lies in ('a'..'j')"
end


if (('a'..'j') === 'z')
  puts "z lies in ('a'..'j')"
end
```

This will produce the following result:

```
5 lies in (1..10)
c lies in ('a'..'j')
```

18. ITERATORS

Iterators are nothing but methods supported by *collections*. Objects that store a group of data members are called collections. In Ruby, arrays and hashes can be termed collections.

Iterators return all the elements of a collection, one after the other. We will be discussing two iterators here, *each* and *collect*. Let's look at these in detail.

Ruby each Iterator

The each iterator returns all the elements of an array or a hash.

Syntax

```
collection.each do |variable|
   code
end
```

Executes *code* for each element in *collection*. Here, *collection* could be an array or a ruby hash.

Example

```
#!/usr/bin/ruby


ary = [1,2,3,4,5]
ary.each do |i|
   puts i
end
```

This will produce the following result:

```
1
2
3
4
5
```

You always associate the *each* iterator with a block. It returns each value of the array, one by one, to the block. The value is stored in the variable **i** and then displayed on the screen.

Ruby collect Iterator

The *collect* iterator returns all the elements of a collection.

Syntax

```
collection = collection.collect
```

The *collect* method need not always be associated with a block. The *collect* method returns the entire collection, regardless of whether it is an array or a hash.

Example

```
#!/usr/bin/ruby


a = [1,2,3,4,5]
b = Array.new
b = a.collect
puts b
```

This will produce the following result:

```
1
2
3
4
5
```

NOTE: The *collect* method is not the right way to do copying between arrays. There is another method called a *clone*, which should be used to copy one array into another array.

You normally use the collect method when you want to do something with each of the values to get the new array. For example, this code produces an array *b* containing 10 times each value in *a*.

```
#!/usr/bin/ruby


a = [1,2,3,4,5]
b = a.collect{|x| 10*x}
puts b
```

This will produce the following result:

```
10
20
30
40
50
```

19. FILE I/O

Ruby provides a whole set of I/O-related methods implemented in the Kernel module. All the I/O methods are derived from the class IO.

The class *IO* provides all the basic methods, such as *read, write, gets, puts, readline, getc,* and *printf*.

This chapter will cover all the basic I/O functions available in Ruby. For more functions, please refer to Ruby Class *IO*.

The puts Statement

In the previous chapters, you have assigned values to variables and then printed the output using *puts* statement.

The *puts* statement instructs the program to display the value stored in the variable. This will add a new line at the end of each line it writes.

Example

```
#!/usr/bin/ruby


val1 = "This is variable one"
val2 = "This is variable two"
puts val1
puts val2
```

This will produce the following result:

```
This is variable one
This is variable two
```

The gets Statement

The *gets* statement can be used to take any input from the user from standard screen called STDIN.

Example

The following code shows you how to use the gets statement. This code will prompt the user to enter a value, which will be stored in a variable val and finally will be printed on STDOUT.

```
#!/usr/bin/ruby


puts "Enter a value :"

val = gets

puts val
```

This will produce the following result:

```
Enter a value :

This is entered value

This is entered value
```

The putc Statement

Unlike the *puts* statement, which outputs the entire string onto the screen, the *putc* statement can be used to output one character at a time.

Example

The output of the following code is just the character H:

```
#!/usr/bin/ruby


str="Hello Ruby!"

putc str
```

This will produce the following result:

```
H
```

The print Statement

The *print* statement is similar to the *puts* statement. The only difference is that the *puts* statement goes to the next line after printing the contents, whereas with the *print* statement the cursor is positioned on the same line.

Example

```
#!/usr/bin/ruby


print "Hello World"

print "Good Morning"
```

This will produce the following result:

```
Hello WorldGood Morning
```

Opening and Closing Files

Until now, you have been reading and writing to the standard input and output. Now, we will see how to play with actual data files.

The File.new Method

You can create a *File* object using *File.new* method for reading, writing, or both, according to the mode string. Finally, you can use *File.close* method to close that file.

Syntax

```
aFile = File.new("filename", "mode")
   # ... process the file
aFile.close
```

The File.open Method

You can use *File.open* method to create a new file object and assign that file object to a file. However, there is one difference in between *File.open* and *File.new* methods. The difference is that the *File.open* method can be associated with a block, whereas you cannot do the same using the *File.new* method.

```
File.open("filename", "mode") do |aFile|
   # ... process the file
end
```

Here is a list of The Different Modes of opening a File:

Modes	Description
r	Read-only mode. The file pointer is placed at the beginning of the file. This is the default mode.
r+	Read-write mode. The file pointer will be at the beginning of the file.
w	Write-only mode. Overwrites the file if the file exists. If the file does not exist, creates a new file for writing.
w+	Read-write mode. Overwrites the existing file if the file exists. If the file does not exist, creates a new file for reading and writing.
a	Write-only mode. The file pointer is at the end of the file if the file exists. That is, the file is in the append mode. If the file does not exist, it creates a new file for writing.
a+	Read and write mode. The file pointer is at the end of the file if the file exists. The file opens in the append mode. If the file does not exist, it creates a new file for reading and writing.

Reading and Writing Files

The same methods that we've been using for 'simple' I/O are available for all file objects. So, gets reads a line from standard input, and *aFile.gets* reads a line from the file object aFile.

However, I/O objects provides additional set of access methods to make our lives easier.

The sysread Method

You can use the method *sysread* to read the contents of a file. You can open the file in any of the modes when using the method sysread. For example:

Following is the input text file:

```
This is a simple text file for testing purpose.
```

Now let's try to read this file:

```
#!/usr/bin/ruby

aFile = File.new("input.txt", "r")
if aFile
   content = aFile.sysread(20)
   puts content
else
   puts "Unable to open file!"
end
```

This statement will output the first 20 characters of the file. The file pointer will now be placed at the 21st character in the file.

The syswrite Method

You can use the method syswrite to write the contents into a file. You need to open the file in write mode when using the method syswrite. For example:

```
#!/usr/bin/ruby

aFile = File.new("input.txt", "r+")
if aFile
   aFile.syswrite("ABCDEF")
else
   puts "Unable to open file!"
end
```

This statement will write "ABCDEF" into the file.

The each_byte Method

This method belongs to the class *File*. The method *each_byte* is always associated with a block. Consider the following code sample:

```
#!/usr/bin/ruby

aFile = File.new("input.txt", "r+")
if aFile
   aFile.syswrite("ABCDEF")
```

```
   aFile.each_byte {|ch| putc ch; putc ?. }
else
   puts "Unable to open file!"
end
```

Characters are passed one by one to the variable *ch* and then displayed on the screen as follows:

```
s. .a. .s.i.m.p.l.e. .t.e.x.t. .f.i.l.e. .f.o.r. .t.e.s.t.i.n.g.
.p.u.r.p.o.s.e...
.
.
```

The IO.readlines Method

The class *File* is a subclass of the class IO. The class IO also has some methods, which can be used to manipulate files.

One of the IO class methods is *IO.readlines*. This method returns the contents of the file line by line. The following code displays the use of the method *IO.readlines*:

```
#!/usr/bin/ruby


arr = IO.readlines("input.txt")
puts arr[0]
puts arr[1]
```

In this code, the variable arr is an array. Each line of the file *input.txt* will be an element in the array arr. Therefore, arr[0] will contain the first line, whereas arr[1] will contain the second line of the file.

The IO.foreach Method

This method also returns output line by line. The difference between the method *foreach* and the method *readlines* is that the method *foreach* is associated with a block. However, unlike the method *readlines*, the method *foreach* does not return an array. For example:

```
#!/usr/bin/ruby
```

```
IO.foreach("input.txt"){|block| puts block}
```

This code will pass the contents of the file *test* line by line to the variable block, and then the output will be displayed on the screen.

Renaming and Deleting Files

You can rename and delete files programmatically with Ruby with the *rename* and *delete* methods.

Following is the example to rename an existing file *test1.txt*:

```
#!/usr/bin/ruby


# Rename a file from test1.txt to test2.txt
File.rename( "test1.txt", "test2.txt" )
```

Following is the example to delete an existing file *test2.txt*:

```
#!/usr/bin/ruby


# Delete file test2.txt
File.delete("text2.txt")
```

File Modes and Ownership

Use the *chmod* method with a mask to change the mode or permissions/access list of a file:

Following is the example to change mode of an existing file *test.txt* to a mask value:

```
#!/usr/bin/ruby


file = File.new( "test.txt", "w" )
file.chmod( 0755 )
```

Following is the table, which can help you to choose different mask for *chmod* method:

Mask	Description
0700	rwx mask for owner
0400	r for owner
0200	w for owner
0100	x for owner
0070	rwx mask for group
0040	r for group
0020	w for group
0010	x for group
0007	rwx mask for other
0004	r for other
0002	w for other
0001	x for other
4000	Set user ID on execution
2000	Set group ID on execution
1000	Save swapped text, even after use

File Inquiries

The following command tests whether a file exists before opening it:

```
#!/usr/bin/ruby


File.open("file.rb") if File::exists?( "file.rb" )
```

The following command inquire whether the file is really a file:

```
#!/usr/bin/ruby


# This returns either true or false
File.file?( "text.txt" )
```

The following command finds out if the given file name is a directory:

```
#!/usr/bin/ruby


# a directory
File::directory?( "/usr/local/bin" ) # => true


# a file
File::directory?( "file.rb" ) # => false
```

The following command finds whether the file is readable, writable or executable:

```
#!/usr/bin/ruby


File.readable?( "test.txt" )   # => true
File.writable?( "test.txt" )   # => true
File.executable?( "test.txt" ) # => false
```

The following command finds whether the file has zero size or not:

```
#!/usr/bin/ruby


File.zero?( "test.txt" )      # => true
```

The following command returns size of the file:

```
#!/usr/bin/ruby

File.size?( "text.txt" )     # => 1002
```

The following command can be used to find out a type of file:

```
#!/usr/bin/ruby

File::ftype( "test.txt" )     # => file
```

The ftype method identifies the type of the file by returning one of the following: *file, directory, characterSpecial, blockSpecial, fifo, link, socket, or unknown.*

The following command can be used to find when a file was created, modified, or last accessed :

```
#!/usr/bin/ruby

File::ctime( "test.txt" ) # => Fri May 09 10:06:37 -0700 2008
File::mtime( "text.txt" ) # => Fri May 09 10:44:44 -0700 2008
File::atime( "text.txt" ) # => Fri May 09 10:45:01 -0700 2008
```

Directories in Ruby

All files are contained within various directories, and Ruby has no problem handling these too. Whereas the *File* class handles files, directories are handled with the *Dir* class.

Navigating Through Directories

To change directory within a Ruby program, use *Dir.chdir* as follows. This example changes the current directory to */usr/bin*.

```
Dir.chdir("/usr/bin")
```

You can find out what the current directory is with *Dir.pwd*:

```
puts Dir.pwd # This will return something like /usr/bin
```

You can get a list of the files and directories within a specific directory using *Dir.entries*:

```
puts Dir.entries("/usr/bin").join(' ')
```

Dir.entries returns an array with all the entries within the specified directory. *Dir.foreach* provides the same feature:

```
Dir.foreach("/usr/bin") do |entry|
   puts entry
end
```

An even more concise way of getting directory listings is by using Dir's class array method:

```
Dir["/usr/bin/*"]
```

Creating a Directory

The *Dir.mkdir* can be used to create directories:

```
Dir.mkdir("mynewdir")
```

You can also set permissions on a new directory (not one that already exists) with mkdir:

NOTE: The mask 755 sets permissions owner, group, world [anyone] to rwxr-xr-x where r = read, w = write, and x = execute.

```
Dir.mkdir( "mynewdir", 755 )
```

Deleting a Directory

The *Dir.delete* can be used to delete a directory. The *Dir.unlink* and *Dir.rmdir* performs exactly the same function and are provided for convenience.

```
Dir.delete("testdir")
```

Creating Files & Temporary Directories

Temporary files are those that might be created briefly during a program's execution but aren't a permanent store of information.

Dir.tmpdir provides the path to the temporary directory on the current system, although the method is not available by default. To make *Dir.tmpdir* available it's necessary to use require 'tmpdir'.

You can use *Dir.tmpdir* with *File.join* to create a platform-independent temporary file:

```
require 'tmpdir'
   tempfilename = File.join(Dir.tmpdir, "tingtong")
   tempfile = File.new(tempfilename, "w")
   tempfile.puts "This is a temporary file"
   tempfile.close
   File.delete(tempfilename)
```

This code creates a temporary file, writes data to it, and deletes it. Ruby's standard library also includes a library called *Tempfile* that can create temporary files for you:

```
require 'tempfile'
   f = Tempfile.new('tingtong')
   f.puts "Hello"
   puts f.path
   f.close
```

Built-in Functions

Here are the ruby built-in functions to process files and directories:

- **File Class and Methods**.
- **Dir Class and Methods**.

File Class and Methods

A *File* represents n *stdio* object that connects to a regular file and returns an instance of this class for regular files.

Class Methods

SN	Methods with Description
1	**File::atime(path)** Returns the last access time for *path*.

2	**File::basename(path[, suffix])** Returns the filename at the end of *path*. If *suffix* is specified, it's deleted from the end of the filename. e.g. File.basename("/home/users/bin/ruby.exe") #=> "ruby.exe"
3	**File::blockdev?(path)** Returns true if path is a block device.
4	**File::chardev?(path)** Returns true if path is a character device.
5	**File::chmod(mode, path...)** Changes the permission mode of the specified files.
6	**File::chown(owner, group, path...)** Changes the owner and group of the specified files.
7	**File::ctime(path)** Returns the last node change time for path.
8	**File::delete(path...)** **File::unlink(path...)** Deletes the specified files.
9	**File::directory?(path)** Returns true if path is a directory.
10	**File::dirname(path)** Returns the directory portion of path, without the final filename.
11	**File::executable?(path)** Returns true if path is executable.
12	**File::executable_real?(path)** Returns true if path is executable with real user permissions.
13	**File::exist?(path)**

	Returns true if path exists.
14	**File::expand_path(path[, dir])** Returns the absolute path of path, expanding ~ to the process owner's home directory, and ~user to the user's home directory. Relative paths are resolved from the directory specified by dir, or the current working directory if dir is omitted.
15	**File::file?(path)** Returns true if path is a regular file.
16	**File::ftype(path)** Returns one of the following strings representing a file type: **file** - Regular file **directory** - Directory **characterSpecial** - Character special file **blockSpecial** - Block special file **fifo** - Named pipe (FIFO) **link** - Symbolic link **socket** - Socket **unknown** - Unknown file type
17	**File::grpowned?(path)** Returns true if path is owned by the user's group.
18	**File::join(item...)** Returns a string consisting of the specified items joined together with File::Separator separating each item. e.g., File::join("", "home", "usrs", "bin") # => "/home/usrs/bin"
19	**File::link(old, new)** Creates a hard link to file old.
20	**File::lstat(path)** Same as stat, except that it returns information on symbolic links themselves, not the files they point to.

21	**File::mtime(path)** Returns the last modification time for path.
22	**File::new(path[, mode="r"])** **File::open(path[, mode="r"])** **File::open(path[, mode="r"]) {|f| ...}** Opens a file. If a block is specified, the block is executed with the new file passed as an argument. The file is closed automatically when the block exits. These methods differ from Kernel.open in that even if path begins with |, the following string isn't run as a command.
23	**File::owned?(path)** Returns true if path is owned by the effective user.
24	**File::pipe?(path)** Returns true if path is a pipe.
25	**File::readable?(path)** Returns true if path is readable.
26	**File::readable_real?(path)** Returns true if path is readable with real user permissions.
27	**File::readlink(path)** Returns the file pointed to by path.
28	**File::rename(old, new)** Changes the filename from old to new.
29	**File::setgid?(path)** Returns true if path's set-group-id permission bit is set.
30	**File::setuid?(path)** Returns true if path's set-user-id permission bit is set.
31	**File::size(path)** Returns the file size of path.

32	**File::size?(path)** Returns the file size of path, or nil if it's 0.
33	**File::socket?(path)** Returns true if path is a socket.
34	**File::split(path)** Returns an array containing the contents of path split into File::dirname(path) and File::basename(path).
35	**File::stat(path)** Returns a File::Stat object with information on path.
36	**File::sticky?(path)** Returns true if path's sticky bit is set.
37	**File::symlink(old, new)** Creates a symbolic link to file old.
38	**File::symlink?(path)** Returns true if path is a symbolic link.
39	**File::truncate(path, len)** Truncates the specified file to len bytes.
40	**File::unlink(path...)** Deletes a file given at the path.
41	**File::umask([mask])** Returns the current umask for this process if no argument is specified. If an argument is specified, the umask is set, and the old umask is returned.
42	**File::utime(atime, mtime, path...)** Changes the access and modification times of the specified files.
43	**File::writable?(path)** Returns true if path is writable.

44	**File::writable_real?(path)** Returns true if path is writable with real user permissions.
45	**File::zero?(path)** Returns true if the file size of path is 0.

Instance Methods

Assuming **f** is an instance of **File** class:

SN	Methods with Description
1	**f.atime** Returns the last access time for f.
2	**f.chmode(mode)** Changes the permission mode of f.
3	**f.chown(owner, group)** Changes the owner and group of f.
4	**f.ctime** Returns the last inode change time for f.
5	**f.flock(op)** Calls flock(2). op may be 0 or a logical or of the File class constants LOCK_EX, LOCK_NB, LOCK_SH, and LOCK_UN.
6	**f.lstat** Same as stat, except that it returns information on symbolic links themselves, not the files they point to.
7	**f.mtime** Returns the last modification time for f.

8	**f.path** Returns the pathname used to create f.
9	**f.reopen(path[, mode="r"])** Reopens the file.
10	**f.truncate(len)** Truncates f to len bytes.

Directory Class and Methods

A **Dir** is a class to represent a directory stream that gives filenames in the directory in the operating system. Dir class also holds directory related operations, such as wild card filename matching, changing current working directory, etc. as class methods.

Class Methods

SN	Method with Description
1	**Dir[pat]** **Dir::glob(pat)** Returns an array of filenames matching the specified wild card pattern pat : ***** - Matches any string including the null string ****** - Matches any string recursively **?** - Matches any single character **[...]** - Matches any one of enclosed characters **{a,b...}** - Matches any one of strings Dir["foo.*"] # matches "foo.c", "foo.rb", etc. Dir["foo.?"] # matches "foo.c", "foo.h", etc.
2	**Dir::chdir(path)** Changes the current directory.

3	**Dir::chroot(path)** Changes the root directory (only allowed by super user). Not available on all platforms.
4	**Dir::delete(path)** Deletes the directory specified by path. The directory must be empty.
5	**Dir::entries(path)** Returns an array of filenames in directory path.
6	**Dir::foreach(path) {| f| ...}** Executes the block once for each file in the directory specified by path.
7	**Dir::getwd** **Dir::pwd** Returns the current directory.
8	**Dir::mkdir(path[, mode=0777])** Creates the directory specified by path. Permission mode may be modified by the value of File::umask and is ignored on Win32 platforms.
9	**Dir::new(path)** **Dir::open(path)** **Dir::open(path) {| dir| ...}** Returns a new directory object for path. If open is given a block, a new directory object is passed to the block, which closes the directory object before terminating.
10	**Dir::pwd** See Dir::getwd.
11	**Dir::rmdir(path)** **Dir::unlink(path)** **Dir::delete(path)** Deletes the directory specified by path. The directory must be empty.

Instance Methods

Assuming **d** is an instance of **Dir** class:

SN	Method with Description
1	**d.close** Closes the directory stream.
2	**d.each {| f| ...}** Executes the block once for each entry in d.
3	**d.pos** d.tell Returns the current position in d.
4	**d.pos= offset** Sets the position in the directory stream.
5	**d.pos= pos** **d.seek(po s)** Moves to a position in d. pos must be a value returned by d.pos or 0.
6	**d.read** Returns the next entry from d.
7	**d.rewind** Moves position in d to the first entry.
8	**d.seek(po s)** See d.pos=pos.
9	**d.tell** See d.pos.

20. EXCEPTIONS

The execution and the exception always go together. If you are opening a file, which does not exist, then if you did not handle this situation properly, then your program is considered to be of bad quality.

The program stops if an exception occurs. So exceptions are used to handle various type of errors, which may occur during a program execution and take appropriate action instead of halting program completely.

Ruby provide a nice mechanism to handle exceptions. We enclose the code that could raise an exception in a *begin/end* block and use *rescue* clauses to tell Ruby the types of exceptions we want to handle.

Syntax

```
begin
# -
rescue OneTypeOfException
# -
rescue AnotherTypeOfException
# -
else
# Other exceptions
ensure
# Always will be executed
end
```

Everything from *begin* to *rescue* is protected. If an exception occurs during the execution of this block of code, control is passed to the block between *rescue* and *end*.

For each *rescue* clause in the *begin* block, Ruby compares the raised Exception against each of the parameters in turn. The match will succeed if the exception named in the rescue clause is the same as the type of the currently thrown exception, or is a superclass of that exception.

In an event, that an exception does not match any of the error types specified, we are allowed to use an *else* clause after all the *rescue* clauses.

Example

```
#!/usr/bin/ruby


begin
   file = open("/unexistant_file")
   if file
      puts "File opened successfully"
   end
rescue
      file = STDIN
end
print file, "==", STDIN, "\n"
```

This will produce the following result. You can see that *STDIN* is substituted to *file* because *open* failed.

```
#<IO:0xb7d16f84>==#<IO:0xb7d16f84>
```

Using retry Statement

You can capture an exception using *rescue* block and then use *retry* statement to execute *begin* block from the beginning.

Syntax

```
begin
    # Exceptions raised by this code will
     # be caught by the following rescue clause
rescue
    # This block will capture all types of exceptions
    retry  # This will move control to the beginning of begin
end
```

Example

```
#!/usr/bin/ruby

begin
   file = open("/unexistant_file")
   if file
      puts "File opened successfully"
   end
rescue
   fname = "existant_file"
   retry
end
```

The following is the flow of the process:

- An exception occurred at open.
- Went to rescue. fname was re-assigned.
- By retry went to the beginning of the begin.
- This time file opens successfully.
- Continued the essential process.

NOTE: Notice that if the file of re-substituted name does not exist this example code retries infinitely. Be careful if you use *retry* for an exception process.

Using raise Statement

You can use *raise* statement to raise an exception. The following method raises an exception whenever it's called. It's second message will be printed.

Syntax

```
raise

OR

raise "Error Message"

OR
```

```
raise ExceptionType, "Error Message"

OR

raise ExceptionType, "Error Message" condition
```

The first form simply re-raises the current exception (or a RuntimeError if there is no current exception). This is used in exception handlers that need to intercept an exception before passing it on.

The second form creates a new *RuntimeError* exception, setting its message to the given string. This exception is then raised up the call stack.

The third form uses the first argument to create an exception and then sets the associated message to the second argument.

The fourth form is similar to the third form but you can add any conditional statement like *unless* to raise an exception.

Example

```
#!/usr/bin/ruby

begin
    puts 'I am before the raise.'
    raise 'An error has occurred.'
    puts 'I am after the raise.'
rescue
    puts 'I am rescued.'
end
puts 'I am after the begin block.'
```

This will produce the following result:

```
I am before the raise.
I am rescued.
I am after the begin block.
```

One more example showing the usage of *raise*:

```
#!/usr/bin/ruby


begin
  raise 'A test exception.'
rescue Exception => e
  puts e.message
  puts e.backtrace.inspect
end
```

This will produce the following result:

```
A test exception.
["main.rb:4"]
```

Using ensure Statement

Sometimes, you need to guarantee that some processing is done at the end of a block of code, regardless of whether an exception was raised. For example, you may have a file open on entry to the block and you need to make sure it gets closed as the block exits.

The *ensure* clause does just this. *ensure* goes after the last rescue clause and contains a chunk of code that will always be executed as the block terminates. It doesn't matter if the block exits normally, if it raises and rescues an exception, or if it is terminated by an uncaught exception, the *ensure* block will get run.

Syntax

```
begin
   #.. process
   #..raise exception
rescue
   #.. handle error
ensure
   #.. finally ensure execution
   #.. This will always execute.
end
```

Example

```
begin
  raise 'A test exception.'
rescue Exception => e
  puts e.message
  puts e.backtrace.inspect
ensure
  puts "Ensuring execution"
end
```

This will produce the following result:

```
A test exception.
["main.rb:4"]
Ensuring execution
```

Using else Statement

If the *else* clause is present, it goes after the *rescue* clauses and before any *ensure*.

The body of an *else* clause is executed only if no exceptions are raised by the main body of code.

Syntax

```
begin
   #.. process
   #..raise exception
rescue
   # .. handle error
else
   #.. executes if there is no exception
ensure
   #.. finally ensure execution
   #.. This will always execute.
end
```

Example

```
begin
 # raise 'A test exception.'
 puts "I'm not raising exception"
rescue Exception => e
  puts e.message
  puts e.backtrace.inspect
else
   puts "Congratulations-- no errors!"
ensure
  puts "Ensuring execution"
end
```

This will produce the following result:

```
I'm not raising exception
Congratulations-- no errors!
Ensuring execution
```

Raised error message can be captured using $! variable.

Catch and Throw

While the exception mechanism of raise and rescue is great for abandoning the execution when things go wrong, it's sometimes nice to be able to jump out of some deeply nested construct during normal processing. This is where catch and throw come in handy.

The *catch* defines a block that is labeled with the given name (which may be a Symbol or a String). The block is executed normally until a throw is encountered.

Syntax

```
throw :lablename
#.. this will not be executed
catch :lablename do
#.. matching catch will be executed after a throw is encountered.
end
```

```
OR

throw :lablename condition
#.. this will not be executed
catch :lablename do
#.. matching catch will be executed after a throw is encountered.
end
```

Example

The following example uses a throw to terminate interaction with the user if '!' is typed in response to any prompt.

```
def promptAndGet(prompt)
   print prompt
   res = readline.chomp
   throw :quitRequested if res == "!"
   return res
end

catch :quitRequested do
   name = promptAndGet("Name: ")
   age = promptAndGet("Age: ")
   sex = promptAndGet("Sex: ")
   # ..
   # process information
end
promptAndGet("Name:")
```

You should try the above program on your machine because it needs manual interaction. This will produce the following result:

```
Name: Ruby on Rails
Age: 3
Sex: !
Name:Just Ruby
```

Class Exception

Ruby's standard classes and modules raise exceptions. All the exception classes form a hierarchy, with the class Exception at the top. The next level contains seven different types:

- Interrupt
- NoMemoryError
- SignalException
- ScriptError
- StandardError
- SystemExit

There is one other exception at this level, **Fatal**, but the Ruby interpreter only uses this internally.

Both ScriptError and StandardError have a number of subclasses, but we do not need to go into the details here. The important thing is that if we create our own exception classes, they need to be subclasses of either class Exception or one of its descendants.

Let's look at an example:

```
class FileSaveError < StandardError
   attr_reader :reason
   def initialize(reason)
      @reason = reason
   end
end
```

Now, look at the following example, which will use this exception:

```
File.open(path, "w") do |file|
begin
    # Write out the data ...
rescue
    # Something went wrong!
    raise FileSaveError.new($!)
end
end
```

The important line here is raise *FileSaveError.new($!)*. We call raise to signal that an exception has occurred, passing it a new instance of FileSaveError, with the reason being that specific exception caused the writing of the data to fail.

21. RUBY OBJECT ORIENTED

Ruby is a pure object-oriented language and everything appears to Ruby as an object. Every value in Ruby is an object, even the most primitive things: strings, numbers and even true and false. Even a class itself is an *object* that is an instance of the *Class* class. This chapter will take you through all the major functionalities related to Object Oriented Ruby.

A class is used to specify the form of an object and it combines data representation and methods for manipulating that data into one neat package. The data and methods within a class are called members of the class.

Ruby Class Definition

When you define a class, you define a blueprint for a data type. This doesn't actually define any data, but it does define what the class name means, that is, what an object of the class will consist of and what operations can be performed on such an object.

A class definition starts with the keyword **class** followed by the **class name** and is delimited with an **end**. For example, we defined the Box class using the keyword class as follows:

```
class Box

   code

end
```

The name must begin with a capital letter and by convention names that contain more than one word are run together with each word capitalized and no separating characters (CamelCase).

Define Ruby Objects

A class provides the blueprints for objects, so basically an object is created from a class. We declare objects of a class using **new** keyword. Following statements declare two objects of class Box:

```
box1 = Box.new

box2 = Box.new
```

The initialize Method

The **initialize method** is a standard Ruby class method and works almost same way as **constructor** works in other object oriented programming languages. The initialize method is useful when you want to initialize some class variables at the time of object creation. This method may take a list of parameters and like any other ruby method it would be preceded by **def** keyword as shown below:

```
class Box
   def initialize(w,h)
      @width, @height = w, h
   end
end
```

The instance Variables

The **instance variables** are kind of class attributes and they become properties of objects once objects are created using the class. Every object's attributes are assigned individually and share no value with other objects. They are accessed using the @ operator within the class but to access them outside of the class we use **public** methods, which are called **accessor methods**. If we take the above defined class **Box** then @width and @height are instance variables for the class Box.

```
class Box
   def initialize(w,h)
      # assign instance avriables
      @width, @height = w, h
   end
end
```

The accessor & setter Methods

To make the variables available from outside the class, they must be defined within **accessor methods**, these accessor methods are also known as a getter methods. Following example shows the usage of accessor methods:

```
#!/usr/bin/ruby -w

# define a class
class Box
```

```
   # constructor method
   def initialize(w,h)
      @width, @height = w, h
   end

   # accessor methods
   def printWidth
      @width
   end

   def printHeight
      @height
   end
end

# create an object
box = Box.new(10, 20)

# use accessor methods
x = box.printWidth()
y = box.printHeight()

puts "Width of the box is : #{x}"
puts "Height of the box is : #{y}"
```

When the above code is executed, it produces the following result:

```
Width of the box is : 10
Height of the box is : 20
```

Similar to accessor methods, which are used to access the value of the variables, Ruby provides a way to set the values of those variables from outside of the class using **setter methods**, which are defined as below:

```
#!/usr/bin/ruby -w
```

```
# define a class
class Box
   # constructor method
   def initialize(w,h)
      @width, @height = w, h
   end

   # accessor methods
   def getWidth
      @width
   end
   def getHeight
      @height
   end

   # setter methods
   def setWidth=(value)
      @width = value
   end
   def setHeight=(value)
      @height = value
   end
end

# create an object
box = Box.new(10, 20)

# use setter methods
box.setWidth = 30
box.setHeight = 50

# use accessor methods
```

```
x = box.getWidth()
y = box.getHeight()

puts "Width of the box is : #{x}"
puts "Height of the box is : #{y}"
```

When the above code is executed, it produces the following result:

```
Width of the box is : 30
Height of the box is : 50
```

The instance Methods

The **instance methods** are also defined in the same way as we define any other method using **def** keyword and they can be used using a class instance only as shown below. Their functionality is not limited to access the instance variables, but also they can do a lot more as per your requirement.

```
#!/usr/bin/ruby -w

# define a class
class Box
   # constructor method
   def initialize(w,h)
      @width, @height = w, h
   end
   # instance method
   def getArea
      @width * @height
   end
end

# create an object
box = Box.new(10, 20)

# call instance methods
a = box.getArea()
```

```
puts "Area of the box is : #{a}"
```

When the above code is executed, it produces the following result:

```
Area of the box is : 200
```

The class Methods and Variables

The **class variables** is a variable, which is shared between all instances of a class. In other words, there is one instance of the variable and it is accessed by object instances. Class variables are prefixed with two @ characters (@@). A class variable must be initialized within the class definition as shown below.

A class method is defined using **def self.methodname()**, which ends with end delimiter and would be called using the class name as **classname.methodname** as shown in the following example:

```
#!/usr/bin/ruby -w


class Box
   # Initialize our class variables
   @@count = 0
   def initialize(w,h)
      # assign instance avriables
      @width, @height = w, h

      @@count += 1
   end

   def self.printCount()
      puts "Box count is : #@@count"
   end
end

# create two object
box1 = Box.new(10, 20)
box2 = Box.new(30, 100)
```

```
# call class method to print box count
Box.printCount()
```

When the above code is executed, it produces the following result:

```
Box count is : 2
```

The to_s Method

Any class you define should have a **to_s** instance method to return a string representation of the object. Following is a simple example to represent a Box object in terms of width and height:

```
#!/usr/bin/ruby -w


class Box
   # constructor method
   def initialize(w,h)
      @width, @height = w, h
   end
   # define to_s method
   def to_s
      "(w:#@width,h:#@height)"  # string formatting of the object.
   end
end


# create an object
box = Box.new(10, 20)


# to_s method will be called in reference of string automatically.
puts "String representation of box is : #{box}"
```

When the above code is executed, it produces the following result:

```
String representation of box is : (w:10,h:20)
```

Access Control

Ruby gives you three levels of protection at instance methods level, which may be **public, private, or protected**. Ruby does not apply any access control over instance and class variables.

- **Public Methods:** Public methods can be called by anyone. Methods are public by default except for initialize, which is always private.
- **Private Methods:** Private methods cannot be accessed, or even viewed from outside the class. Only the class methods can access private members.
- **Protected Methods:** A protected method can be invoked only by objects of the defining class and its subclasses. Access is kept within the family.

Following is a simple example to show the syntax of all the three access modifiers:

```
#!/usr/bin/ruby -w

# define a class
class Box
   # constructor method
   def initialize(w,h)
      @width, @height = w, h
   end

   # instance method by default it is public
   def getArea
      getWidth() * getHeight
   end

   # define private accessor methods
   def getWidth
      @width
   end
   def getHeight
      @height
   end
```

```
   # make them private
   private :getWidth, :getHeight

   # instance method to print area
   def printArea
      @area = getWidth() * getHeight
      puts "Big box area is : #@area"
   end
   # make it protected
   protected :printArea
end

# create an object
box = Box.new(10, 20)

# call instance methods
a = box.getArea()
puts "Area of the box is : #{a}"

# try to call protected or methods
box.printArea()
```

When the above code is executed, it produces the following result. Here, first method is called successfully but second method gave a problem.

```
Area of the box is : 200
test.rb:42: protected method `printArea' called for #
<Box:0xb7f11280 @height=20, @width=10> (NoMethodError)
```

Class Inheritance

One of the most important concepts in object-oriented programming is that of inheritance. Inheritance allows us to define a class in terms of another class, which makes it easier to create and maintain an application.

Inheritance also provides an opportunity to reuse the code functionality and fast implementation time but unfortunately Ruby does not support multiple levels of inheritances but Ruby supports **mixins**. A mixin is like a specialized implementation of multiple inheritance in which only the interface portion is inherited.

When creating a class, instead of writing completely new data members and member functions, the programmer can designate that the new class should inherit the members of an existing class. This existing class is called the **base class or superclass**, and the new class is referred to as the **derived class or sub-class**.

Ruby also supports the concept of subclassing, i.e., inheritance and following example explains the concept. The syntax for extending a class is simple. Just add a < character and the name of the superclass to your class statement. For example, following define a class *BigBox* as a subclass of *Box*:

```
#!/usr/bin/ruby -w

# define a class
class Box
   # constructor method
   def initialize(w,h)
      @width, @height = w, h
   end
   # instance method
   def getArea
      @width * @height
   end
end

# define a subclass
class BigBox < Box

   # add a new instance method
   def printArea
      @area = @width * @height
      puts "Big box area is : #@area"
   end
end
```

```
# create an object
box = BigBox.new(10, 20)

# print the area
box.printArea()
```

When the above code is executed, it produces the following result:

```
Big box area is : 200
```

Methods Overriding

Though you can add new functionality in a derived class, but sometimes you would like to change the behavior of already defined method in a parent class. You can do so simply by keeping the method name same and overriding the functionality of the method as shown below in the example:

```
#!/usr/bin/ruby -w

# define a class
class Box
   # constructor method
   def initialize(w,h)
      @width, @height = w, h
   end
   # instance method
   def getArea
      @width * @height
   end
end

# define a subclass
class BigBox < Box

   # change existing getArea method as follows
   def getArea
```

```
    @area = @width * @height
    puts "Big box area is : #@area"
  end
end

# create an object
box = BigBox.new(10, 20)

# print the area using overriden method.
box.getArea()
```

Operator Overloading

We'd like the + operator to perform vector addition of two Box objects using +, the * operator to multiply a Box width and height by a scalar, and the unary - operator to do negate the width and height of the Box. Here is a version of the Box class with mathematical operators defined:

```
class Box
  def initialize(w,h) # Initialize the width and height
    @width,@height = w, h
  end

  def +(other)         # Define + to do vector addition
    Box.new(@width + other.width, @height + other.height)
  end

  def -@               # Define unary minus to negate width and height
    Box.new(-@width, -@height)
  end

  def *(scalar)        # To perform scalar multiplication
    Box.new(@width*scalar, @height*scalar)
  end
end
```

Freezing Objects

Sometimes, we want to prevent an object from being changed. The freeze method in Object allows us to do this, effectively turning an object into a constant. Any object can be frozen by invoking **Object.freeze**. A frozen object may not be modified: you can't change its instance variables.

You can check if a given object is already frozen or not using **Object.frozen?** method, which returns true in case the object is frozen otherwise a false value is return. Following example clears the concept:

```
#!/usr/bin/ruby -w


# define a class
class Box
   # constructor method
   def initialize(w,h)
      @width, @height = w, h
   end

   # accessor methods
   def getWidth
      @width
   end
   def getHeight
      @height
   end

   # setter methods
   def setWidth=(value)
      @width = value
   end
   def setHeight=(value)
      @height = value
   end
end
```

```
# create an object
box = Box.new(10, 20)

# let us freez this object
box.freeze
if( box.frozen? )
   puts "Box object is frozen object"
else
   puts "Box object is normal object"
end

# now try using setter methods
box.setWidth = 30
box.setHeight = 50

# use accessor methods
x = box.getWidth()
y = box.getHeight()

puts "Width of the box is : #{x}"
puts "Height of the box is : #{y}"
```

When the above code is executed, it produces the following result:

```
Box object is frozen object
test.rb:20:in `setWidth=': can't modify frozen object (TypeError)
        from test.rb:39
```

Class Constants

You can define a constant inside a class by assigning a direct numeric or string value to a variable, which is defined without using either @ or @@. By convention, we keep constant names in upper case.

Once a constant is defined, you cannot change its value but you can access a constant directly inside a class much like a variable but if you want to access a constant outside of the class then you would have to use **classname::constant** as shown in the below example.

```
#!/usr/bin/ruby -w

# define a class
class Box
   BOX_COMPANY = "TATA Inc"
   BOXWEIGHT = 10
   # constructor method
   def initialize(w,h)
      @width, @height = w, h
   end
   # instance method
   def getArea
      @width * @height
   end
end

# create an object
box = Box.new(10, 20)

# call instance methods
a = box.getArea()
puts "Area of the box is : #{a}"
puts Box::BOX_COMPANY
puts "Box weight is: #{Box::BOXWEIGHT}"
```

When the above code is executed, it produces the following result:

```
Area of the box is : 200
TATA Inc
Box weight is: 10
```

Class constants are inherited and can be overridden like instance methods.

Create Object Using Allocate

There may be a situation when you want to create an object without calling its constructor **initialize** i.e. using new method, in such case you can call *allocate,* which will create an uninitialized object for you as in the following example:

```
#!/usr/bin/ruby -w

# define a class
class Box
   attr_accessor :width, :height

   # constructor method
   def initialize(w,h)
      @width, @height = w, h
   end

   # instance method
   def getArea
      @width * @height
   end
end

# create an object using new
box1 = Box.new(10, 20)

# create another object using allocate
box2 = Box.allocate

# call instance method using box1
a = box1.getArea()
puts "Area of the box is : #{a}"

# call instance method using box2
a = box2.getArea()
```

```
puts "Area of the box is : #{a}"
```

When the above code is executed, it produces the following result:

```
Area of the box is : 200
test.rb:14: warning: instance variable @width not initialized
test.rb:14: warning: instance variable @height not initialized
test.rb:14:in `getArea': undefined method `*'
   for nil:NilClass (NoMethodError) from test.rb:29
```

Class Information

If class definitions are executable code, this implies that they execute in the context of some object: self must reference something. Let's find out what it is.

```
#!/usr/bin/ruby -w


class Box
   # print class information
   puts "Type of self = #{self.type}"
   puts "Name of self = #{self.name}"
end
```

When the above code is executed, it produces the following result:

```
Type of self = Class
Name of self = Box
```

This means that a class definition is executed with that class as the current object. This means that methods in the metaclass and its superclasses will be available during the execution of the method definition.

22. REGULAR EXPRESSIONS

A *regular expression* is a special sequence of characters that helps you match or find other strings or sets of strings using a specialized syntax held in a pattern.

A *regular expression literal* is a pattern between slashes or between arbitrary delimiters followed by %r as follows:

Syntax

```
/pattern/
/pattern/im    # option can be specified
%r!/usr/local! # general delimited regular expression
```

Example

```
#!/usr/bin/ruby

line1 = "Cats are smarter than dogs";
line2 = "Dogs also like meat";

if ( line1 =~ /Cats(.*)/ )
  puts "Line1 contains Cats"
end
if ( line2 =~ /Cats(.*)/ )
  puts "Line2 contains  Dogs"
end
```

This will produce the following result:

```
Line1 contains Cats
```

Regular-Expression Modifiers

Regular expression literals may include an optional modifier to control various aspects of matching. The modifier is specified after the second slash character, as shown previously and may be represented by one of these characters:

Modifier	Description
i	Ignores case when matching text.
o	Performs #{} interpolations only once, the first time the regexp literal is evaluated.
x	Ignores whitespace and allows comments in regular expressions.
m	Matches multiple lines, recognizing newlines as normal characters.
u,e,s,n	Interprets the regexp as Unicode (UTF-8), EUC, SJIS, or ASCII. If none of these modifiers is specified, the regular expression is assumed to use the source encoding.

Like string literals delimited with %Q, Ruby allows you to begin your regular expressions with %r followed by a delimiter of your choice. This is useful when the pattern you are describing contains a lot of forward slash characters that you don't want to escape:

```
# Following matches a single slash character, no escape required
%r|/|

# Flag characters are allowed with this syntax, too
%r[</(.*)>]i
```

Regular-Expression Patterns

Except for control characters, **(+ ? . * ^ $ ( ) [ ] { } | \)**, all characters match themselves. You can escape a control character by preceding it with a backslash.

Following table lists the regular expression syntax that is available in Ruby.

Pattern	Description
^	Matches beginning of line.

$	Matches end of line.
.	Matches any single character except newline. Using m option allows it to match newline as well.
[...]	Matches any single character in brackets.
[^...]	Matches any single character not in brackets
re*	Matches 0 or more occurrences of preceding expression.
re+	Matches 1 or more occurrence of preceding expression.
re?	Matches 0 or 1 occurrence of preceding expression.
re{ n}	Matches exactly n number of occurrences of preceding expression.
re{ n,}	Matches n or more occurrences of preceding expression.
re{ n, m}	Matches at least n and at most m occurrences of preceding expression.
a| b	Matches either a or b.
(re)	Groups regular expressions and remembers matched text.
(?imx)	Temporarily toggles on i, m, or x options within a regular expression. If in parentheses, only that area is affected.
(?-imx)	Temporarily toggles off i, m, or x options within a regular expression. If in parentheses, only that area is affected.
(?: re)	Groups regular expressions without remembering matched text.
(?imx: re)	Temporarily toggles on i, m, or x options within parentheses.

(?-imx: re)	Temporarily toggles off i, m, or x options within parentheses.
(?#...)	Comment.
(?= re)	Specifies position using a pattern. Doesn't have a range.
(?! re)	Specifies position using pattern negation. Doesn't have a range.
(?> re)	Matches independent pattern without backtracking.
\w	Matches word characters.
\W	Matches nonword characters.
\s	Matches whitespace. Equivalent to [\t\n\r\f].
\S	Matches nonwhitespace.
\d	Matches digits. Equivalent to [0-9].
\D	Matches nondigits.
\A	Matches beginning of string.
\Z	Matches end of string. If a newline exists, it matches just before newline.
\z	Matches end of string.
\G	Matches point where last match finished.
\b	Matches word boundaries when outside brackets. Matches backspace (0x08) when inside brackets.
\B	Matches nonword boundaries.

\n, \t, etc.	Matches newlines, carriage returns, tabs, etc.
\1...\9	Matches nth grouped subexpression.
\10	Matches nth grouped subexpression if it matched already. Otherwise refers to the octal representation of a character code.

Regular-Expression Examples

Literal Characters

Example	Description
/ruby/	Matches "ruby".
¥	Matches Yen sign. Multibyte characters are supported in Ruby 1.9 and Ruby 1.8.

Character Classes

Example	Description
/[Rr]uby/	Matches "Ruby" or "ruby".
/rub[ye]/	Matches "ruby" or "rube".
/[aeiou]/	Matches any one lowercase vowel.
/[0-9]/	Matches any digit; same as /[0123456789]/.
/[a-z]/	Matches any lowercase ASCII letter.
/[A-Z]/	Matches any uppercase ASCII letter.
/[a-zA-Z0-9]/	Matches any of the above.

/[^aeiou]/	Matches anything other than a lowercase vowel.
/[^0-9]/	Matches anything other than a digit.

Special Character Classes

Example	Description
/./	Matches any character except newline.
/./m	In multiline mode, matches newline, too.
/\d/	Matches a digit: /[0-9]/.
/\D/	Matches a nondigit: /[^0-9]/.
/\s/	Matches a whitespace character: /[\t\r\n\f]/.
/\S/	Matches nonwhitespace: /[^ \t\r\n\f]/.
/\w/	Matches a single word character: /[A-Za-z0-9_]/.
/\W/	Matches a nonword character: /[^A-Za-z0-9_]/.

Repetition Cases

Example	Description
/ruby?/	Matches "rub" or "ruby": the y is optional.
/ruby*/	Matches "rub" plus 0 or more ys.
/ruby+/	Matches "rub" plus 1 or more ys.
/\d{3}/	Matches exactly 3 digits.

/\d{3,}/	Matches 3 or more digits.
/\d{3,5}/	Matches 3, 4, or 5 digits.

Nongreedy Repetition

This matches the smallest number of repetitions:

Example	Description
/<.*>/	Greedy repetition: matches "<ruby>perl>".
/<.*?>/	Nongreedy: matches "<ruby>" in "<ruby>perl>".

Grouping with Parentheses

Example	Description
/\D\d+/	No group: + repeats \d
/(\D\d)+/	Grouped: + repeats \D\d pair
/([Rr]uby(,)?)+/	Match "Ruby", "Ruby, ruby, ruby", etc.

Back References

This matches a previously matched group again:

Example	Description
/([Rr])uby&\1ails/	Matches ruby&rails or Ruby&Rails.
/(['"])(?:(?!\1).)*\1/	Single or double-quoted string. \1 matches whatever the 1st group matched . \2 matches whatever the 2nd group matched, etc.

Alternatives

<table>
<tr><th>Example</th><th>Description</th></tr>
<tr><td>/ruby|rube/</td><td>Matches "ruby" or "rube".</td></tr>
<tr><td>/rub(y|le))/</td><td>Matches "ruby" or "ruble".</td></tr>
<tr><td>/ruby(!+|\?)/</td><td>"ruby" followed by one or more ! or one ?</td></tr>
</table>

Anchors

It needs to specify match position.

Example	Description
/^Ruby/	Matches "Ruby" at the start of a string or internal line.
/Ruby$/	Matches "Ruby" at the end of a string or line.
/\ARuby/	Matches "Ruby" at the start of a string.
/Ruby\Z/	Matches "Ruby" at the end of a string.
/\bRuby\b/	Matches "Ruby" at a word boundary.
/\brub\B/	\B is nonword boundary: matches "rub" in "rube" and "ruby" but not alone.
/Ruby(?=!)/	Matches "Ruby", if followed by an exclamation point.
/Ruby(?!!)/	Matches "Ruby", if not followed by an exclamation point.

Special Syntax with Parentheses

Example	Description
/R(?#comment)/	Matches "R". All the rest is a comment.
/R(?i)uby/	Case-insensitive while matching "uby".
/R(?i:uby)/	Same as above.
/rub(?:y|le))/	Group only without creating \1 backreference.

Search and Replace

Some of the most important String methods that use regular expressions are **sub** and **gsub**, and their in-place variants **sub!** and **gsub!**.

All of these methods perform a search-and-replace operation using a Regexp pattern. The **sub** & **sub!** replaces the first occurrence of the pattern and **gsub** & **gsub!** replaces all occurrences.

The **sub** and **gsub** returns a new string, leaving the original unmodified where as **sub!** and**gsub!** modify the string on which they are called.

Following is the example:

```
#!/usr/bin/ruby


phone = "2004-959-559 #This is Phone Number"


# Delete Ruby-style comments
phone = phone.sub!(/#.*$/, "")
puts "Phone Num : #{phone}"


# Remove anything other than digits
phone = phone.gsub!(/\D/, "")
puts "Phone Num : #{phone}"
```

This will produce the following result:

```
Phone Num : 2004-959-559

Phone Num : 2004959559
```

Following is another example:

```
#!/usr/bin/ruby

text = "rails are rails, really good Ruby on Rails"

# Change "rails" to "Rails" throughout
text.gsub!("rails", "Rails")

# Capitalize the word "Rails" throughout
text.gsub!(/\brails\b/, "Rails")

puts "#{text}"
```

This will produce the following result:

```
Rails are Rails, really good Ruby on Rails
```

23. DBI

This chapter teaches you how to access a database using Ruby. The *Ruby DBI* module provides a database-independent interface for Ruby scripts similar to that of the Perl DBI module.

DBI stands for Database Independent Interface for Ruby, which means DBI provides an abstraction layer between the Ruby code and the underlying database, allowing you to switch database implementations really easily. It defines a set of methods, variables, and conventions that provide a consistent database interface, independent of the actual database being used.

DBI can interface with the following:

- ADO (ActiveX Data Objects)
- DB2
- Frontbase
- mSQL
- MySQL
- ODBC
- Oracle
- OCI8 (Oracle)
- PostgreSQL
- Proxy/Server
- SQLite
- SQLRelay

Architecture of a DBI Application

DBI is independent of any database available in the backend. You can use DBI whether you are working with Oracle, MySQL or Informix, etc. This is clear from the following architecture diagram.

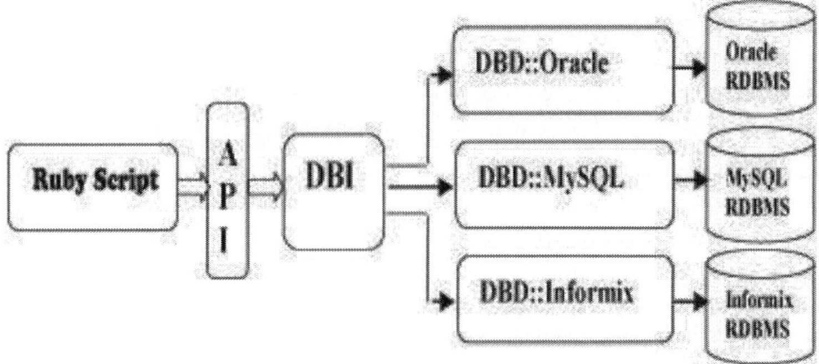

The general architecture for Ruby DBI uses two layers:

- The database interface (DBI) layer. This layer is database independent and provides a set of common access methods that are used the same way regardless of the type of database server with which you're communicating.
- The database driver (DBD) layer. This layer is database dependent; different drivers provide access to different database engines. There is one driver for MySQL, another for PostgreSQL, another for InterBase, another for Oracle, and so forth. Each driver interprets requests from the DBI layer and maps them onto requests appropriate for a given type of database server.

Prerequisites

If you want to write Ruby scripts to access MySQL databases, you'll need to have the Ruby MySQL module installed.

This module acts as a DBD as explained above and can be downloaded fromhttp://www.tmtm.org/en/mysql/ruby/.

Obtaining and Installing Ruby/DBI

You can download and install the Ruby DBI module from the following location:

http://rubyforge.org/projects/ruby-dbi/

Before starting this installation make sure you have the root privilege. Now, follow the steps given below:

Step 1

```
$ tar zxf dbi-0.2.0.tar.gz
```

Step 2

Go in distribution directory *dbi-0.2.0* and configure it using the *setup.rb* script in that directory. The most general configuration command looks like this, with no arguments following the config argument. This command configures the distribution to install all drivers by default.

```
$ ruby setup.rb config
```

To be more specific, provide a --with option that lists the particular parts of the distribution you want to use. For example, to configure only the main DBI module and the MySQL DBD-level driver, issue the following command:

```
$ ruby setup.rb config --with=dbi,dbd_mysql
```

Step 3

Final step is to build the driver and install it using the following commands:

```
$ ruby setup.rb setup
$ ruby setup.rb install
```

Database Connection

Assuming we are going to work with MySQL database, before connecting to a database make sure of the following:

- You have created a database TESTDB.
- You have created EMPLOYEE in TESTDB.
- This table is having fields FIRST_NAME, LAST_NAME, AGE, SEX, and INCOME.
- User ID "testuser" and password "test123" are set to access TESTDB.
- Ruby Module DBI is installed properly on your machine.
- You have gone through MySQL to understand MySQL Basics.

Following is the example of connecting with MySQL database "TESTDB"

```
#!/usr/bin/ruby -w


require "dbi"


begin
```

```
     # connect to the MySQL server
     dbh = DBI.connect("DBI:Mysql:TESTDB:localhost", "testuser", "test123")
     # get server version string and display it
     row = dbh.select_one("SELECT VERSION()")
     puts "Server version: " + row[0]
rescue DBI::DatabaseError => e
     puts "An error occurred"
     puts "Error code:    #{e.err}"
     puts "Error message: #{e.errstr}"
ensure
     # disconnect from server
     dbh.disconnect if dbh
end
```

While running this script, it produces the following result at our Linux machine.

```
Server version: 5.0.45
```

If a connection is established with the data source, then a Database Handle is returned and saved into **dbh** for further use otherwise **dbh** is set to nil value and *e.err* and *e::errstr* return error code and an error string respectively.

Finally, before coming out it, ensure that database connection is closed and resources are released.

INSERT Operation

INSERT operation is required when you want to create your records into a database table.

Once a database connection is established, we are ready to create tables or records into the database tables using **do** method or **prepare** and **execute** method.

Using do Statement

Statements that do not return rows can be issued by invoking the **do** database handle method. This method takes a statement string argument and returns a count of the number of rows affected by the statement.

```
dbh.do("DROP TABLE IF EXISTS EMPLOYEE")
dbh.do("CREATE TABLE EMPLOYEE (
```

```
    FIRST_NAME  CHAR(20) NOT NULL,
    LAST_NAME  CHAR(20),
    AGE INT,
    SEX CHAR(1),
    INCOME FLOAT )" );
```

Similarly, you can execute the SQL *INSERT* statement to create a record into the EMPLOYEE table.

```
#!/usr/bin/ruby -w

require "dbi"

begin
     # connect to the MySQL server
     dbh = DBI.connect("DBI:Mysql:TESTDB:localhost",
                       "testuser", "test123")
     dbh.do( "INSERT INTO EMPLOYEE(FIRST_NAME,
                  LAST_NAME,
                  AGE,
             SEX,
             INCOME)
          VALUES ('Mac', 'Mohan', 20, 'M', 2000)" )
     puts "Record has been created"
     dbh.commit
rescue DBI::DatabaseError => e
     puts "An error occurred"
     puts "Error code:    #{e.err}"
     puts "Error message: #{e.errstr}"
     dbh.rollback
ensure
     # disconnect from server
     dbh.disconnect if dbh
end
```

Using prepare and execute

You can use *prepare* and *execute* methods of DBI class to execute the SQL statement through Ruby code.

Record creation takes the following steps:

- Preparing SQL statement with INSERT statement. This will be done using the **prepare** method.
- Executing SQL query to select all the results from the database. This will be done using the **execute** method.
- Releasing Statement handle. This will be done using **finish** API
- If everything goes fine, then **commit** this operation otherwise you can **rollback** the complete transaction.

Following is the syntax to use these two methods:

```
sth = dbh.prepare(statement)
sth.execute
   ... zero or more SQL operations ...
sth.finish
```

These two methods can be used to pass **bind** values to SQL statements. There may be a case when values to be entered is not given in advance. In such a case, binding values are used. A question mark (**?**) is used in place of actual values and then actual values are passed through execute() API.

Following is the example to create two records in the EMPLOYEE table:

```
#!/usr/bin/ruby -w


require "dbi"


begin
     # connect to the MySQL server
     dbh = DBI.connect("DBI:Mysql:TESTDB:localhost",
                       "testuser", "test123")
     sth = dbh.prepare( "INSERT INTO EMPLOYEE(FIRST_NAME,
                   LAST_NAME,
                   AGE,
              SEX,
```

```
             INCOME)
                  VALUES (?, ?, ?, ?, ?)" )
     sth.execute('John', 'Poul', 25, 'M', 2300)
     sth.execute('Zara', 'Ali', 17, 'F', 1000)
     sth.finish
     dbh.commit
     puts "Record has been created"
rescue DBI::DatabaseError => e
     puts "An error occurred"
     puts "Error code:    #{e.err}"
     puts "Error message: #{e.errstr}"
     dbh.rollback
ensure
     # disconnect from server
     dbh.disconnect if dbh
end
```

If there are multiple INSERTs at a time, then preparing a statement first and then executing it multiple times within a loop is more efficient than invoking do each time through the loop

READ Operation

READ Operation on any database means to fetch some useful information from the database.

Once our database connection is established, we are ready to make a query into this database. We can use either **do** method or **prepare** and **execute** methods to fetch values from a database table.

Record fetching takes following steps:

- Preparing SQL query based on required conditions. This will be done using the **prepare** method.
- Executing SQL query to select all the results from the database. This will be done using the **execute** method.
- Fetching all the results one by one and printing those results. This will be done using the **fetch** method.
- Releasing Statement handle. This will be done using the **finish** method.

Following is the procedure to query all the records from EMPLOYEE table having salary more than 1000.

```
#!/usr/bin/ruby -w

require "dbi"

begin
     # connect to the MySQL server
     dbh = DBI.connect("DBI:Mysql:TESTDB:localhost",
                        "testuser", "test123")
     sth = dbh.prepare("SELECT * FROM EMPLOYEE
                       WHERE INCOME > ?")
     sth.execute(1000)

     sth.fetch do |row|
        printf "First Name: %s, Last Name : %s\n", row[0], row[1]
        printf "Age: %d, Sex : %s\n", row[2], row[3]
        printf "Salary :%d \n\n", row[4]
     end
     sth.finish
rescue DBI::DatabaseError => e
     puts "An error occurred"
     puts "Error code:    #{e.err}"
     puts "Error message: #{e.errstr}"
ensure
     # disconnect from server
     dbh.disconnect if dbh
end
```

This will produce the following result:

```
First Name: Mac, Last Name : Mohan
```

```
Age: 20, Sex : M
Salary :2000

First Name: John, Last Name : Poul
Age: 25, Sex : M
Salary :2300
```

There are more short cut methods to fetch records from the database. If you are interested then go through the **Fetching the Result** otherwise proceed to the next section.

Fetching the Result

DBI provides several different methods to fetch records from the database. Assuming **dbh** is a database handle and **sth** is a statement handle:

S.N.	Methods with Description
1	**db.select_one(stmt, *bindvars) => aRow | nil** Executes the *stmt* statement with the *bindvars* binding beforehand to parameter markers. Returns the first row or *nil* if the result-set is empty.
2	**db.select_all(stmt, *bindvars) => [aRow, ...] | nil** **db.select_all(stmt, *bindvars){ |aRow| aBlock }** Executes the *stmt* statement with the *bindvars* binding beforehand to parameter markers. Calling this method without block returns an array containing all rows. If a block is given, this will be called for each row.
3	**sth.fetch => aRow | nil** Returns the *next* row. Returns *nil* if no further rows are in the result-set.
4	**sth.fetch { |aRow| aBlock }** Invokes the given block for the remaining rows of the result-set.
5	**sth.fetch_all => [aRow, ...]** Returns all remaining rows of the result-set collected in an array.

6	**sth.fetch_many(count) => [aRow, ...]** Returns the next *count* rows collected in an [aRow, ...] array.
7	**sth.fetch_scroll(direction, offset=1) => aRow | nil** Returns the row specified by the *direction* parameter and *offset*. Parameter *offset*is discarded for all but SQL_FETCH_ABSOLUTE and SQL_FETCH_RELATIVE. See a table below for possible values of *direction* parameter.
8	**sth.column_names => anArray** Returns the names of the columns.
9	**column_info => [aColumnInfo, ...]** Returns an array of DBI::ColumnInfo objects. Each object stores information about one column and contains its name, type, precision and more.
10	**sth.rows => rpc** Returns the Row Processed *Count* of the executed statement or *nil* if no such exist.
11	**sth.fetchable? => true | false** Returns *true* if it's possible to fetch rows, otherwise *false*.
12	**sth.cancel** Frees the resources held by the result-set. After calling this method, it is no longer possible to fetch rows until you again call *execute*.
13	**sth.finish** Frees the resources held by the prepared statement. After calling this method no further methods can be called onto this object.

The direction Parameter

Following values could be used for the direction Parameter of the *fetch_scroll* Method:

Constant	Description
DBI::SQL_FETCH_FIRST	Fetches first row.
DBI::SQL_FETCH_LAST	Fetches last row.
DBI::SQL_FETCH_NEXT	Fetches next row.
DBI::SQL_FETCH_PRIOR	Fetches previous row.
DBI::SQL_FETCH_ABSOLUTE	Fetches row at position offset.
DBI::SQL_FETCH_RELATIVE	Fetches the row that is offset rows away from the current.

Example

The following example shows how to get the metadata for a statement. Consider the EMPLOYEE table, which we created in the last chapter.

```
#!/usr/bin/ruby -w

require "dbi"

begin
     # connect to the MySQL server
     dbh = DBI.connect("DBI:Mysql:TESTDB:localhost",
                         "testuser", "test123")
     sth = dbh.prepare("SELECT * FROM EMPLOYEE
                         WHERE INCOME > ?")
     sth.execute(1000)
     if sth.column_names.size == 0 then
        puts "Statement has no result set"
        printf "Number of rows affected: %d\n", sth.rows
     else
        puts "Statement has a result set"
        rows = sth.fetch_all
```

```
        printf "Number of rows: %d\n", rows.size
        printf "Number of columns: %d\n", sth.column_names.size
        sth.column_info.each_with_index do |info, i|
          printf "--- Column %d (%s) ---\n", i, info["name"]
          printf "sql_type:         %s\n", info["sql_type"]
          printf "type_name:        %s\n", info["type_name"]
          printf "precision:        %s\n", info["precision"]
          printf "scale:            %s\n", info["scale"]
          printf "nullable:         %s\n", info["nullable"]
          printf "indexed:          %s\n", info["indexed"]
          printf "primary:          %s\n", info["primary"]
          printf "unique:           %s\n", info["unique"]
          printf "mysql_type:       %s\n", info["mysql_type"]
          printf "mysql_type_name:  %s\n", info["mysql_type_name"]
          printf "mysql_length:     %s\n", info["mysql_length"]
          printf "mysql_max_length: %s\n", info["mysql_max_length"]
          printf "mysql_flags:      %s\n", info["mysql_flags"]
      end
   end
   sth.finish
rescue DBI::DatabaseError => e
     puts "An error occurred"
     puts "Error code:    #{e.err}"
     puts "Error message: #{e.errstr}"
ensure
     # disconnect from server
     dbh.disconnect if dbh
end
```

This will produce the following result:

```
Statement has a result set
Number of rows: 5
```

```
Number of columns: 5
--- Column 0 (FIRST_NAME) ---
sql_type:         12
type_name:        VARCHAR
precision:        20
scale:            0
nullable:         true
indexed:          false
primary:          false
unique:           false
mysql_type:       254
mysql_type_name:  VARCHAR
mysql_length:     20
mysql_max_length: 4
mysql_flags:      0
--- Column 1 (LAST_NAME) ---
sql_type:         12
type_name:        VARCHAR
precision:        20
scale:            0
nullable:         true
indexed:          false
primary:          false
unique:           false
mysql_type:       254
mysql_type_name:  VARCHAR
mysql_length:     20
mysql_max_length: 5
mysql_flags:      0
--- Column 2 (AGE) ---
sql_type:         4
type_name:        INTEGER
precision:        11
```

```
scale:           0
nullable:        true
indexed:         false
primary:         false
unique:          false
mysql_type:      3
mysql_type_name: INT
mysql_length:    11
mysql_max_length: 2
mysql_flags:     32768
--- Column 3 (SEX) ---
sql_type:        12
type_name:       VARCHAR
precision:       1
scale:           0
nullable:        true
indexed:         false
primary:         false
unique:          false
mysql_type:      254
mysql_type_name: VARCHAR
mysql_length:    1
mysql_max_length: 1
mysql_flags:     0
--- Column 4 (INCOME) ---
sql_type:        6
type_name:       FLOAT
precision:       12
scale:           31
nullable:        true
indexed:         false
primary:         false
unique:          false
```

```
mysql_type:       4
mysql_type_name:  FLOAT
mysql_length:     12
mysql_max_length: 4
mysql_flags:      32768
```

Update Operation

UPDATE Operation on any database means to update one or more records, which are already available in the database. Following is the procedure to update all the records having SEX as 'M'. Here, we will increase AGE of all the males by one year. This will take three steps:

- Preparing SQL query based on required conditions. This will be done using the **prepare** method.
- Executing SQL query to select all the results from the database. This will be done using the **execute** method.
- Releasing Statement handle. This will be done using the **finish** method.
- If everything goes fine then **commit** this operation otherwise you can **rollback** the complete transaction.

```
#!/usr/bin/ruby -w


require "dbi"


begin
     # connect to the MySQL server
     dbh = DBI.connect("DBI:Mysql:TESTDB:localhost",
                          "testuser", "test123")
     sth = dbh.prepare("UPDATE EMPLOYEE SET AGE = AGE + 1
                          WHERE SEX = ?")
     sth.execute('M')
     sth.finish
     dbh.commit
rescue DBI::DatabaseError => e
     puts "An error occurred"
     puts "Error code:    #{e.err}"
```

```
     puts "Error message: #{e.errstr}"
     dbh.rollback
ensure
     # disconnect from server
     dbh.disconnect if dbh
end
```

DELETE Operation

DELETE operation is required when you want to delete some records from your database. Following is the procedure to delete all the records from EMPLOYEE where AGE is more than 20. This operation will take following steps.

- Preparing SQL query based on required conditions. This will be done using the **prepare** method.
- Executing SQL query to delete required records from the database. This will be done using the **execute** method.
- Releasing Statement handle. This will be done using the **finish** method.
- If everything goes fine then **commit** this operation otherwise you can **rollback** the complete transaction.

```
#!/usr/bin/ruby -w

require "dbi"

begin
     # connect to the MySQL server
     dbh = DBI.connect("DBI:Mysql:TESTDB:localhost",
                        "testuser", "test123")
     sth = dbh.prepare("DELETE FROM EMPLOYEE
                       WHERE AGE > ?")
     sth.execute(20)
     sth.finish
     dbh.commit
rescue DBI::DatabaseError => e
     puts "An error occurred"
```

```
     puts "Error code:    #{e.err}"
     puts "Error message: #{e.errstr}"
     dbh.rollback
ensure
     # disconnect from server
     dbh.disconnect if dbh
end
```

Performing Transactions

Transactions are a mechanism that ensures data consistency. Transactions should have the following four properties:

- **Atomicity:** Either a transaction completes or nothing happens at all.
- **Consistency:** A transaction must start in a consistent state and leave the system is a consistent state.
- **Isolation:** Intermediate results of a transaction are not visible outside the current transaction.
- **Durability:** Once a transaction was committed, the effects are persistent, even after a system failure.

The DBI provides two methods to either *commit* or *rollback* a transaction. There is one more method called *transaction*, which can be used to implement transactions. There are two simple approaches to implement transactions:

Approach I

The first approach uses DBI's *commit* and *rollback* methods to explicitly commit or cancel the transaction:

```
dbh['AutoCommit'] = false # Set auto commit to false.
begin
  dbh.do("UPDATE EMPLOYEE SET AGE = AGE+1
          WHERE FIRST_NAME = 'John'")
  dbh.do("UPDATE EMPLOYEE SET AGE = AGE+1
          WHERE FIRST_NAME = 'Zara'")
  dbh.commit
rescue
  puts "transaction failed"
```

```
    dbh.rollback
  end
  dbh['AutoCommit'] = true
```

Approach II

The second approach uses the *transaction* method. This is simpler, because it takes a code block containing the statements that make up the transaction. The *transaction* method executes the block, then invokes *commit* or *rollback* automatically, depending on whether the block succeeds or fails:

```
  dbh['AutoCommit'] = false # Set auto commit to false.
  dbh.transaction do |dbh|
    dbh.do("UPDATE EMPLOYEE SET AGE = AGE+1
            WHERE FIRST_NAME = 'John'")
    dbh.do("UPDATE EMPLOYEE SET AGE = AGE+1
            WHERE FIRST_NAME = 'Zara'")
  end
  dbh['AutoCommit'] = true
```

COMMIT Operation

Commit is the operation, which gives a green signal to database to finalize the changes, and after this operation, no change can be reverted back.

Here is a simple example to call the **commit** method.

```
    dbh.commit
```

ROLLBACK Operation

If you are not satisfied with one or more of the changes and you want to revert back those changes completely, then use the **rollback** method.

Here is a simple example to call the **rollback** method.

```
    dbh.rollback
```

Disconnecting Database

To disconnect Database connection, use disconnect API.

```
dbh.disconnect
```

If the connection to a database is closed by the user with the disconnect method, any outstanding transactions are rolled back by the DBI. However, instead of depending on any of DBI's implementation details, your application would be better off calling the commit or rollback explicitly.

Handling Errors

There are many sources of errors. A few examples are a syntax error in an executed SQL statement, a connection failure, or calling the fetch method for an already canceled or finished statement handle.

If a DBI method fails, DBI raises an exception. DBI methods may raise any of several types of exception but the two most important exception classes are *DBI::InterfaceError* and *DBI::DatabaseError*.

Exception objects of these classes have three attributes named *err*, *errstr*, and *state*, which represent the error number, a descriptive error string, and a standard error code. The attributes are explained below:

- **err:** Returns an integer representation of the occurred error or *nil* if this is not supported by the DBD.The Oracle DBD for example returns the numerical part of an *ORA-XXXX* error message.
- **errstr:** Returns a string representation of the occurred error.
- **state:** Returns the SQLSTATE code of the occurred error.The SQLSTATE is a five-character-long string. Most DBDs do not support this and return nil instead.

You have seen following code above in most of the examples:

```
rescue DBI::DatabaseError => e
     puts "An error occurred"
     puts "Error code:    #{e.err}"
     puts "Error message: #{e.errstr}"
     dbh.rollback
ensure
     # disconnect from server
     dbh.disconnect if dbh
end
```

To get debugging information about what your script is doing as it executes, you can enable tracing. To do this, you must first load the dbi/trace module and then call the *trace* method that controls the trace mode and output destination:

```
require "dbi/trace"

..............


trace(mode, destination)
```

The mode value may be 0 (off), 1, 2, or 3, and the destination should be an IO object. The default values are 2 and STDERR, respectively.

Code Blocks with Methods

There are some methods that create handles. These methods can be invoked with a code block. The advantage of using code block along with methods is that they provide the handle to the code block as its parameter and automatically cleans up the handle when the block terminates. There are few examples to understand the concept.

- **DBI.connect:** This method generates a database handle and it is recommended to call *disconnect* at the end of the block to disconnect the database.
- **dbh.prepare:** This method generates a statement handle and it is recommended to *finish* at the end of the block. Within the block, you must invoke *execute* method to execute the statement.
- **dbh.execute:** This method is similar except we don't need to invoke execute within the block. The statement handle is automatically executed.

Example 1

DBI.connect can take a code block, passes the database handle to it, and automatically disconnects the handle at the end of the block as follows.

```
dbh = DBI.connect("DBI:Mysql:TESTDB:localhost",

                   "testuser", "test123") do |dbh|
```

Example 2

dbh.prepare can take a code block, passes the statement handle to it, and automatically calls finish at the end of the block as follows.

```
dbh.prepare("SHOW DATABASES") do |sth|

       sth.execute

       puts "Databases: " + sth.fetch_all.join(", ")

end
```

Example 3

dbh.execute can take a code block, passes the statement handle to it, and automatically calls finish at the end of the block as follows:

```
dbh.execute("SHOW DATABASES") do |sth|
   puts "Databases: " + sth.fetch_all.join(", ")
end
```

DBI *transaction* method also takes a code block, which has been described above.

Driver-specific Functions and Attributes

The DBI lets the database drivers provide additional database-specific functions, which can be called by the user through the *func* method of any Handle object.

Driver-specific attributes are supported and can be set or gotten using the **[]=** or **[]**methods.

DBD::Mysql implements the following driver-specific functions:

S.N.	Functions with Description
1	**dbh.func(:createdb, db_name)** Creates a new database.
2	**dbh.func(:dropdb, db_name)** Drops a database.
3	**dbh.func(:reload)** Performs a reload operation.
4	**dbh.func(:shutdown)** Shuts down the server.
5	**dbh.func(:insert_id) => Fixnum** Returns the most recent AUTO_INCREMENT value for a connection.
6	**dbh.func(:client_info) => String** Returns MySQL client information in terms of version.

7	**dbh.func(:client_version) => Fixnum** Returns client information in terms of version. It's similar to :client_info but it return a fixnum instead of sting.
8	**dbh.func(:host_info) => String** Returns host information.
9	**dbh.func(:proto_info) => Fixnum** Returns protocol being used for the communication.
10	**dbh.func(:server_info) => String** Returns MySQL server information in terms of version.
11	**dbh.func(:stat) => String** Returns current state of the database.
12	**dbh.func(:thread_id) => Fixnum** Returns current thread ID.

Example

```
#!/usr/bin/ruby


require "dbi"
begin
   # connect to the MySQL server
   dbh = DBI.connect("DBI:Mysql:TESTDB:localhost",
                          "testuser", "test123")
   puts dbh.func(:client_info)
   puts dbh.func(:client_version)
   puts dbh.func(:host_info)
   puts dbh.func(:proto_info)
   puts dbh.func(:server_info)
   puts dbh.func(:thread_id)
   puts dbh.func(:stat)
rescue DBI::DatabaseError => e
   puts "An error occurred"
```

```
   puts "Error code:    #{e.err}"
   puts "Error message: #{e.errstr}"
ensure
   dbh.disconnect if dbh
end
```

This will produce the following result:

```
5.0.45
50045
Localhost via UNIX socket
10
5.0.45
150621
Uptime: 384981  Threads: 1  Questions: 1101078  Slow queries: 4 \
Opens: 324  Flush tables: 1  Open tables: 64  \
Queries per second avg: 2.860
```

24. WEB APPLICATIONS

Ruby is a general-purpose language; it can't properly be called a *web language* at all. Even so, web applications and web tools in general are among the most common uses of Ruby.

Not only can you write your own SMTP server, FTP daemon, or Web server in Ruby, but you can also use Ruby for more usual tasks such as CGI programming or as a replacement for PHP.

Please spend few minutes with CGI Programming for more detail on CGI Programming.

Writing CGI Scripts

The most basic Ruby CGI script looks like this:

```
#!/usr/bin/ruby


puts "HTTP/1.0 200 OK"
puts "Content-type: text/html\n\n"
puts "<html><body>This is a test</body></html>"
```

If you call this script *test.cgi* and uploaded it to a Unix-based Web hosting provider with the right permissions, you could use it as a CGI script.

For example, if you have the Web site http://www.example.com/ hosted with a Linux Web hosting provider and you upload *test.cgi* to the main directory and give it execute permissions, then visiting http://www.example.com/test.cgi should return an HTML page saying ***This is a test***.

Here when *test.cgi* is requested from a Web browser, the Web server looks for *test.cgi* on the Web site, and then executes it using the Ruby interpreter. The Ruby script returns a basic HTTP header and then returns a basic HTML document.

Using cgi.rb

Ruby comes with a special library called **cgi** that enables more sophisticated interactions than those with the preceding CGI script.

Let's create a basic CGI script that uses cgi:

```
#!/usr/bin/ruby
```

```
require 'cgi'


cgi = CGI.new
puts cgi.header
puts "<html><body>This is a test</body></html>"
```

Here, you created a CGI object and used it to print the header line for you.

Form Processing

Using class CGI gives you access to HTML query parameters in two ways. Suppose we are given a URL of /cgi-bin/test.cgi?FirstName=Zara&LastName=Ali.

You can access the parameters *FirstName* and *LastName* using CGI#[] directly as follows:

```
#!/usr/bin/ruby


require 'cgi'
cgi = CGI.new
cgi['FirstName'] # =>  ["Zara"]
cgi['LastName']  # =>  ["Ali"]
```

There is another way to access these form variables. This code will give you a hash of all the key and values:

```
#!/usr/bin/ruby


require 'cgi'
cgi = CGI.new
h = cgi.params  # =>  {"FirstName"=>["Zara"],"LastName"=>["Ali"]}
h['FirstName']  # =>  ["Zara"]
h['LastName']   # =>  ["Ali"]
```

Following is the code to retrieve all the keys:

```
#!/usr/bin/ruby


require 'cgi'
cgi = CGI.new
cgi.keys         # =>  ["FirstName", "LastName"]
```

If a form contains multiple fields with the same name, the corresponding values will be returned to the script as an array. The [] accessor returns just the first of these.index the result of the params method to get them all.

In this example, assume the form has three fields called "name" and we entered three names "Zara", "Huma" and "Nuha":

```
#!/usr/bin/ruby


require 'cgi'
cgi = CGI.new
cgi['name']        # => "Zara"
cgi.params['name'] # => ["Zara", "Huma", "Nuha"]
cgi.keys           # => ["name"]
cgi.params         # => {"name"=>["Zara", "Huma", "Nuha"]}
```

Note: Ruby will take care of GET and POST methods automatically. There is no separate treatment for these two different methods.

An associated, but basic, form that could send the correct data would have the HTML code like so:

```
<html>
<body>
<form method="POST" action="http://www.example.com/test.cgi">
First Name :<input type="text" name="FirstName" value="" />
<br />
Last Name :<input type="text" name="LastName" value="" />


<input type="submit" value="Submit Data" />
</form>
</body>
</html>
```

Creating Forms and HTML

CGI contains a huge number of methods used to create HTML. You will find one method per tag. In order to enable these methods, you must create a CGI object by calling CGI.new.

To make tag nesting easier, these methods take their content as code blocks. The code blocks should return a *String*, which will be used as the content for the tag. For example:

```
#!/usr/bin/ruby


require "cgi"
cgi = CGI.new("html4")
cgi.out{
   cgi.html{
      cgi.head{ "\n"+cgi.title{"This Is a Test"} } +
      cgi.body{ "\n"+
         cgi.form{"\n"+
            cgi.hr +
            cgi.h1 { "A Form: " } + "\n"+
            cgi.textarea("get_text") +"\n"+
            cgi.br +
            cgi.submit
         }
      }
   }
}
```

NOTE: The *form* method of the CGI class can accept a method parameter, which will set the HTTP method (GET, POST, and so on...) to be used on form submittal. The default, used in this example, is POST.

This will produce the following result:

```
Content-Type: text/html
Content-Length: 302
```

```
<!DOCTYPE HTML PUBLIC "-//W3C//DTD HTML 4.0 Final//EN">
<HTML>
<HEAD>
<TITLE>This Is a Test</TITLE>
</HEAD>
<BODY>
<FORM METHOD="post" ENCTYPE="application/x-www-form-urlencoded">
<HR>
<H1>A Form: </H1>
<TEXTAREA COLS="70" NAME="get_text" ROWS="10"></TEXTAREA>
<BR>
<INPUT TYPE="submit">
</FORM>
</BODY>
</HTML>
```

Quoting Strings

When dealing with URLs and HTML code, you must be careful to quote certain characters. For instance, a slash character (/) has special meaning in a URL, so it must be **escaped** if it's not part of the pathname.

For example, any / in the query portion of the URL will be translated to the string %2F and must be translated back to a / for you to use it. Space and ampersand are also special characters. To handle this, CGI provides the routines **CGI.escape** and **CGI.unescape**.

```
#!/usr/bin/ruby


require 'cgi'
puts CGI.escape(Zara Ali/A Sweet & Sour Girl")
```

This will produce the following result:

```
Zara+Ali%2FA Sweet+%26+Sour+Girl")
#!/usr/bin/ruby
```

```
require 'cgi'
puts CGI.escapeHTML('<h1>Zara Ali/A Sweet & Sour Girl</h1>')
```

This will produce the following result:

```
&lt;h1&gt;Zara Ali/A Sweet & Sour Girl&lt;/h1&gt;'
```

Useful Methods in CGI Class

Here is the list of methods related to CGI class:

- The **Ruby CGI** - Methods related to Standard CGI library.

Ruby CGI

CGI Class Methods

Here is a list of CGI Class methods:

SN	Methods with Description
1	**CGI::new([level="query"])** Creates a CGI object. Level may be one of the following options. If one of the HTML levels is specified, the following methods are defined for generating output conforming to that level: **query:** No HTML output generated **html3:** HTML3.2 **html4:** HTML4.0 Strict **html4Tr:** HTML4.0 Transitional **html4Fr:** HTML4.0 Frameset
2	**CGI::escape(str)** Escapes an unsafe string using URL-encoding.
3	**CGI::unescape(str)** Expands a string that has been escaped using URL-encoding.

4	**CGI::escapeHTML(str)** Escapes HTML special characters, including: & < >.
5	**CGI::unescapeHTML(str)** Expands escaped HTML special characters, including: & < >.
6	**CGI::escapeElement(str[, element...])** Escapes HTML special characters in the specified HTML elements.
7	**CGI::unescapeElement(str, element[, element...])** Expands escaped HTML special characters in the specified HTML elements.
8	**CGI::parse(query)** Parses the query and returns a hash containing its key-value pairs.
9	**CGI::pretty(string[, leader=" "])** Returns a neatly formatted version of the HTML string. If *leader* is specified, it's written at the beginning of each line. The default value for *leader* is two spaces.
10	**CGI::rfc1123_date(time)** Formats the data and time according to RFC-1123 (for example, Tue, 2 Jun 2008 00:00:00 GMT).

CGI Instance Methods

Assuming **c** is an instance created by *CGI::new*. Now, here is a list of methods, which can be applied to this instance:

SN	Methods with Description
1	**c[name]** Returns an array containing the value of the field name corresponding to *name*.

2	**c.checkbox(name[, value[, check=false]])** **c.checkbox(options)** Returns an HTML string defining a checkbox field. Tag attributes may be specified in a hash passed as an argument.
3	**c.checkbox_group(name, value...)** **c.checkbox_group(options)** Returns an HTML string defining a checkbox group. Tag attributes may be specified in a hash passed as an argument.
4	**c.file_field(name[, size=20[, max]])** **c.file_field(options)** Returns an HTML string defining a file field.
5	**c.form([method="post"[, url]]) { ...}** **c.form(options)** Returns an HTML string defining a form. If a block is specified, the string produced by its output creates the contents of the form. Tag attributes may be specified in a hash passed as an argument.
6	**c.cookies** Returns a hash containing a CGI::Cookie object containing keys and values from a cookie.
7	**c.header([header])** Returns a CGI header containing the information in header. If header is a hash, its key-value pairs are used to create the header.
8	**c.hidden(name[, value])** **c.hidden(options)** Returns an HTML string defining a HIDDEN field. Tag attributes may be specified in a hash passed as an argument.
9	**c.image_button(url[, name[, alt]])** **c.image_button(options)** Returns an HTML string defining an image button. Tag attributes may be specified in a hash passed as an argument.

10	**c.keys** Returns an array containing the field names from the form.
11	**c.key?(name)** **c.has_key?(name)** **c.include?(name)** Returns true if the form contains the specified field name.
12	**c.multipart_form([url[, encode]]) { ...}** **c.multipart_form(options) { ...}** Returns an HTML string defining a multipart form. If a block is specified, the string produced by its output creates the contents of the form. Tag attributes may be specified in a hash passed as an argument.
13	**c.out([header]) { ...}** Generates HTML output. Uses the string produced by the block's output to create the body of the page.
14	**c.params** Returns a hash containing field names and values from the form.
15	**c.params= hash** Sets field names and values in the form using a hash.
16	**c.password_field(name[, value[, size=40[, max]]])** **c.password_field(options)** Returns an HTML string defining a password field. Tag attributes may be specified in a hash passed as an argument.
17	**c.popup_menu(name, value...)** **c.popup_menu(options)** **c.scrolling_list(name, value...)** **c.scrolling_list(options)** Returns an HTML string defining a pop-up menu. Tag attributes may be specified in a hash passed as an argument.
18	**c.radio_button(name[, value[, checked=false]])**

	c.radio_button(options) Returns an HTML string defining a radio button. Tag attributes may be specified in a hash passed as an argument.
19	**c.radio_group(name, value...)** **c.radio_group(options)** Returns an HTML string defining a radio button group. Tag attributes may be specified in a hash passed as an argument.
20	**c.reset(name[, value])** **c.reset(options)** Returns an HTML string defining a reset button. Tag attributes may be specified in a hash passed as an argument.
21	**c.text_field(name[, value[, size=40[, max]]])** **c.text_field(options)** Returns an HTML string defining a text field. Tag attributes may be specified in a hash passed as an argument.
22	**c.textarea(name[, cols=70[, rows=10]]) { ...}** **c.textarea(options) { ...}** Returns an HTML string defining a text area. If a block is specified, the string produced by its output creates the contents of the text area. Tag attributes may be specified in a hash passed as an argument.

HTML Generation Methods

You can create any HTML tag by using the corresponding HTML tag name along with any CGI instance. For example:

```
#!/usr/bin/ruby


require "cgi"
cgi = CGI.new("html4")
cgi.out{
   cgi.html{
      cgi.head{ "\n"+cgi.title{"This Is a Test"} } +
```

```
        cgi.body{ "\n"+
          cgi.form{"\n"+
            cgi.hr +
            cgi.h1 { "A Form: " } + "\n"+
            cgi.textarea("get_text") +"\n"+
            cgi.br +
            cgi.submit
          }
        }
    }
}
```

CGI Object Attributes

You can access any of the following attributes using a CGI instance:

Attribute	Returned Value
accept	Acceptable MIME type
accept_charset	Acceptable character set
accept_encoding	Acceptable encoding
accept_language	Acceptable language
auth_type	Authentication type
raw_cookie	Cookie data (raw string)
content_length	Content length
content_type	Content type
From	Client e-mail address

gateway_interface	CGI version string
path_info	Extra path
path_translated	Converted extra path
Query_string	Query string
referer	Previously accessed URL
remote_addr	Client host address
remote_host	Client hostname
remote_ident	Client name
remote_user	Authenticated user
request_method	Request method (GET, POST, etc.)
script_name	Program name
server_name	Server name
server_port	Server port
server_protocol	Server protocol
server_software	Server software
user_agent	User agent

Cookies and Sessions

We have explained these two concepts in different sections. Please follow the sections:

- The **Ruby CGI Cookies** - How to handle CGI Cookies.

- The **Ruby CGI Sessions** - How to manage CGI sessions.

Ruby CGI Cookies

HTTP protocol is a stateless protocol. But for a commercial website, it is required to maintain session information among different pages. For example, one user registration ends after completing many pages. But how to maintain user's session information across all the web pages.

In many situations, using cookies is the most efficient method of remembering and tracking preferences, purchases, commissions, and other information required for better visitor experience or site statistics.

How It Works?

Your server sends some data to the visitor's browser in the form of a cookie. The browser may accept the cookie. If it does, it is stored as a plain text record on the visitor's hard drive. Now, when the visitor arrives at another page on your site, the cookie is available for retrieval. Once retrieved, your server knows/remembers what was stored.

Cookies are a plain text data record of five variable-length fields:

- **Expires:** The date the cookie will expire. If this is blank, the cookie will expire when the visitor quits the browser.
- **Domain:** The domain name of your site.
- **Path:** The path to the directory or web page that sets the cookie. This may be blank if you want to retrieve the cookie from any directory or page.
- **Secure:** If this field contains the word "secure", then the cookie may only be retrieved with a secure server. If this field is blank, no such restriction exists.
- **Name=Value:** Cookies are set and retrieved in the form of key and value pairs.

Handling Cookies in Ruby

You can create a named cookie object and store any textual information in it. To send it down to the browser, set a **cookie** header in the call to *CGI.out*.

```
#!/usr/bin/ruby


require "cgi"

cgi = CGI.new("html4")
```

```
cookie = CGI::Cookie.new('name' => 'mycookie',
                         'value' => 'Zara Ali',
                         'expires' => Time.now + 3600)
cgi.out('cookie' => cookie) do
   cgi.head + cgi.body { "Cookie stored" }
end
```

The next time the user comes back to this page, you can retrieve the cookie values set as shown below:

```
#!/usr/bin/ruby

require "cgi"
cgi = CGI.new("html4")
cookie = cgi.cookies['mycookie']
cgi.out('cookie' => cookie) do
   cgi.head + cgi.body { cookie[0] }
end
```

Cookies are represented using a separate object of class CGI::Cookie, containing the following accessors:

Attribute	Returned Value
name	Cookie name
value	An array of cookie values
path	The cookie's path
domain	The domain
expires	The expiration time (as a Time object)
secure	True if secure cookie

Ruby CGI Sessions

A CGI::Session maintains a persistent state for Web users in a CGI environment. Sessions should be closed after use, as this ensures that their data is written out to the store. When you've permanently finished with a session, you should delete it.

```
#!/usr/bin/ruby

require 'cgi'
require 'cgi/session'
cgi = CGI.new("html4")

sess = CGI::Session.new( cgi, "session_key" => "a_test",
                              "prefix" => "rubysess.")
lastaccess = sess["lastaccess"].to_s
sess["lastaccess"] = Time.now
if cgi['bgcolor'][0] =~ /[a-z]/
  sess["bgcolor"] = cgi['bgcolor']
end

cgi.out{
  cgi.html {
    cgi.body ("bgcolor" => sess["bgcolor"]){
      "The background of this page"    +
      "changes based on the 'bgcolor'" +
      "each user has in session."      +
      "Last access time: #{lastaccess}"
    }
  }
}
```

Accessing "/cgi-bin/test.cgi?bgcolor=red" would turn the page red for a single user for each successive hit until a new "bgcolor" was specified via the URL.

Session data is stored in a temporary file for each session, and the prefix parameter assigns a string to be prepended to the filename, making your sessions easy to identify on the filesystem of the server.

CGI::Session still lacks many features, such as the capability to store objects other than Strings, session storage across multiple servers.

Class CGI::Session

A CGI::Session maintains a persistent state for web users in a CGI environment. Sessions may be memory-resident or may be stored on disk.

Class Methods

Ruby class *Class CGI::Session* provides a single class method to create a session:

```
CGI::Session::new( cgi[, option])
```

Starts a new CGI session and returns the corresponding CGI::Session object. *option* may be an option hash specifying one or more of the following:

- **session_key:** Key name holding the session ID. Default is _session_id.
- **session_id:** Unique session ID. Generated automatically
- **new_session:** If true, create a new session id for this session. If false, use an existing session identified by session_id. If omitted, use an existing session if available, otherwise create a new one.
- **database_manager:** Class to use to save sessions; may be CGI::Session::FileStore or CGI::Session::MemoryStore. Default is FileStore.
- **tmpdir:** For FileStore, directory for session files.
- **prefix:** For FileStore, prefix of session filenames.

Instance Methods

SN	Methods with Description
1	**[ ]** Returns the value for the given key. See example above.
2	**[ ]=** Sets the value for the given key. See example above.
3	**delete**

	Calls the delete method of the underlying database manager. For FileStore, deletes the physical file containing the session. For MemoryStore, removes the session from memory.
4	**update** Calls the update method of the underlying database manager. For FileStore, writes the session data out to disk. Has no effect with MemoryStore.

Web Hosting Servers

You could check the following topic on the internet to host your website on a Unix-based Server:

- **Unix-based Web hosting**

25. SENDING EMAIL

Simple Mail Transfer Protocol (SMTP) is a protocol, which handles sending e-mail and routing e-mail between mail servers.

Ruby provides Net::SMTP class for Simple Mail Transfer Protocol (SMTP) client-side connection and provides two class methods *new* and *start*.

- The **new** takes two parameters:
  - The *server name* defaulting to localhost.
  - The *port number* defaulting to the well-known port 25.
- The **start** method takes these parameters:
  - The *server* - IP name of the SMTP server, defaulting to localhost.
  - The *port* - Port number, defaulting to 25.
  - The *domain* - Domain of the mail sender, defaulting to ENV["HOSTNAME"].
  - The *account* - Username, default is nil.
  - The *password* - User password, defaulting to nil.
  - The *authtype* - Authorization type, defaulting to *cram_md5.*

An SMTP object has an instance method called sendmail, which will typically be used to do the work of mailing a message. It takes three parameters:

- The *source* - A string or array or anything with an *each* iterator returning one string at a time.
- The *sender* - A string that will appear in the *from* field of the email.
- The *recipients* - A string or an array of strings representing the recipients' addressee(s).

Example

Here is a simple way to send one email using Ruby script. Try it once:

```
require 'net/smtp'


message = <<MESSAGE_END
From: Private Person <me@fromdomain.com>
To: A Test User <test@todomain.com>
```

```
Subject: SMTP e-mail test


This is a test e-mail message.
MESSAGE_END


Net::SMTP.start('localhost') do |smtp|
  smtp.send_message message, 'me@fromdomain.com',
                             'test@todomain.com'
end
```

Here, you have placed a basic e-mail in message, using a document, taking care to format the headers correctly. E-mails require a **From**, **To**, and **Subject** header, separated from the body of the e-mail with a blank line.

To send the mail you use Net::SMTP to connect to the SMTP server on the local machine and then use the send_message method along with the message, the from address, and the destination address as parameters (even though the from and to addresses are within the e-mail itself, these aren't always used to route mail).

If you're not running an SMTP server on your machine, you can use the Net::SMTP to communicate with a remote SMTP server. Unless you're using a webmail service (such as Hotmail or Yahoo! Mail), your e-mail provider will have provided you with outgoing mail server details that you can supply to Net::SMTP, as follows:

```
Net::SMTP.start('mail.your-domain.com')
```

This line of code connects to the SMTP server on port 25 of mail.your-domain.com without using any username or password. If you need to, though, you can specify port number and other details. For example:

```
Net::SMTP.start('mail.your-domain.com',
                25,
                'localhost',
                'username', 'password' :plain)
```

This example connects to the SMTP server at mail.your-domain.com using a username and password in plain text format. It identifies the client's hostname as localhost.

Sending an HTML e-mail using Ruby

When you send a text message using Ruby then all the content will be treated as simple text. Even if you will include HTML tags in a text message, it will be displayed as simple text and HTML tags will not be formatted according to HTML syntax. But Ruby Net::SMTP provides option to send an HTML message as actual HTML message.

While sending an email message you can specify a Mime version, content type and character set to send an HTML email.

Example

Following is the example to send HTML content as an email. Try it once:

```
require 'net/smtp'

message = <<MESSAGE_END
From: Private Person <me@fromdomain.com>
To: A Test User <test@todomain.com>
MIME-Version: 1.0
Content-type: text/html
Subject: SMTP e-mail test

This is an e-mail message to be sent in HTML format

<b>This is HTML message.</b>
<h1>This is headline.</h1>
MESSAGE_END

Net::SMTP.start('localhost') do |smtp|
  smtp.send_message message, 'me@fromdomain.com',
                             'test@todomain.com'
end
```

Sending Attachments as an e-mail

To send an email with mixed content requires to set **Content-type** header to **multipart/mixed**. Then text and attachment sections can be specified within **boundaries**.

A boundary is started with two hyphens followed by a unique number, which cannot appear in the message part of the email. A final boundary denoting the email's final section must also end with two hyphens.

Attached files should be encoded with the **pack("m")** function to have base64 encoding before transmission.

Example

Following is the example, which will send a file **/tmp/test.txt** as an attachment.

```
require 'net/smtp'

filename = "/tmp/test.txt"
# Read a file and encode it into base64 format
filecontent = File.read(filename)
encodedcontent = [filecontent].pack("m")   # base64

marker = "AUNIQUEMARKER"

body =<<EOF
This is a test email to send an attachement.
EOF

# Define the main headers.
part1 =<<EOF
From: Private Person <me@fromdomain.net>
To: A Test User <test@todmain.com>
Subject: Sending Attachement
MIME-Version: 1.0
Content-Type: multipart/mixed; boundary=#{marker}
--#{marker}
EOF

# Define the message action
part2 =<<EOF
Content-Type: text/plain
Content-Transfer-Encoding:8bit
```

```
#{body}
--#{marker}
EOF

# Define the attachment section
part3 =<<EOF
Content-Type: multipart/mixed; name=\"#{filename}\"
Content-Transfer-Encoding:base64
Content-Disposition: attachment; filename="#{filename}"

#{encodedcontent}
--#{marker}--
EOF

mailtext = part1 + part2 + part3

# Let's put our code in safe area
begin
  Net::SMTP.start('localhost') do |smtp|
     smtp.sendmail(mailtext, 'me@fromdomain.net',
                          ['test@todmain.com'])
  end
rescue Exception => e
  print "Exception occured: " + e
end
```

NOTE: You can specify multiple destinations inside the array but they should be separated by comma.

26. SOCKET PROGRAMMING

Ruby provides two levels of access to network services. At a low level, you can access the basic socket support in the underlying operating system, which allows you to implement clients and servers for both connection-oriented and connectionless protocols.

Ruby also has libraries that provide higher-level access to specific application-level network protocols, such as FTP, HTTP, and so on.

This chapter gives you an understanding on most famous concept in Networking - Socket Programming.

What are Sockets?

Sockets are the endpoints of a bidirectional communications channel. Sockets may communicate within a process, between processes on the same machine, or between processes on different continents.

Sockets may be implemented over a number of different channel types: Unix domain sockets, TCP, UDP, and so on. The *socket* library provides specific classes for handling the common transports as well as a generic interface for handling the rest.

Sockets have their own vocabulary:

Term	Description
domain	The family of protocols that will be used as the transport mechanism. These values are constants such as PF_INET, PF_UNIX, PF_X25, and so on.
type	The type of communications between the two endpoints, typically SOCK_STREAM for connection-oriented protocols and SOCK_DGRAM for connectionless protocols.
protocol	Typically zero, this may be used to identify a variant of a protocol within a domain and type.
hostname	The identifier of a network interface: A string, which can be a host name, a dotted-quad address, or an

	IPV6 address in colon (and possibly dot) notation A string "<broadcast>", which specifies an INADDR_BROADCAST address. A zero-length string, which specifies INADDR_ANY, or An Integer, interpreted as a binary address in host byte order.
port	Each server listens for clients calling on one or more ports. A port may be a Fixnum port number, a string containing a port number, or the name of a service.

A Simple Client

Here we will write a very simple client program, which will open a connection to a given port and given host. Ruby class **TCPSocket** provides *open* function to open such a socket.

The **TCPSocket.open(hosname, port)** opens a TCP connection to *hostname* on the *port*.

Once you have a socket open, you can read from it like any IO object. When done, remember to close it, as you would close a file.

The following code is a very simple client that connects to a given host and port, reads any available data from the socket, and then exits:

```
require 'socket'      # Sockets are in standard library


hostname = 'localhost'
port = 2000


s = TCPSocket.open(hostname, port)


while line = s.gets   # Read lines from the socket
  puts line.chop      # And print with platform line terminator
end
s.close               # Close the socket when done
```

A Simple Server

To write Internet servers, we use the **TCPServer** class. A TCPServer object is a factory for TCPSocket objects.

Now call **TCPServer.open(hostname, port** function to specify a *port* for your service and create a **TCPServer** object.

Next, call the *accept* method of the returned TCPServer object. This method waits until a client connects to the port you specified, and then returns a *TCPSocket* object that represents the connection to that client.

```
require 'socket'               # Get sockets from stdlib

server = TCPServer.open(2000)  # Socket to listen on port 2000
loop {                         # Servers run forever
  client = server.accept       # Wait for a client to connect
  client.puts(Time.now.ctime)  # Send the time to the client
  client.puts "Closing the connection. Bye!"
  client.close                 # Disconnect from the client
}
```

Now, run this server in background and then run the above client to see the result.

Multi-Client TCP Servers

Most servers on the Internet are designed to deal with large numbers of clients at any one time.

Ruby's *Thread* class makes it easy to create a multithreaded server.one that accepts requests and immediately creates a new thread of execution to process the connection while allowing the main program to await more connections:

```
require 'socket'                # Get sockets from stdlib

server = TCPServer.open(2000)   # Socket to listen on port 2000
loop {                          # Servers run forever
  Thread.start(server.accept) do |client|
    client.puts(Time.now.ctime) # Send the time to the client
     client.puts "Closing the connection. Bye!"
    client.close                # Disconnect from the client
```

```
  end
}
```

In this example, you have a permanent loop, and when server.accept responds, a new thread is created and started immediately to handle the connection that has just been accepted, using the connection object passed into the thread. However, the main program immediately loops back and awaits new connections.

Using Ruby threads in this way means the code is portable and will run in the same way on Linux, OS X, and Windows.

A Tiny Web Browser

We can use the socket library to implement any Internet protocol. Here, for example, is a code to fetch the content of a web page:

```
require 'socket'

host = 'www.webhost.com'            # The web server
port = 80                           # Default HTTP port
path = "/index.htm"                 # The file we want

# This is the HTTP request we send to fetch a file
request = "GET #{path} HTTP/1.0\r\n\r\n"

socket = TCPSocket.open(host,port)  # Connect to server
socket.print(request)               # Send request
response = socket.read              # Read complete response
# Split response at first blank line into headers and body
headers,body = response.split("\r\n\r\n", 2)
print body                          # And display it
```

To implement the similar web client, you can use a pre-built library like **Net::HTTP** for working with HTTP. Here is the code that does the equivalent of the previous code:

```
require 'net/http'                  # The library we need
```

```
host = 'www.webhost.com'     # The web server
path = '/index.htm'                 # The file we want

http = Net::HTTP.new(host)          # Create a connection
headers, body = http.get(path)      # Request the file
if headers.code == "200"            # Check the status code
  print body
else
  puts "#{headers.code} #{headers.message}"
end
```

Please check similar libraries to work with FTP, SMTP, POP, and IMAP protocols.

Further Readings

We have given you a quick start on Socket Programming. It is a big subject, so it is recommended that you go through **Ruby Socket Library and Class Methods** to find more details.

27. XML, XSLT, XPATH

What is XML?

The Extensible Markup Language (XML) is a markup language much like HTML or SGML. This is recommended by the World Wide Web Consortium and available as an open standard.

XML is a portable, open source language that allows programmers to develop applications that can be read by other applications, regardless of operating system and/or developmental language.

XML is extremely useful for keeping track of small to medium amounts of data without requiring a SQL-based backbone.

XML Parser Architectures and APIs

There are two different flavors available for XML parsers:

- **SAX-like (Stream interfaces):** Here you register callbacks for events of interest and then let the parser proceed through the document. This is useful when your documents are large or you have memory limitations, it parses the file as it reads it from disk, and the entire file is never stored in memory.
- **DOM-like (Object tree interfaces):** This is World Wide Web Consortium recommendation wherein the entire file is read into memory and stored in a hierarchical (tree-based) form to represent all the features of an XML document.

SAX obviously can't process information as fast as DOM can when working with large files. On the other hand, using DOM exclusively can really kill your resources, especially if used on a lot of small files.

SAX is read-only, while DOM allows changes to the XML file. Since these two different APIs literally complement each other there is no reason why you can't use them both for large projects.

Parsing and Creating XML using Ruby

The most common way to manipulate XML is with the REXML library by Sean Russell. Since 2002, REXML has been part of the standard Ruby distribution.

REXML is a pure-Ruby XML processor conforming to the XML 1.0 standard. It is a *nonvalidating* processor, passing all of the OASIS nonvalidating conformance tests.

REXML parser has the following advantages over other available parsers:

- It is written 100 percent in Ruby.
- It can be used for both SAX and DOM parsing.
- It is lightweight, less than 2000 lines of code.
- Methods and classes are really easy-to-understand.
- SAX2-based API and Full XPath support.
- Shipped with Ruby installation and no separate installation is required.

For all our XML code examples, let's use a simple XML file as an input:

```
<collection shelf="New Arrivals">
<movie title="Enemy Behind">
   <type>War, Thriller</type>
   <format>DVD</format>
   <year>2003</year>
   <rating>PG</rating>
   <stars>10</stars>
   <description>Talk about a US-Japan war</description>
</movie>
<movie title="Transformers">
   <type>Anime, Science Fiction</type>
   <format>DVD</format>
   <year>1989</year>
   <rating>R</rating>
   <stars>8</stars>
   <description>A schientific fiction</description>
</movie>
   <movie title="Trigun">
   <type>Anime, Action</type>
   <format>DVD</format>
   <episodes>4</episodes>
   <rating>PG</rating>
```

```
    <stars>10</stars>
    <description>Vash the Stampede!</description>
</movie>
<movie title="Ishtar">
    <type>Comedy</type>
    <format>VHS</format>
    <rating>PG</rating>
    <stars>2</stars>
    <description>Viewable boredom</description>
</movie>
</collection>
```

DOM-like Parsing

Let's first parse our XML data in *tree fashion*. We begin by requiring the **rexml/document** library; often we do an include REXML to import into the top-level namespace for convenience.

```
#!/usr/bin/ruby -w

require 'rexml/document'
include REXML

xmlfile = File.new("movies.xml")
xmldoc = Document.new(xmlfile)

# Now get the root element
root = xmldoc.root
puts "Root element : " + root.attributes["shelf"]

# This will output all the movie titles.
xmldoc.elements.each("collection/movie"){
    |e| puts "Movie Title : " + e.attributes["title"]
}
```

```
# This will output all the movie types.
xmldoc.elements.each("collection/movie/type") {
   |e| puts "Movie Type : " + e.text
}

# This will output all the movie description.
xmldoc.elements.each("collection/movie/description") {
   |e| puts "Movie Description : " + e.text
}
```

This will produce the following result:

```
Root element : New Arrivals
Movie Title : Enemy Behind
Movie Title : Transformers
Movie Title : Trigun
Movie Title : Ishtar
Movie Type : War, Thriller
Movie Type : Anime, Science Fiction
Movie Type : Anime, Action
Movie Type : Comedy
Movie Description : Talk about a US-Japan war
Movie Description : A schientific fiction
Movie Description : Vash the Stampede!
Movie Description : Viewable boredom
```

SAX-like Parsing

To process the same data, *movies.xml*, file in a *stream-oriented* way we will define a *listener* class whose methods will be the target of *callbacks* from the parser.

NOTE: It is not suggested to use SAX-like parsing for a small file, this is just for a demo example.

```
#!/usr/bin/ruby -w
```

```
require 'rexml/document'
require 'rexml/streamlistener'
include REXML


class MyListener
  include REXML::StreamListener
  def tag_start(*args)
    puts "tag_start: #{args.map {|x| x.inspect}.join(', ')}"
  end

  def text(data)
    return if data =~ /^\w*$/     # whitespace only
    abbrev = data[0..40] + (data.length > 40 ? "..." : "")
    puts "  text   :   #{abbrev.inspect}"
  end
end

list = MyListener.new
xmlfile = File.new("movies.xml")
Document.parse_stream(xmlfile, list)
```

This will produce the following result:

```
tag_start: "collection", {"shelf"=>"New Arrivals"}
tag_start: "movie", {"title"=>"Enemy Behind"}
tag_start: "type", {}
  text   :   "War, Thriller"
tag_start: "format", {}
tag_start: "year", {}
tag_start: "rating", {}
tag_start: "stars", {}
tag_start: "description", {}
  text   :   "Talk about a US-Japan war"
```

```
tag_start: "movie", {"title"=>"Transformers"}
tag_start: "type", {}
  text   :   "Anime, Science Fiction"
tag_start: "format", {}
tag_start: "year", {}
tag_start: "rating", {}
tag_start: "stars", {}
tag_start: "description", {}
  text   :   "A schientific fiction"
tag_start: "movie", {"title"=>"Trigun"}
tag_start: "type", {}
  text   :   "Anime, Action"
tag_start: "format", {}
tag_start: "episodes", {}
tag_start: "rating", {}
tag_start: "stars", {}
tag_start: "description", {}
  text   :   "Vash the Stampede!"
tag_start: "movie", {"title"=>"Ishtar"}
tag_start: "type", {}
tag_start: "format", {}
tag_start: "rating", {}
tag_start: "stars", {}
tag_start: "description", {}
  text   :   "Viewable boredom"
```

XPath and Ruby

An alternative way to view XML is XPath. This is a kind of pseudo-language that describes how to locate specific elements and attributes in an XML document, treating that document as a logical ordered tree.

REXML has XPath support via the *XPath* class. It assumes tree-based parsing (document object model) as we have seen above.

```
#!/usr/bin/ruby -w
```

```
require 'rexml/document'
include REXML

xmlfile = File.new("movies.xml")
xmldoc = Document.new(xmlfile)

# Info for the first movie found
movie = XPath.first(xmldoc, "//movie")
p movie

# Print out all the movie types
XPath.each(xmldoc, "//type") { |e| puts e.text }

# Get an array of all of the movie formats.
names = XPath.match(xmldoc, "//format").map {|x| x.text }
p names
```

This will produce the following result:

```
<movie title='Enemy Behind'> ... </>
War, Thriller
Anime, Science Fiction
Anime, Action
Comedy
["DVD", "DVD", "DVD", "VHS"]
```

XSLT and Ruby

There are two XSLT parsers available that Ruby can use. A brief description of each is given here.

Ruby-Sablotron:

This parser is written and maintained by Masayoshi Takahashi. This is written primarily for Linux OS and requires the following libraries:

- Sablot

- Iconv
- Expat

You can find this module at **Ruby-Sablotron**.

XSLT4R

XSLT4R is written by Michael Neumann and can be found at the RAA in the Library section under XML. XSLT4R uses a simple commandline interface, though it can alternatively be used within a third-party application to transform an XML document.

XSLT4R needs XMLScan to operate, which is included within the XSLT4R archive and which is also a 100 percent Ruby module. These modules can be installed using standard Ruby installation method (i.e., ruby install.rb).

XSLT4R has the following syntax:

```
ruby xslt.rb stylesheet.xsl document.xml [arguments]
```

If you want to use XSLT4R from within an application, you can include XSLT and input the parameters you need. Here is the example:

```
require "xslt"

stylesheet = File.readlines("stylesheet.xsl").to_s
xml_doc = File.readlines("document.xml").to_s
arguments = { 'image_dir' => '/....' }

sheet = XSLT::Stylesheet.new( stylesheet, arguments )

# output to StdOut
sheet.apply( xml_doc )

# output to 'str'
str = ""
sheet.output = [ str ]
sheet.apply( xml_doc )
```

Further Reading

- For a complete detail on REXML Parser, please refer to standard documentation for **REXML Parser Documentation**.
- You can download XSLT4R from **RAA Repository**.

28. WEB SERVICES

What is SOAP?

The Simple Object Access Protocol (SOAP), is a cross-platform and language-independent RPC protocol based on XML and, usually (but not necessarily) HTTP.

It uses XML to encode the information that makes the remote procedure call, and HTTP to transport that information across a network from clients to servers and vice versa.

SOAP has several advantages over other technologies like COM, CORBA etc: for example, its relatively cheap deployment and debugging costs, its extensibility and ease-of-use, and the existence of several implementations for different languages and platforms.

Please refer to our simple example **SOAP** to understand it in detail.

This chapter makes you familiar with the SOAP implementation for Ruby (SOAP4R). This is a basic example, so if you need a deep detail, you would need to refer other resources.

Installing SOAP4R

SOAP4R is the SOAP implementation for Ruby developed by Hiroshi Nakamura and can be downloaded from:

NOTE: There may be a great chance that you already have installed this component.

```
Download SOAP
```

If you are aware of **gem** utility then you can use the following command to install SOAP4R and related packages.

```
$ gem install soap4r --include-dependencies
```

If you are working on Windows, then you need to download a zipped file from the above location and need to install it using the standard installation method by running *ruby install.rb*.

Writing SOAP4R Servers

SOAP4R supports two different types of servers:

- CGI/FastCGI based (SOAP::RPC::CGIStub)
- Standalone (SOAP::RPC:StandaloneServer)

This chapter gives detail on writing a stand alone server. The following steps are involved in writing a SOAP server.

Step 1 - Inherit SOAP::RPC::StandaloneServer Class

To implement your own stand alone server you need to write a new class, which will be child of *SOAP::StandaloneServer* as follows:

```
class MyServer < SOAP::RPC::StandaloneServer
  ...............
end
```

NOTE: If you want to write a FastCGI based server then you need to take *SOAP::RPC::CGIStub* as parent class, rest of the procedure will remain the same.

Step 2 - Define Handler Methods

Second step is to write your Web Services methods, which you would like to expose to the outside world.

They can be written as simple Ruby methods. For example, let's write two methods to add two numbers and divide two numbers:

```
class MyServer < SOAP::RPC::StandaloneServer
   ...............

   # Handler methods
   def add(a, b)
      return a + b
   end
   def div(a, b)
      return a / b
   end
end
```

Step 3 - Expose Handler Methods

Next step is to add our defined methods to our server. The *initialize* method is used to expose service methods with one of the two following methods:

```
class MyServer < SOAP::RPC::StandaloneServer
   def initialize(*args)
      add_method(receiver, methodName, *paramArg)
   end
end
```

Here is the description of the parameters:

Paramter	Description
receiver	The object that contains the methodName method. You define the service methods in the same class as the methodDef method, this parameter is *self*.
methodName	The name of the method that is called due to an RPC request.
paramArg	Specifies, when given, the parameter names and parameter modes.

To understand the usage of *inout* or *out* parameters, consider the following service method that takes two parameters (inParam and inoutParam), returns one normal return value (retVal) and two further parameters: *inoutParam* and *outParam*:

```
def aMeth(inParam, inoutParam)
   retVal = inParam + inoutParam
   outParam = inParam . inoutParam
   inoutParam = inParam * inoutParam
   return retVal, inoutParam, outParam
end
```

Now, we can expose this method as follows:

```
add_method(self, 'aMeth', [
    %w(in inParam),
```

```
    %w(inout inoutParam),
    %w(out outParam),
    %w(retval return)
])
```

Step 4 - Start the Server

The final step is to start your server by instantiating one instance of the derived class and calling **start** method.

```
myServer = MyServer.new('ServerName',
                        'urn:ruby:ServiceName', hostname, port)

myServer.start
```

Here is the description of required parameters :

Paramter	Description
ServerName	A server name, you can give what you like most.
urn:ruby:ServiceName	Here *urn:ruby* is constant but you can give a unique *ServiceName* name for this server.
hostname	Specifies the hostname on which this server will listen.
port	An available port number to be used for the web service.

Example

Now, using the above steps, let us write one standalone server:

```
require "soap/rpc/standaloneserver"

begin
   class MyServer < SOAP::RPC::StandaloneServer
```

```
      # Expose our services
      def initialize(*args)
         add_method(self, 'add', 'a', 'b')
         add_method(self, 'div', 'a', 'b')
      end

      # Handler methods
      def add(a, b)
         return a + b
      end
      def div(a, b)
         return a / b
      end
   end
   server = MyServer.new("MyServer",
            'urn:ruby:calculation', 'localhost', 8080)
   trap('INT'){
      server.shutdown
   }
   server.start
rescue => err
   puts err.message
end
```

When executed, this server application starts a standalone SOAP server on *localhost* and listens for requests on *port* 8080. It exposes one service methods, *add* and *div*, which takes two parameters and return the result.

Now, you can run this server in background as follows:

```
$ ruby MyServer.rb&
```

Writing SOAP4R Clients

The *SOAP::RPC::Driver* class provides support for writing SOAP client applications. This chapter describes this class and demonstrate its usage on the basis of an application.

Following is the bare minimum information you would need to call a SOAP service:

- The URL of the SOAP service (SOAP Endpoint URL).
- The namespace of the service methods (Method Namespace URI).
- The names of the service methods and their parameters.

Now, we will write a SOAP client which would call service methods defined in above example, named *add* and *div*.

Here are the main steps to create a SOAP client.

Step 1 - Create a SOAP Driver Instance

We create an instance of *SOAP::RPC::Driver* by calling its new method as follows:

```
SOAP::RPC::Driver.new(endPoint, nameSpace, soapAction)
```

Here is the description of required parameters :

Paramter	Description
endPoint	URL of the SOAP server to connect with.
nameSpace	The namespace to use for all RPCs done with this SOAP::RPC::Driver object.
soapAction	A value for the SOAPAction field of the HTTP header. If *nil* this defaults to the empty string "".

Step 2 - Add Service Methods

To add a SOAP service method to a *SOAP::RPC::Driver*, we can call the following method using *SOAP::RPC::Driver* instance:

```
driver.add_method(name, *paramArg)
```

Here is the description of the parameters:

Paramter	Description
name	The name of the remote web service method.

paramArg	Specifies the names of the remote procedures' parameters.

Step 3 - Invoke SOAP service

The final step is to invoice SOAP service using *SOAP::RPC::Driver* instance as follows:

```
result = driver.serviceMethod(paramArg...)
```

Here *serviceMethod* is the actual web service method and *paramArg...* is the list parameters required to pass in the service method.

Example

Based on the above steps, we will write a SOAP client as follows:

```
#!/usr/bin/ruby -w

require 'soap/rpc/driver'

NAMESPACE = 'urn:ruby:calculation'
URL = 'http://localhost:8080/'

begin
   driver = SOAP::RPC::Driver.new(URL, NAMESPACE)

   # Add remote sevice methods
   driver.add_method('add', 'a', 'b')

   # Call remote service methods
   puts driver.add(20, 30)
rescue => err
   puts err.message
end
```

29. TK GUIDE

Introduction

The standard graphical user interface (GUI) for Ruby is Tk. Tk started out as the GUI for the Tcl scripting language developed by John Ousterhout.

Tk has the unique distinction of being the only cross-platform GUI. Tk runs on Windows, Mac, and Linux and provides a native look-and-feel on each operating system.

The basic component of a Tk-based application is called a widget. A component is also sometimes called a window, since, in Tk, "window" and "widget" are often used interchangeably.

Tk applications follow a widget hierarchy where any number of widgets may be placed within another widget, and those widgets within another widget, ad infinitum. The main widget in a Tk program is referred to as the root widget and can be created by making a new instance of the TkRoot class.

- Most Tk-based applications follow the same cycle: create the widgets, place them in the interface, and finally, bind the events associated with each widget to a method.
- There are three geometry managers; *place, grid* and *pack* that are responsible for controlling the size and location of each of the widgets in the interface.

Installation

The Ruby Tk bindings are distributed with Ruby but Tk is a separate installation. Windows users can download a single click Tk installation from **ActiveState's ActiveTcl**.

Mac and Linux users may not need to install it because there is a great chance that its already installed along with OS but if not, you can download prebuilt packages or get the source from the **Tcl Developer Xchange**.

Simple Tk Application

A typical structure for Ruby/Tk programs is to create the main or **root** window (an instance of TkRoot), add widgets to it to build up the user interface, and then start the main event loop by calling **Tk.mainloop**.

The traditional *Hello, World!* example for Ruby/Tk looks something like this:

```
require 'tk'


root = TkRoot.new { title "Hello, World!" }
TkLabel.new(root) do
   text 'Hello, World!'
   pack { padx 15 ; pady 15; side 'left' }
end
Tk.mainloop
```

Here, after loading the tk extension module, we create a root-level frame using *TkRoot.new*. We then make a *TkLabel* widget as a child of the root frame, setting several options for the label. Finally, we pack the root frame and enter the main GUI event loop.

If you would run this script, it would produce the following result:

Ruby/Tk Widget Classes

There is a list of various Ruby/Tk classes, which can be used to create a desired GUI using Ruby/Tk.

- **TkFrame** Creates and manipulates frame widgets.
- **TkButton** Creates and manipulates button widgets.
- **TkLabel** Creates and manipulates label widgets.
- **TkEntry** Creates and manipulates entry widgets.
- **TkCheckButton** Creates and manipulates checkbutton widgets.
- **TkRadioButton** Creates and manipulates radiobutton widgets.
- **TkListbox** Creates and manipulates listbox widgets.
- **TkComboBox** Creates and manipulates listbox widgets.
- **TkMenu** Creates and manipulates menu widgets.
- **TkMenubutton** Creates and manipulates menubutton widgets.
- **Tk.messageBox** Creates and manipulates a message dialog.

- **TkScrollbar** Creates and manipulates scrollbar widgets.
- **TkCanvas** Creates and manipulates canvas widgets.
- **TkScale** Creates and manipulates scale widgets.
- **TkText** Creates and manipulates text widgets.
- **TkToplevel** Creates and manipulates toplevel widgets.
- **TkSpinbox** Creates and manipulates Spinbox widgets.
- **TkProgressBar** Creates and manipulates Progress Bar widgets.
- **Dialog Box** Creates and manipulates Dialog Box widgets.
- **Tk::Tile::Notebook** Display several windows in limited space with notebook metaphor.
- **Tk::Tile::Paned** Displays a number of subwindows, stacked either vertically or horizontally.
- **Tk::Tile::Separator** Displays a horizontal or vertical separator bar.
- **Ruby/Tk Font, Colors and Images** Understanding Ruby/Tk Fonts, Colors and Images

TkFrame

Description

A *frame* is a widget that displays just as a simple rectangle. Frames are primarily used as a container for other widgets, which are under the control of a geometry manager such as grid.

The only features of a frame are its background color and an optional 3-D border to make the frame appear raised or sunken.

Syntax

Here is a simple syntax to create a Frame Widget:

```
TkFrame.new {
  .....Standard Options....
  .....Widget-specific Options....
}
```

Standard Options

- borderwidth
- highlightbackground
- highlightthickness
- takefocus
- highlightcolor
- relief
- cursor

These options have been described in the previous chapter.

Widget-Specific Options

SN	Options with Description
1	**background** => String This option is the same as the standard **background** option except that its value may also be specified as an undefined value. In this case, the widget will display no background or border, and no colors will be consumed from its colormap for its background and border.
2	**colormap** => String Specifies a colormap to use for the window. The value may be either *new*, in which case a new colormap is created for the window and its children, or the name of another window (which must be on the same screen), in which case the new window will use the colormap from the specified window. If the **colormap** option is not specified, the new window uses the same colormap as its parent.
3	**container** => Boolean The value must be a boolean. If true, it means that this window will be used as a container in which some other application will be embedded. The window will support the appropriate window manager protocols for things like geometry requests. The window should not have any children of its own in this application.
4	**height** => Integer

	Specifies the desired height for the window in pixels or points.
5	**width** => Integer Specifies the desired width for the window in pixels or points.

Event Bindings

When a new frame is created, it has no default event bindings: frames are not intended to be interactive.

Examples

```
require "tk"


f1 = TkFrame.new {
  relief 'sunken'
  borderwidth 3
  background "red"
  padx 15
  pady 20
  pack('side' => 'left')
}
f2 = TkFrame.new {
  relief 'groove'
  borderwidth 1
  background "yellow"
  padx 10
  pady 10
  pack('side' => 'right')
}


TkButton.new(f1) {
  text 'Button1'
  command {print "push button1!!\n"}
  pack('fill' => 'x')
```

```
}
TkButton.new(f1) {
  text 'Button2'
  command {print "push button2!!\n"}
  pack('fill' => 'x')
}
TkButton.new(f2) {
  text 'Quit'
  command 'exit'
  pack('fill' => 'x')
}
Tk.mainloop
```

This will produce the following result:

TkButton

Description

A **button** is very much designed for the user to interact with, and in particular, press to perform some action. A button is a widget that displays a textual string, bitmap or image. If text is displayed, it must all be in a single font, but it can occupy multiple lines on the screen.

A button can display itself in either of three different ways, according to the *state* option. It can be made to appear *raised*, *sunken*, or *flat* and it can be made to flash.

Syntax

Here is a simple syntax to create this widget:

```
TkButton.new(root) {
  .....Standard Options....
  .....Widget-specific Options....
}
```

Standard Options

- activebackground
- activeforeground
- anchor
- background
- bitmap
- borderwidth
- cursor
- disabledforeground
- font
- foreground
- highlightbackground
- highlightcolor
- highlightthickness
- image
- justify
- padx
- pady
- relief
- repeatdelay
- repeatinterval
- takefocus
- text

- textvariable
- underline
- wraplength

These options have been described in the previous chapter.

Widget-Specific Options

SN	Options with Description
1	**command** => String Specifies a Ruby command to associate with the button. This *command* is typically invoked when mouse button 1 is released over the button window. Here you can associate a Ruby method to be executed against mouse click. I have done it in the example given below.
2	**compound** => String Specifies whether the button should display both an image and text, and if so, where the image should be placed relative to the text. Valid values for this option are **bottom**, **center**, **left**, **none**, **right** and **top**. The default value is **none**, meaning that the button will display either an image or text, depending on the values of the*image* and *bitmap* options.
3	**height** => Integer Specifies a desired height for the button.
4	**state** => String Specifies one of three states for the button: *normal, active, or disabled*. In normal state the button is displayed using the *foreground* and *background* options. The active state is typically used when the pointer is over the button. In active state the button is displayed using the *activeforeground* and *activebackground* options. Disabled state means that the button should be insensitive:
5	**width** => Integer Specifies a desired width for the button.

Event Bindings

Ruby/Tk automatically creates class bindings for buttons that give them the following default behavior:

- A button activates whenever the mouse passes over it and deactivates whenever the mouse leaves the button.
- A button's relief is changed to sunken whenever mouse button 1 is pressed over the button, and the relief is restored to its original value when button 1 is later released.
- If mouse button 1 is pressed over a button and later released over the button, the button is invoked. However, if the mouse is not over the button when button 1 is released, then no invocation occurs.
- When a button has the input focus, the space key causes the button to be invoked.

If the button's state is *disabled* then none of the above actions occur: the button is completely non-responsive.

Examples

```
require 'tk'


def myproc
  puts "The user says OK."
  exit
end


root = TkRoot.new
btn_OK = TkButton.new(root) do
  text "OK"
  borderwidth 5
  underline 0
  state "normal"
  cursor "watch"
  font TkFont.new('times 20 bold')
  foreground  "red"
  activebackground "blue"
  relief      "groove"
```

```
  command (proc {myproc})
  pack("side" => "right",  "padx"=> "50", "pady"=> "10")
end
Tk.mainloop
```

This will produce the following result if you will click over this button then ruby method *myproc* would be executed.

TkLabel

Description

A **label** is a widget that displays text or images, typically that the user will just view but not otherwise interact with. Labels are used for such things as identifying controls or other parts of the user interface, providing textual feedback or results, etc.

A label can display a textual string, bitmap or image. If text is displayed, it must all be in a single font, but it can occupy multiple lines on the screen (if it contains newlines or if wrapping occurs because of the *wraplength* option) and one of the characters may optionally be underlined using the *underline* option.

Syntax

Here is a simple syntax to create this widget:

```
TkLabel.new(root) {
  .....Standard Options....
  .....Widget-specific Options....
}
```

Standard Options

- anchor

- background
- bitmap
- borderwidth
- cursor
- font
- foreground
- highlightbackground
- highlightcolor
- highlightthickness
- image
- justify
- padx
- pady
- relief
- takefocus
- text
- textvariable
- underline
- wraplength

These options have been described in the previous chapter.

Widget-Specific Options

SN	Options with Description
1	**height** => Integer Specifies a desired height for the label.
2	**width** => Integer Specifies a desired width for the label.

Event Bindings

When a new label is created, it has no default event bindings: labels are not intended to be interactive.

Examples

```
require 'tk'


$resultsVar = TkVariable.new
root = TkRoot.new
root.title = "Window"
Lbl = TkLabel.new(root) do
  textvariable
  borderwidth 5
  font TkFont.new('times 20 bold')
  foreground  "red"
  relief      "groove"
  pack("side" => "right",  "padx"=> "50", "pady"=> "50")
end


Lbl['textvariable'] = $resultsVar
$resultsVar.value = 'New value to display'


Tk.mainloop
```

This will produce the following result:

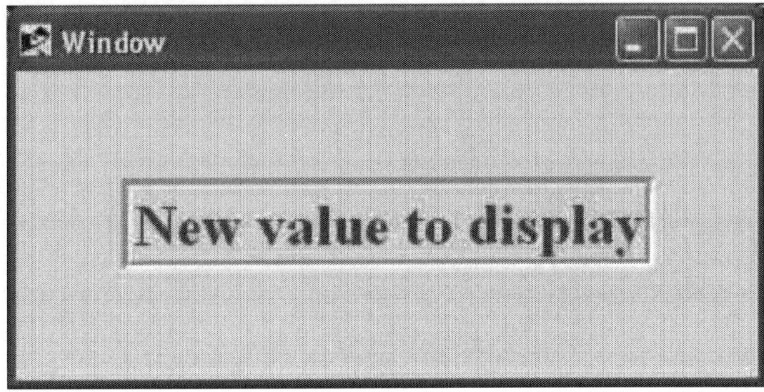

TkEntry

Description

A **Entry** presents the user with a single-line text field that they can use to type in a value. These can be just about anything: their name, a city, a password, social security number, and so on.

Syntax

Here is a simple syntax to create this widget:

```
TkEntry.new{
  .....Standard Options....
  .....Widget-specific Options....
}
```

Standard Options

- background
- borderwidth
- cursor
- exportselection
- font
- foreground
- highlightbackground
- highlightcolor
- highlightthickness
- justify
- relief
- selectbackground
- selectborderwidth
- selectforeground
- takefocus
- textvariable

- xscrollcommand

These options have been described in the previous chapter.

Widget-Specific Options

SN	Options with Description
1	**disabledbackground** => String Specifies the background color to use when the entry is disabled. If this option is the empty string, the normal background color is used.
2	**disabledforeground** => String Specifies the foreground color to use when the entry is disabled. If this option is the empty string, the normal foreground color is used.
3	**readonlybackground** => String Specifies the background color to use when the entry is read-only. If this option is the empty string, the normal background color is used.
4	**show** => String If this option is specified, then the true contents of the entry are not displayed in the window. Instead, each character in the entry's value will be displayed as the first character in the value of this option, such as ``*''. This is useful, for example, if the entry is to be used to enter a password. If characters in the entry are selected and copied elsewhere, the information copied will be what is displayed, not the true contents of the entry.
5	**state** => String Specifies one of three states for the entry: **normal**, **disabled**, or **readonly**. If the entry is **readonly**, then the value may not be changed using widget commands and no insertion cursor will be displayed, even if the input focus is in the widget; the contents of the widget may still be selected. If the entry is **disabled**, the value may not be changed, no insertion cursor will be displayed, the contents will not be selectable, and the entry may be displayed in a different color.
6	**validate** => String Specifies the mode in which validation should operate: **none**, **focus**, **focusin**,**focusout**, **key**, or **all**. It defaults to **none**. When you want

	validation, you must explicitly state which mode you wish to use.
7	**validatecommand** => String Specifies a script to eval when you want to validate the input into the entry widget.
8	**width** => Integer Specifies an integer value indicating the desired width of the entry window, in average-size characters of the widget's font. If the value is less than or equal to zero, the widget picks a size just large enough to hold its current text.

Validation of Entry

We can validate the entered value by setting the *validatecommand* option to a callback, which will be evaluated according to the *validate* option as follows:

- **none:** Default. This means no validation will occur.
- **focus:** validatecommand will be called when the entry receives or loses focus.
- **focusin:** validatecommand will be called when the entry receives focus.
- **focusout:** validatecommand will be called when the entry loses focus.
- **key:** validatecommand will be called when the entry is edited.
- **all:** validatecommand will be called for all above conditions.

Manipulating Entries

The following useful methods are available to manipulate the content of an entry:

- **delete(first, ?last?):** Deletes one or more elements of the entry. First is the index of the first character to delete, and last is the index of the character just after the last one to delete. If last isn't specified it defaults to first+1, i.e. a single character is deleted. This command returns an empty string.
- **get:** Returns the entry's string.
- **icursor(index):** Arrange for the insertion cursor to be displayed just before the character given by index. Returns an empty string.
- **index(index):** Returns the numerical index corresponding to index.

- **insert(index, string):** Insert the characters of string just before the character indicated by index. Returns an empty string.
- **xview(args):** This command is used to query and change the horizontal position of the text in the widget's window.

Event Bindings

Ruby/Tk automatically creates class bindings for entries that give them the following default behavior:

- Clicking mouse button 1 positions the insertion cursor just before the character underneath the mouse cursor, sets the input focus to this widget, and clears any selection in the widget. Dragging with mouse button 1 strokes out a selection between the insertion cursor and the character under the mouse.
- Double-clicking with mouse button 1 selects the word under the mouse and positions the insertion cursor at the beginning of the word. Dragging after a double click will stroke out a selection consisting of whole words.
- Triple-clicking with mouse button 1 selects all of the text in the entry and positions the insertion cursor before the first character.
- The ends of the selection can be adjusted by dragging with mouse button 1 while the Shift key is down; this will adjust the end of the selection that was nearest to the mouse cursor when button 1 was pressed. If the button is double-clicked before dragging then the selection will be adjusted in units of whole words.
- Clicking mouse button 1 with the Control key down will position the insertion cursor in the entry without affecting the selection.
- If any normal printing characters are typed in an entry, they are inserted at the point of the insertion cursor.
- The view in the entry can be adjusted by dragging with mouse button 2. If mouse button 2 is clicked without moving the mouse, the selection is copied into the entry at the position of the insertion cursor.
- If the mouse is dragged out of the entry on the left or right sides while button 1 is pressed, the entry will automatically scroll to make more text visible (if there is more text off-screen on the side where the mouse left the window).
- The Left and Right keys move the insertion cursor one character to the left or right; they also clear any selection in the entry and set the selection anchor. If Left or Right is typed with the Shift key down, then the insertion cursor moves and the selection is extended to include the new character. Control-Left and Control-Right move the insertion cursor by words, and Control-Shift-Left and Control-Shift-Right move the

insertion cursor by words and also extend the selection. Control-b and Control-f behave the same as Left and Right, respectively. Meta-b and Meta-f behave the same as Control-Left and Control-Right, respectively.

- The Home key, or Control-a, will move the insertion cursor to the beginning of the entry and clear any selection in the entry. Shift-Home moves the insertion cursor to the beginning of the entry and also extends the selection to that point.
- The End key, or Control-e, will move the insertion cursor to the end of the entry and clear any selection in the entry. Shift-End moves the cursor to the end and extends the selection to that point.
- The Select key and Control-Space set the selection anchor to the position of the insertion cursor. They don't affect the current selection. Shift-Select and Control-Shift-Space adjust the selection to the current position of the insertion cursor, selecting from the anchor to the insertion cursor if there was not any selection previously.
- Control-/ selects all the text in the entry.
- Control-\ clears any selection in the entry.
- The F16 key (labelled Copy on many Sun workstations) or Meta-w copies the selection in the widget to the clipboard, if there is a selection.
- The F20 key (labelled Cut on many Sun workstations) or Control-w copies the selection in the widget to the clipboard and deletes the selection. If there is no selection in the widget then these keys have no effect.
- The F18 key (labelled Paste on many Sun workstations) or Control-y inserts the contents of the clipboard at the position of the insertion cursor.
- The Delete key deletes the selection, if there is one in the entry. If there is no selection, it deletes the character to the right of the insertion cursor.
- The BackSpace key and Control-h delete the selection, if there is one in the entry. If there is no selection, it deletes the character to the left of the insertion cursor.
- Control-d deletes the character to the right of the insertion cursor.
- Meta-d deletes the word to the right of the insertion cursor.
- Control-k deletes all the characters to the right of the insertion cursor.
- Control-w deletes the word to the left of the insertion cursor.
- Control-t reverses the order of the two characters to the right of the insertion cursor.

If the entry is disabled using the **state** option, then the entry's view can still be adjusted and text in the entry can still be selected, but no insertion cursor will be displayed and no text modifications will take place.

Examples

```
require 'tk'

root = TkRoot.new
root.title = "Window"

entry1 = TkEntry.new(root)
entry2 = TkEntry.new(root) do
     show '*'
end

variable1 = TkVariable.new
variable2 = TkVariable.new
entry1.textvariable = variable1
entry2.textvariable = variable2
variable1.value = "Enter any text value"
variable2.value = "Enter any confidential value"

entry1.place('height' => 25,
            'width'  => 150,
            'x'      => 10,
            'y'      => 10)

entry2.place('height' => 25,
            'width'  => 150,
            'x'      => 10,
            'y'      => 40)

Tk.mainloop
```

This will produce the following result:

TkCheckButton

Description

A **Checkbutton** is like a regular button, except that not only can the user press it, which will invoke a command callback, but it also holds a binary value of some kind (i.e., a toggle). Checkbuttons are used all the time when a user is asked to choose between, e.g., two different values for an option.

A checkbutton can display a textual string, bitmap or image. If text is displayed, it must all be in a single font, but it can occupy multiple lines on the screen (if it contains newlines or if wrapping occurs because of the *wraplength* option) and one of the characters may optionally be underlined using the *underline* option.

A checkbutton has all of the behavior of a simple button, including the following: it can display itself in either of three different ways, according to the state option; it can be made to appear raised, sunken, or flat; it can be made to flash; and it invokes a Tcl command whenever mouse button 1 is clicked over the checkbutton.

Syntax

Here is a simple syntax to create this widget:

```
TkCheckButton.new(root) {
  .....Standard Options....
  .....Widget-specific Options....
}
```

Standard Options

- activebackground
- activeforeground
- anchor

- background
- bitmap
- borderwidth
- compound
- cursor
- disabledforeground
- font
- foreground
- highlightbackground
- highlightcolor
- highlightthickness
- image
- justify
- padx
- pady
- relief
- takefocus
- text
- textvariable
- underline
- wraplength

These options have been described in the previous chapter.

Widget-Specific Options

SN	Options with Description
1	**command** => String Specifies a Ruby command to associate with the button. This command is typically invoked when mouse button 1 is released over the button window. Here you can associate a Ruby method to be executed against mouse click. Built in function which can be called using command option:

	deselect: Deselects the checkbutton and sets the associated variable to its "off" value. **flash:** Flashes the checkbutton. This is accomplished by redisplaying the checkbutton several times, alternating between active and normal colors. **select:** Selects the checkbutton and sets the associated variable to its "on" value. **toggle:** Toggles the selection state of the button, redisplaying it and modifying its associated variable to reflect the new state.
2	**height** => Integer Specifies a desired height for the button.
3	**indicatoron** => Boolean Specifies whether or not the indicator should be drawn. Must be a proper boolean value. If *false*, the *relief* option is ignored and the widget's relief is always sunken if the widget is selected and raised otherwise.
4	**offvalue** => Integer Specifies value to store in the button's associated variable whenever this button is deselected. Defaults to 0.
5	**onvalue** => Integer Specifies value to store in the button's associated variable whenever this button is selected. Defaults to 1.
6	**selectcolor** => String Specifies a background color to use when the button is selected. If *indicatoron* is true, then the color applies to the indicator. If *indicatoron* is false, this color is used as the background for the entire widget, in place of *background* or*activebackground*, whenever the widget is selected.
7	**selectimage** => Image Specifies an image to display (in place of the image option) when the checkbutton is selected. This option is ignored unless the image option has been specified.
8	**state** => String

	Specifies one of three states for the button: *normal, active, or disabled*. In normal state the button is displayed using the *foreground* and *background* options. The active state is typically used when the pointer is over the button. In active state the button is displayed using the *activeforeground* and *activebackground* options. Disabled state means that the button should be insensitive.
9	**variable** => Variable Specifies name of global variable to set to indicate whether or not this button is selected. Defaults to the name of the button within its parent.
10	**width** => Integer Specifies a desired width for the button.

Event Bindings

Ruby/Tk automatically creates class bindings for checkbuttons that give them the following default behavior:

- A checkbutton activates whenever the mouse passes over it and deactivates whenever the mouse leaves the checkbutton.
- When mouse button 1 is pressed over a checkbutton it is invoked (its selection state toggles and the command associated with the button is invoked, if there is one).
- When a checkbutton has the input focus, the space key causes the checkbutton to be invoked.

If the checkbutton's state is *disabled* then none of the above actions occur: the checkbutton is completely non-responsive.

Examples

```
require 'tk'


root = TkRoot.new
root.title = "Window"


CkhButton1 = TkCheckButton.new(root) do
  text "Orange"
  indicatoron "true"
```

```
  background  "red"
  relief "groove"
  height 2
  width 2
  onvalue 'Orange'
  place('height' => 25,'width'  => 100, 'x' => 10, 'y'=> 10)
  command (select)
end
CkhButton2 = TkCheckButton.new(root) do
  text "Banana"
  background  "red"
  relief "groove"
  height 2
  width 2
  onvalue 'Banana'
  place('height' => 25,'width' => 100, 'x' => 10, 'y'=> 40)
end
Tk.mainloop
```

This will produce the following result:

TkRadioButton

Description

A **radiobutton** lets you choose between one of a number of mutually exclusive choices, unlike a checkbutton, it is not limited to just two choices. Radiobuttons are always used together in a set and are good when the number of choices is fairly small.

A radiobutton can display a textual string, bitmap or image and a diamond or circle called an *indicator*. If text is displayed, it must all be in a single font, but it can occupy multiple lines on the screen (if it contains newlines or if wrapping occurs because of the *wraplength* option) and one of the characters may optionally be underlined using the *underline* option.

A checkbutton has all of the behavior of a simple button, including the following: it can display itself in either of three different ways, according to the state option; it can be made to appear raised, sunken, or flat; it can be made to flash; and it invokes a Tcl command whenever mouse button 1 is clicked over the checkbutton.

Syntax

Here is a simple syntax to create this widget:

```
TkRadiobutton.new(root) {
  .....Standard Options....
  .....Widget-specific Options....
}
```

Standard Options

- activebackground
- activeforeground
- anchor
- background
- bitmap
- borderwidth
- compound
- cursor
- disabledforeground
- font
- foreground
- highlightbackground
- highlightcolor
- highlightthickness

- image
- justify
- padx
- pady
- relief
- takefocus
- text
- textvariable
- underline
- wraplength

These options have been described in the previous chapter.

Widget-Specific Options

SN	Options with Description
1	**command** => String Specifies a Ruby command to associate with the button. This command is typically invoked when mouse button 1 is released over the button window. Here you can associate a Ruby method to be executed against mouse click. Built in function which can be called using command option: **deselect:** Deselects the checkbutton and sets the associated variable to its "off" value. **flash:** Flashes the checkbutton. This is accomplished by redisplaying the checkbutton several times, alternating between active and normal colors. **select:** Selects the checkbutton and sets the associated variable to its "on" value. **toggle:** Toggles the selection state of the button, redisplaying it and modifying its associated variable to reflect the new state.
2	**height** => Integer Specifies a desired height for the button.
3	**indicatoron** => Boolean Specifies whether or not the indicator should be drawn. Must be a proper

	boolean value. If *false*, the *relief* option is ignored and the widget's relief is always sunken if the widget is selected and raised otherwise.
4	**offvalue** => Integer Specifies value to store in the button's associated variable whenever this button is deselected. Defaults to 0.
5	**onvalue** => Integer Specifies value to store in the button's associated variable whenever this button is selected. Defaults to 1.
6	**selectcolor** => String Specifies a background color to use when the button is selected. If *indicatoron* is true then the color applicies to the indicator. If *indicatoron* is false, this color is used as the background for the entire widget, in place of *background* or*activebackground*, whenever the widget is selected.
7	**selectimage** => Image Specifies an image to display (in place of the image option) when the checkbutton is selected. This option is ignored unless the image option has been specified.
8	**state** => String Specifies one of three states for the button: *normal, active, or disabled*. In normal state the button is displayed using the *foreground* and *background* options. The active state is typically used when the pointer is over the button. In active state the button is displayed using the *activeforeground* and *activebackground* options. Disabled state means that the button should be insensitive.
9	**variable** => Variable Specifies name of global variable to set to indicate whether or not this button is selected. Defaults to the name of the button within its parent.
10	**width** => Integer Specifies a desired width for the button.

Event Bindings

Ruby/Tk automatically creates class bindings for Radiobutton that gives them the following default behavior:

- A Radiobutton activates whenever the mouse passes over it and deactivates whenever the mouse leaves the radiobutton.
- When mouse button 1 is pressed over a radiobutton it is invoked (its selection state toggles and the command associated with the button is invoked, if there is one).
- When a radiobutton has the input focus, the space key causes the checkbutton to be invoked.

If the radiobutton's state is *disabled* then none of the above actions occur: the radiobutton is completely non-responsive.

Examples

```
require "tk"


def print_v
  print $v, "\n"
end


$v = TkVariable.new


TkRadioButton.new {
  text 'top'
  variable $v
  value 'top'
  anchor 'w'
  pack('side' => 'top', 'fill' => 'x')
}
TkRadioButton.new {
  text 'middle'
  variable $v
  value 'middle'
  anchor 'w'
  pack('side' => 'top', 'fill' => 'x')
```

```
}
TkRadioButton.new {
  text 'bottom'
  variable $v
  value 'bottom'
  anchor 'w'
  pack('side' => 'top', 'fill' => 'x')
}

TkButton.new {
  text 'Quit'
  command 'exit'
  pack
}

Tk.root.bind "1", proc{print_v}

Tk.mainloop
```

This will produce the following result:

TkListbox

Description

A **radiobutton** displays a list of single-line text items, usually lengthy, and allows the user to browse through the list, selecting one or more.

When first created, a new listbox has no elements. Elements may be added or deleted using provided methods. In addition, one or more elements may be selected from the listed items.

It is not necessary for all the elements to be displayed in the listbox window at once. Listboxes allow scrolling in both directions using the standard *xscrollcommand* and *yscrollcommand* options.

Syntax

Here is a simple syntax to create this widget:

```
TkListbox.new(root) {
  .....Standard Options....
  .....Widget-specific Options....
}
```

Standard Options

- background
- borderwidth
- cursor
- disabledforeground
- exportselection
- font
- foreground
- hight
- highlightbackground
- highlightcolor
- highlightthickness
- offset
- relief
- selectbackground
- selectborderwidth
- selectforeground
- setgrid
- takefocus
- tile

- width
- xscrollcommand
- yscrollcommand

These options have been described in the previous chapter.

Widget-Specific Options

SN	Options with Description
1	**activestyle** => String Specifies the style in which to draw the active element. This must be one of **dotbox**,**none** or **underline**. The default is **underline**.
2	**height** => Integer Specifies the desired height for the window, in lines. If zero or less, then the desired height for the window is made just large enough to hold all the elements in the listbox.
3	**listvariable** => Variable Specifies the reference of a variable. The value of the variable is an array to be displayed inside the widget; if the variable value changes then the widget will automatically update itself to reflect the new value.
4	**selectmode** => String Specifies one of several styles for manipulating the selection. The value of the option may be arbitrary, but the default bindings expect it to be either **single**,**browse**, **multiple**, or **extended**; the default value is **browse**.
5	**state** => String Specifies one of two states for the listbox: **normal** or **disabled**. If the listbox is disabled then items may not be inserted or deleted.
6	**width** => Integer Specifies the desired width for the window in characters. If the font doesn't have a uniform width then the width of the character "0" is used in translating from character units to screen units. If zero or less, then the desired width for the window is made just large enough to hold all the

	elements in the listbox.

Manipulating the Listbox Items

There are various ways to play with a list box:

- The **listvariable:** variable allows you to link a variable (which must hold a list) to the listbox. Each element of this list is a string representing one item in the listbox. So to add, remove, or rearrange items in the listbox, you can simply manipulate this variable as you would any other list.
- The **insert idx item ?item... ?** method is used to add one or more items to the list; "idx" is a 0-based index indicating the position of the item before which the item(s) should be added; specify "end" to put the new items at the end of the list.
- The **delete first ?last?** method is used to delete one or more items from the list; "first" and "last" are indices as per the "insert" method.
- The **get first ?last?** method returns the contents of a single item at the given position, or a list of the items between "first" and "last".
- The **size** method returns the number of items in the list.
- The **curselection** method is used to find out which item or items in the listbox the user has currently selected. This will return the list of indices of all items currently selected; this may be an empty list.
- The **selection clear first ?last?** method is used to deselect either a single item, or any within the range of indices specified.
- The **selection set first ?last?** method is used to select an item, or all items in a range.
- The **xview(args)** method is used to query and change the horizontal position of the information in the widget's window.
- The **yview(?args?)** method is used to query and change the vertical position of the text in the widget's window.

Indices

Many of the methods for listboxes take one or more indices as arguments. An index specifies a particular element of the listbox, in any of the following ways:

- **number:** A decimal number giving the position of the desired character within the text item. 0 refers to the first character, 1 to the next character, and so on.

- **active:** Indicates the element that has the location cursor. This element will be displayed with an underline when the listbox has the keyboard focus, and it is specified with the activate method.
- **anchor:** Indicates the anchor point for the selection, which is set with the selection anchor method.
- **end:** Indicates the end of the listbox. For some commands this means just after the last element; for other commands it means the last element.

Event Bindings

Ruby/Tk creates class bindings for listboxes that give them Motif-like behavior. Much of the behavior of a listbox is determined by its *selectmode* option, which selects one of four ways of dealing with the selection.

- If the selection mode is **single** or **browse**, at most one element can be selected in the listbox at once. In both modes, clicking button 1 on an element selects it and deselects any other selected item. In **browse** mode, it is also possible to drag the selection with button 1.
- If the selection mode is **multiple** or **extended**, any number of elements may be selected at once, including discontiguous ranges. In **multiple** mode, clicking button 1 on an element toggles its selection state without affecting any other elements. In **extended** mode, pressing button 1 on an element selects it, deselects everything else, and sets the anchor to the element under the mouse; dragging the mouse with button 1 down extends the selection to include all the elements between the anchor and the element under the mouse, inclusive.

Most people will probably want to use the *browse* mode for single selections and the *extended* mode for multiple selections; the other modes appear to be useful only in special situations.

In addition to the above behavior, there are many other additional behaviors associated with a listbox, which are not covered in this example:

Example 1

```
require "tk"


root = TkRoot.new
root.title = "Window"
list = TkListbox.new(root) do
```

```
  width 20
  height 10
  setgrid 1
  selectmode 'multiple'
  pack('fill' => 'x')
end

list.insert 0, "yellow", "gray", "green",
  "blue", "red", "black", "white", "cyan",
  "pink", "yellow", "orange", "gray"

Tk.mainloop
```

This will produce the following result:

Example 2

Following is the example using *listvariable* option to populate list items:

```
require "tk"

$names = %w{ yellow gray green
              blue red black white cyan
              pink yellow orange gray}
$colornames = TkVariable.new($names)

root = TkRoot.new
root.title = "Window"
```

```
list = TkListbox.new(root) do
  width 20
  height 10
  setgrid 1
  listvariable $colornames
  pack('fill' => 'x')
end

Tk.mainloop
```

This will produce the following result:

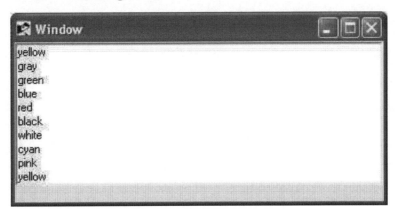

Example 3

Following example explains how to use *TkScrollbar* widget along with list box.

```
require "tk"

$names = %w{ yellow gray green
              blue red black white cyan
              pink yellow orange gray}
$colornames = TkVariable.new($names)

root = TkRoot.new
root.title = "Window"

list = TkListbox.new(root) do
```

```
  listvariable $colornames
  pack('fill' => 'x')
end

list.place('height' => 150,
           'width'  => 100,
           'x'      => 10,
           'y'      => 10)

scroll = TkScrollbar.new(root) do
    orient 'vertical'
    place('height' => 150, 'x' => 110)
end

list.yscrollcommand(proc { |*args|
  scroll.set(*args)
})

scroll.command(proc { |*args|
  list.yview(*args)
})

Tk.mainloop
```

This will produce the following result:

TkComboBox

Description

A **Combobox** combines an entry with a list of choices available to the user. This lets them either choose from a set of values you've provided (e.g., typical settings), but also put in their own value.

Syntax

Here is a simple syntax to create this widget:

```
Tk::BWidget::ComboBox.new(root){
  .....Options....
}
```

Options

Combobox combines the options related to *TkEntry* and *TkListbox* widgets.

Event Bindings

Combobox inherits event bindings from *TkEntry* and *TkListbox* widgets.

Examples

```
require 'tk'
require 'tkextlib/bwidget'

root = TkRoot.new
root.title = "Window"
```

```
combobox = Tk::BWidget::ComboBox.new(root)
combobox.values = [1, 2, 3, 4]
combobox.place('height' => 25,
               'width'  => 100,
               'x'      => 10,
               'y'      => 10)

Tk.mainloop
```

This will produce the following result:

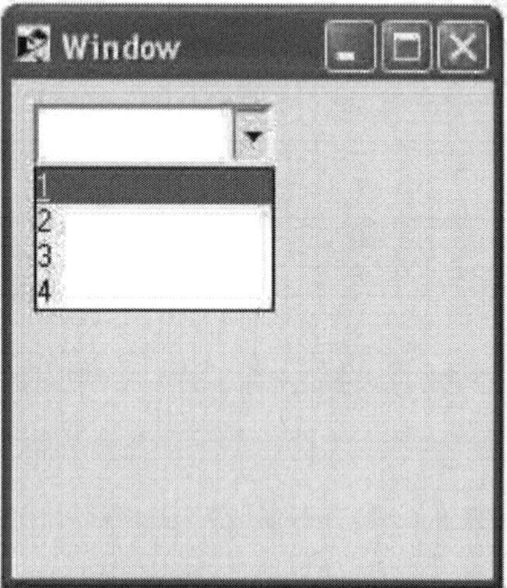

TkMenu

Description

A **menu** is a widget that displays a collection of one-line entries arranged in one or more columns. There exist several different types of entries, each with different properties. Entries of different types may be combined in a single menu. Menu entries are not the same as entry widgets. In fact, menu entries are not even distinct widgets; the entire menu is one widget.

When first created, a new listbox has no elements. Elements may be added or deleted using provided methods. In addition, one or more elements may be selected from the listed items.

It is not necessary for all the elements to be displayed in the listbox window at once. Listboxes allow scrolling in both directions using the standard *xscrollcommand* and *yscrollcommand* options.

Syntax

Here is a simple syntax to create this widget:

```
TkMenu.new(root) {
  .....Standard Options....
  .....Widget-specific Options....
}
```

Standard Options

- activebackground
- background
- disabledforeground
- relief
- activeborderwidth
- borderwidth
- font
- takefocus
- activeforeground
- cursor
- foreground

These options have been described in the previous chapter.

Widget-Specific Options

SN	Options with Description
1	**postcommand** => String If this option is specified then it provides a callback to execute each time the menu is posted. The callback is invoked by the post method before posting the menu.
2	**selectcolor** => String For menu entries that are check buttons or radio buttons, this option specifies the color to display in the indicator when the check button or

	radio button is selected.
3	**tearoff** => Integer This option must have a proper boolean value, which specifies whether or not the menu should include a tear-off entry at the top. If so, it will exist as entry 0 of the menu and the other entries will number starting at 1. The default menu bindings arrange for the menu to be torn off when the tear-off entry is invoked.
4	**tearoffcommand** => String If this option has a non-empty value, then it specifies a Ruby/Tk callback to invoke whenever the menu is torn off. The actual command will consist of the value of this option, followed by a space, followed by the name of the menu window, followed by a space, followed by the name of the name of the torn off menu window. For example, if the option's is "a b" and menu .x.y is torn off to create a new menu .x.tearoff1, then the command "a b .x.y .x.tearoff1" will be invoked.
5	**title** => String The string will be used to title the window created when this menu is torn off. If the title is NULL, then the window will have the title of the menubutton or the text of the cascade item from which this menu was invoked.
6	**type** => String This option can be one of **menubar**,**tearoff**, or **normal**, and is set when the menu is created.

Manipulating the Menus

There are various ways to play with a Menus:

- The **activate(index)** method is used to change the state of the entry indicated by*index* to **active** and redisplay it using its active colors.
- The **add(type, ?option, value, option, value, ...?)** method is used to add a new entry to the bottom of the menu. The new entry's type is given by *type* and must be one of **cascade**, **checkbutton**, **command**, **radiobutton**, or **separator**, or a unique abbreviation of one of the above.

- The **delete(index1?, index2?)** method is used to delete all of the menu entries between *index1* and *index2* inclusive. If *index2* is omitted then it defaults to*index1*.
- The **index(index)** method returns the numerical index corresponding to *index*, or**none** if *index* was specified as **none**.
- The **insert(index, type?, option=>value, ...?)** method is same as the **add** method except that it inserts the new entry just before the entry given by *index*, instead of appending to the end of the menu. The *type*, *option*, and *value* arguments have the same interpretation as for the **add** widget method.
- The **invoke(index)** method is used to invoke the action of the menu entry.
- The **post(x, y)** method is used to arrange for the menu to be displayed on the screen at the root-window coordinates given by x and y.
- The **postcascade(index)** method posts the submenu associated with the cascade entry given by *index*, and unposts any previously posted submenu.
- The **type(index)** method returns the type of the menu entry given by *index*. This is the *type* argument passed to the **add** widget method when the entry was created, such as **command** or **separator**, or **tearoff** for a tear-off entry.
- The **unpost** method unmaps the window so that it is no longer displayed. If a lower-level cascaded menu is posted, unpost that menu. Returns an empty string.
- The **yposition(index)** method returns a decimal string giving the y-coordinate within the menu window of the topmost pixel in the entry specified by *index*.

Menu Configuration

The default bindings support four different ways of using menus:

- **Pulldown Menus:** This is the most common case. You create one menubutton widget for each top-level menu, and typically you arrange a series of menubuttons in a row in a menubar window. You also create the top-level menus and any cascaded submenus, and tie them together with *menu* options in **menubuttons** and cascade menu entries.
- **Popup Menus:** Popup menus typically post in response to a mouse button press or keystroke. You create the popup menus and any cascaded submenus, then you call the **Popup** method at the appropriate time to post the top-level menu.

- **Option Menus:** An option menu consists of a menubutton with an associated menu that allows you to select one of several values. The current value is displayed in the menubutton and is also stored in a global variable. Use the **Optionmenu** class to create option menubuttons and their menus.
- **Torn-off Menus:** You create a torn-off menu by invoking the tear-off entry at the top of an existing menu. The default bindings will create a new menu that is a copy of the original menu and leave it permanently posted as a top-level window. The torn-off menu behaves just the same as the original menu.

Event Bindings

Ruby/Tk automatically creates class bindings for menus that give them the following default behavior:

- When the mouse enters a menu, the entry underneath the mouse cursor activates; as the mouse moves around the menu, the active entry changes to track the mouse.
- When the mouse leaves a menu all of the entries in the menu deactivate, except in the special case where the mouse moves from a menu to a cascaded submenu.
- When a button is released over a menu, the active entry (if any) is invoked. The menu also unposts unless it is a torn-off menu.
- The Space and Return keys invoke the active entry and unpost the menu.
- If any of the entries in a menu have letters underlined with **underline** option, then pressing one of the underlined letters (or its upper-case or lower-case equivalent) invokes that entry and unposts the menu.
- The Escape key aborts a menu selection in progress without invoking any entry. It also unposts the menu unless it is a torn-off menu.
- The Up and Down keys activate the next higher or lower entry in the menu. When one end of the menu is reached, the active entry wraps around to the other end.
- The Left key moves to the next menu to the left. If the current menu is a cascaded submenu, then the submenu is unposted and the current menu entry becomes the cascade entry in the parent. If the current menu is a top-level menu posted from a menubutton, then the current menubutton is unposted and the next menubutton to the left is posted. Otherwise the key has no effect. The left-right order of menubuttons is determined by their stacking order: Tk assumes that the lowest menubutton (which by default is the first one created) is on the left.

- The Right key moves to the next menu to the right. If the current entry is a cascade entry, then the submenu is posted and the current menu entry becomes the first entry in the submenu. Otherwise, if the current menu was posted from a menubutton, then the current menubutton is unposted and the next menubutton to the right is posted.

Disabled menu entries are non-responsive. They don't activate and ignore the mouse button presses and releases.

Examples

```
require "tk"


root = TkRoot.new
root.title = "Window"



menu_click = Proc.new {
  Tk.messageBox(
    'type'    => "ok",
    'icon'    => "info",
    'title'   => "Title",
    'message' => "Message"
  )
}

file_menu = TkMenu.new(root)

file_menu.add('command',
              'label'     => "New...",
              'command'   => menu_click,
              'underline' => 0)
file_menu.add('command',
              'label'     => "Open...",
              'command'   => menu_click,
              'underline' => 0)
file_menu.add('command',
```

```
               'label'     => "Close",
               'command'   => menu_click,
               'underline' => 0)
file_menu.add('separator')
file_menu.add('command',
               'label'     => "Save",
               'command'   => menu_click,
               'underline' => 0)
file_menu.add('command',
               'label'     => "Save As...",
               'command'   => menu_click,
               'underline' => 5)
file_menu.add('separator')
file_menu.add('command',
               'label'     => "Exit",
               'command'   => menu_click,
               'underline' => 3)

menu_bar = TkMenu.new
menu_bar.add('cascade',
              'menu'  => file_menu,
              'label' => "File")

root.menu(menu_bar)

Tk.mainloop
```

This will produce the following result:

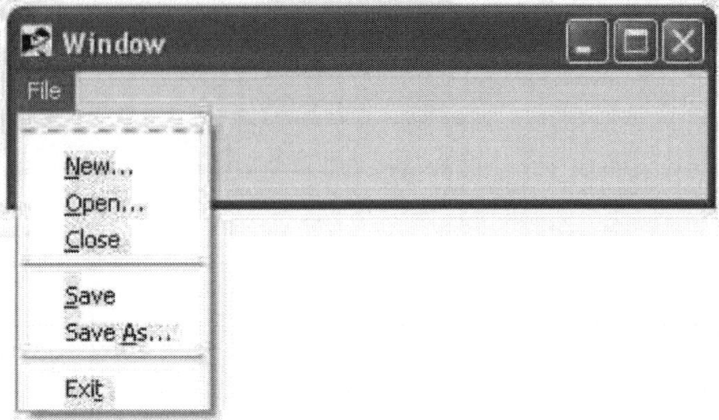

TkMenubutton

Description

A **menubutton** is a widget that displays a textual string, bitmap, or image and is associated with a menu widget. If text is displayed, it must all be in a single font, but it can occupy multiple lines on the screen (if it contains newlines or if wrapping occurs because of the *wraplength* option) and one of the characters may optionally be underlined using the underline option.

In normal usage, pressing mouse button 1 over the menubutton causes the associated menu to be posted just underneath the menubutton. If the mouse is moved over the menu before releasing the mouse button, the button release causes the underlying menu entry to be invoked. When the button is released, the menu is unposted.

Menubuttons are typically organized into groups called menu bars that allow scanning: if the mouse button is pressed over one menubutton and the mouse is moved over another menubutton in the same menu bar without releasing the mouse button, then the menu of the first menubutton is unposted and the menu of the new menubutton is posted instead.

Syntax

Here is a simple syntax to create this widget:

```
TkMenubutton.new(root) {
  .....Standard Options....
  .....Widget-specific Options....
}
```

Standard Options

- activebackground
- cursor
- highlightthickness
- takefocus
- activeforeground
- disabledforeground
- image
- text
- anchor
- font
- justify
- textvariable
- background
- foreground
- padx
- underline
- bitmap
- highlightbackground
- pady
- wraplength
- borderwidth
- highlightcolor
- relief

These options have been described in previous chapter.

Widget-Specific Options

SN	Options with Description
1	**compound** => String

	Specifies whether the button should display both an image and text, and if so, where the image should be placed relative to the text. Valid values for this option are **bottom**, **center**, **left**, **none**, **right** and **top**. The default value is **none**, meaning that the button will display either an image or text, depending on the values of the *image* and *bitmap* options.
2	**direction** => String Specifies where the menu is going to be popup up. **above** tries to pop the menu above the menubutton. **below** tries to pop the menu below the menubutton. **Left** tries to pop the menu to the left of the menubutton. **right** tries to pop the menu to the right of the menu button. **flush** pops the menu directly over the menubutton.
3	**height** => Integer Specifies a desired height for the menubutton.
4	**indicatoron** => Boolean The value must be a proper boolean value. If it is true, then a small indicator rectangle will be displayed on the right side of the menubutton and the default menu bindings will treat this as an option menubutton. If false then no indicator will be displayed.
5	**menu** => String Specifies the path name of the menu associated with this menubutton. The menu must be a child of the menubutton.
6	**state** => String Specifies one of three states for the menubutton: **normal**, **active**, or **disabled**. In normal state the menubutton is displayed using the **foreground** and **background** options.
7	**width** => Integer Specifies a desired width for the menubutton.

Event Bindings

Ruby/Tk automatically creates class bindings for menubuttons that give them the following default behavior:

- A menubutton activates whenever the mouse passes over it and deactivates whenever the mouse leaves it.
- Pressing mouse button 1 over a menubutton posts the menubutton: its relief changes to raised and its associated menu is posted under the menubutton. If the mouse is dragged down into the menu with the button still down, and if the mouse button is then released over an entry in the menu, the menubutton is unposted and the menu entry is invoked.
- If button 1 is pressed over a menubutton and then released over that menubutton, the menubutton stays posted: you can still move the mouse over the menu and click button 1 on an entry to invoke it. Once a menu entry has been invoked, the menubutton unposts itself.
- If button 1 is pressed over a menubutton and then dragged over some other menubutton, the original menubutton unposts itself and the new menubutton posts.
- If button 1 is pressed over a menubutton and released outside any menubutton or menu, the menubutton unposts without invoking any menu entry.
- When a menubutton is posted, its associated menu claims the input focus to allow keyboard traversal of the menu and its submenus.
- If the underline option has been specified for a menubutton then keyboard traversal may be used to post the menubutton: Alt+x, where x is the underlined character (or its lower-case or upper-case equivalent), may be typed in any window under the menubutton's toplevel to post the menubutton.
- The F10 key may be typed in any window to post the first menubutton under its toplevel window that isn't disabled.
- If a menubutton has the input focus, the space and return keys post the menubutton.

If the menubutton's state is **disabled** then none of the above actions occur: the menubutton is completely non-responsive.

Examples

```
require "tk"


mbar = TkFrame.new {
  relief 'raised'
  borderwidth 2
}
```

```
mbar.pack('fill' => 'x')


TkMenubutton.new(mbar) {|mb|
  text "File"
  underline 0
  menu TkMenu.new(mb) {
    add 'command', 'label' => 'New...', 'underline' => 0,
       'command' => proc {print "opening new file\n"}
    add 'command', 'label' => 'Quit',
       'underline' => 0, 'command' => proc{exit}
  }
  pack('side' => 'left', 'padx' => '1m')
}


TkMenubutton.new(mbar) {|mb|
  text "Help"
  underline 0
  menu TkMenu.new(mb) {
    add 'command', 'label' => 'About', 'underline' => 0,
       'command' => proc {print "This is menu example.\n"}
  }
  pack('side' => 'left', 'padx' => '1m')
}


Tk.mainloop
```

This will produce the following result:

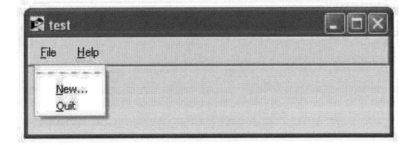

Tk.messageBox

Standard Options

NA

Widget-Specific Options

SN	Options with Description
1	**icon** => String Specify the icon of the messageBox. Valid values are **error**, **info**, **question**, or**warning**.
2	**type** => String Specify the type of the messageBox. Valid values are **abortretryignore**, **ok**,**okcancel**, **retrycancel**, **yesno**, or **yesnocancel**. The type determines the buttons to be shown.
3	**default** => String Specify the default button. This must be one of **abort**, **retry**, **ignore**, **ok**, **cancel**,**yes**, or **no**, depending on the type of the messageBox previously specified.
4	**detail** => String Specify text for the detail region of the messageBox.
5	**message** => String Specify the message text of the messageBox.
6	**title** => String Specify the title of the messageBox.

Event Bindings

NA

Examples

```
require 'tk'

root = TkRoot.new
root.title = "Window"

msgBox = Tk.messageBox(
  'type'    => "ok",
  'icon'    => "info",
  'title'   => "This is title",
  'message' => "This is message"
)
Tk.mainloop
```

This will produce the following result:

TkScrollbar

Description

A **Scrollbar** helps the user to see all parts of another widget, whose content is typically much larger than what can be shown in the available screen space.

A scrollbar displays two arrows, one at each end of the scrollbar, and a slider in the middle portion of the scrollbar. The position and size of the slider indicate which portion of the document is visible in the associated window.

Syntax

Here is a simple syntax to create this widget:

```
TkScrollbar.new{
   .....Standard Options....
   .....Widget-specific Options....
}
```

Standard Options

- activebackground
- highlightbackground
- orient
- takefocus
- background
- highlightcolor
- relief
- troughcolor
- borderwidth
- highlightthickness
- repeatdelay
- cursor
- jump
- repeatinterval

These options have been described in the previous chapter.

Widget-Specific Options

SN	Options with Description
1	**activerelief** => String Specifies the *relief* to use when displaying the element that is active, if any. Elements other than the active element are always displayed with a raised relief.
2	**command** => String Specifies a callback to invoke to change the view in the widget associated with the scrollbar. When a user requests a view change by manipulating the scrollbar, the callback is invoked.
3	**elementborderwidth** => Integer Specifies the width of borders drawn around the internal elements of the scrollbar.
4	**width** => Integer Specifies the desired narrow dimension of the scrollbar window, not including 3-D border, if any. For vertical scrollbars this will be the width and for horizontal scrollbars this will be the height.

Elements of Scrollbar

A scrollbar displays five elements, which are referred in the methods for the scrollbar:

- **arrow1:** The top or left arrow in the scrollbar.
- **trough1:** The region between the slider and arrow1.
- **slider:** The rectangle that indicates what is visible in the associated widget.
- **trough2:** The region between the slider and arrow2.
- **arrow2:** The bottom or right arrow in the scrollbar.

Manipulating Scrollbar

The following useful methods to manipulate the content of a scrollbar:

- **activate(?element?):** Marks the element indicated by *element* as active, which causes it to be displayed as specified by the **activebackground** and **activerelief** options. The only element values understood by this command are **arrow1**, **slider**, or **arrow2**.
- **delta(deltaX, deltaY):** Returns a real number indicating the fractional change in the scrollbar setting that corresponds to a given change in slider position.
- **fraction(x, y):** Returns a real number between 0 and 1 indicating where the point given by x and y lies in the trough area of the scrollbar. The value 0 corresponds to the top or left of the trough, the value 1 corresponds to the bottom or right, 0.5 corresponds to the middle, and so on.
- **get:**Returns the scrollbar settings in the form of a list whose elements are the arguments to the most recent set method.
- **identify(x, y):** Returns the name of the element under the point given by x and y (such as arrow1), or an empty string if the point does not lie in any element of the scrollbar. X and y must be pixel coordinates relative to the scrollbar widget.
- **set(first, last):** This command is invoked by the scrollbar's associated widget to tell the scrollbar about the current view in the widget. The command takes two arguments, each of which is a real fraction between 0 and 1. The fractions describe the range of the document that is visible in the associated widget.

Event Bindings

Ruby/Tk automatically creates class bindings for scrollbars that gives them the following default behavior. If the behavior is different for vertical and horizontal scrollbars, the horizontal behavior is described in parentheses:

- Pressing button 1 over arrow1 causes the view in the associated widget to shift up (left) by one unit so that the document appears to move down (right) one unit. If the button is held down, the action auto-repeats.
- Pressing button 1 over trough1 causes the view in the associated widget to shift up (left) by one screenful so that the document appears to move down (right) one screenful. If the button is held down, the action auto-repeats.
- Pressing button 1 over the slider and dragging causes the view to drag with the slider. If the jump option is true, then the view doesn't drag along with the slider; it changes only when the mouse button is released.
- Pressing button 1 over trough2 causes the view in the associated widget to shift down (right) by one screenful so that the document appears to

move up (left) one screenful. If the button is held down, the action auto-repeats.

- Pressing button 1 over arrow2 causes the view in the associated widget to shift down (right) by one unit so that the document appears to move up (left) one unit. If the button is held down, the action auto-repeats.
- If button 2 is pressed over the trough or the slider, it sets the view to correspond to the mouse position; dragging the mouse with button 2 down causes the view to drag with the mouse. If button 2 is pressed over one of the arrows, it causes the same behavior as pressing button 1.
- If button 1 is pressed with the Control key down, then if the mouse is over arrow1 or trough1 the view changes to the very top (left) of the document; if the mouse is over arrow2 or trough2 the view changes to the very bottom (right) of the document; if the mouse is anywhere else then the button press has no effect.
- In vertical scrollbars the Up and Down keys have the same behavior as mouse clicks over arrow1 and arrow2, respectively. In horizontal scrollbars these keys have no effect.
- In vertical scrollbars Control-Up and Control-Down have the same behavior as mouse clicks over trough1 and trough2, respectively. In horizontal scrollbars these keys have no effect.
- In horizontal scrollbars the Up and Down keys have the same behavior as mouse clicks over arrow1 and arrow2, respectively. In vertical scrollbars these keys have no effect.
- In horizontal scrollbars Control-Up and Control-Down have the same behavior as mouse clicks over trough1 and trough2, respectively. In vertical scrollbars these keys have no effect.
- The Prior and Next keys have the same behavior as mouse clicks over trough1 and trough2, respectively.
- The Home key adjusts the view to the top (left edge) of the document.
- The End key adjusts the view to the bottom (right edge) of the document.

Examples

```
require "tk"


list = scroll = nil


list = TkListbox.new {
  yscroll proc{|idx|
```

```
    scroll.set *idx
  }
  width 20
  height 16
  setgrid 1
  pack('side' => 'left', 'fill' => 'y', 'expand' => 1)
}
scroll = TkScrollbar.new {
  command proc{|idx|
    list.yview *idx
  }
  pack('side' => 'left', 'fill' => 'y', 'expand' => 1)
}

for f in Dir.glob("*")
  list.insert 'end', f
end

Tk.mainloop
```

This will produce the following result:

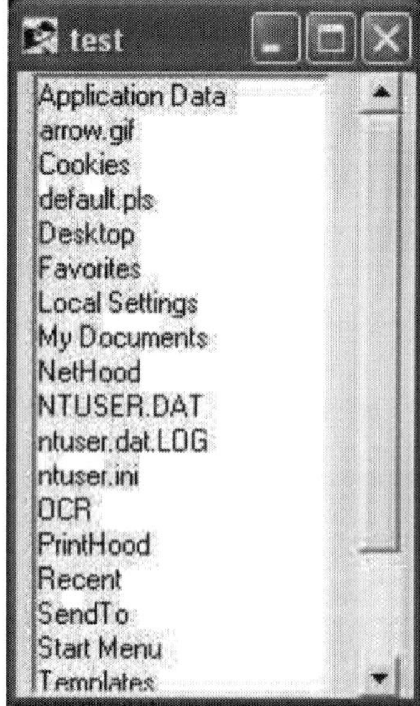

TkCanvas

Description

A **Canvas** widget implements structured graphics. A canvas displays any number of items, which may be things like rectangles, circles, lines, and text.

Items may be manipulated (e.g., moved or re-colored) and callbacks may be associated with items in much the same way that the bind method allows callbacks to be bound to widgets.

Syntax

Here is a simple syntax to create this widget:

```
TkCanvas.new{
  .....Standard Options....
  .....Widget-specific Options....
}
```

Standard Options

- background
- borderwidth
- cursor
- highlightbackground
- highlightcolor
- highlightthickness
- relief
- selectbackground
- selectborderwidth
- selectforeground
- state
- takefocus
- tile
- xscrollcommand
- yscrollcommand

These options have been described in the previous chapter.

Widget-Specific Options

SN	Options with Description
1	**closeenough** =>Integer Specifies a floating-point value indicating how close the mouse cursor must be to an item before it is considered to be **inside** the item. Defaults to 1.0.
2	**confine** =>Boolean Specifies a boolean value that indicates whether or not it should be allowable to set the canvas's view outside the region defined by the *scrollregion* argument. Defaults to true, which means that the view will be constrained within the scroll region.
3	**height** =>Integer Specifies a desired window height that the canvas widget should request from its geometry manager.
4	**scrollregion** =>Coordinates Specifies a list with four coordinates describing the left, top, right, and bottom coordinates of a rectangular region. This region is used for scrolling purposes and is considered to be the boundary of the information in the canvas.
5	**state** =>String Modifies the default state of the canvas where state may be set to one of: **normal, disabled,** or **hidden**. Individual canvas objects all have their own state option, which overrides the default state.
6	**width** =>Integer Specifies a desired window width that the canvas widget should request from its geometry manager.
7	**xscrollincrement** =>Integer Specifies an increment for horizontal scrolling, in any of the usual forms

	permitted for screen distances. If the value of this option is greater than zero, the horizontal view in the window will be constrained so that the canvas x coordinate at the left edge of the window is always an even multiple of xscrollincrement; furthermore, the units for scrolling will also be xscrollincrement.
8	**yscrollincrement** =>Integer Specifies an increment for vertical scrolling, in any of the usual forms permitted for screen distances. If the value of this option is greater than zero, the vertical view in the window will be constrained so that the canvas y coordinate at the top edge of the window is always an even multiple of yscrollincrement; furthermore, the units for scrolling will also be yscrollincrement.

Indices

Indices are used for methods such as inserting text, deleting a range of characters, and setting the insertion cursor position. An index may be specified in any of a number of ways, and different types of items may support different forms for specifying indices.

Text items support the following forms for an index:

- **number:** A decimal number giving the position of the desired character within the text item. 0 refers to the first character, 1 to the next character, and so on.
- **end:** Refers to the character or coordinate just after the last one in the item (same as the number of characters or coordinates in the item).
- **insert:** Refers to the character just before which the insertion cursor is drawn in this item. Not valid for lines and polygons.

Creating Items

When you create a new canvas widget, it will essentially be a large rectangle with nothing on it; truly a blank canvas in other words. To do anything useful with it, you'll need to add items to it.

There are a wide variety of different types of items you can add. Following methods will be used to create different items inside a canvas:

Arc Items

Items of type arc appear on the display as arc-shaped regions. An arc is a section of an oval delimited by two angles. Arcs are created with methods of the following form:

The **TkcArc.new(canvas, x1, y1, x2, y2, ?option, value, option, value, ...?)** method will be used to create an arc.

The arguments x1, y1, x2, and y2 give the coordinates of two diagonally opposite corners of a rectangular region enclosing the oval that defines the arc. Here is the description of other options:

- **extent => degrees:** Specifies the size of the angular range occupied by the arc. If it is greater than 360 or less than -360, then degrees modulo 360 is used as the extent.
- **fill => color:** Fills the region of the arc with color.
- **outline => color:** Color specifies a color to use for drawing the arc's outline.
- **start => degrees:** Specifies the beginning of the angular range occupied by the arc.
- **style => type:** Specifies how to draw the arc. If *type* is **pieslice** (the default) then the arc's region is defined by a section of the oval's perimeter plus two line segments, one between the center of the oval and each end of the perimeter section. If *type* is **chord** then the arc's region is defined by a section of the oval's perimeter plus a single line segment connecting the two end points of the perimeter section. If *type* is **arc** then the arc's region consists of a section of the perimeter alone.
- **tags => tagList:** Specifies a set of tags to apply to the item. TagList consists of a list of tag names, which replace any existing tags for the item. TagList may be an empty list.
- **width => outlineWidth:** Specifies the width of the outline to be drawn around the arc's region.

Bitmap Items

Items of type bitmap appear on the display as images with two colors, foreground and background. Bitmaps are created with methods of the following form:

The **TkcBitmap.new(canvas, x, y, ?option, value, option, value, ...?)** method will be used to create a bitmap.

The arguments x and y specify the coordinates of a point used to position the bitmap on the display. Here is the description of other options:

- **anchor => anchorPos:** AnchorPos tells how to position the bitmap relative to the positioning point for the item. For example, if anchorPos is center then the bitmap is centered on the point; if anchorPos is n then the bitmap will be drawn so that its top center point is at the positioning point. This option defaults to center.
- **background => color:** Specifies a color to use for each of the bitmap pixels whose value is 0.
- **bitmap => bitmap:** Specifies the bitmap to display in the item.
- **foreground => color:** Specifies a color to use for each of the bitmap pixels whose value is 1.
- **tags => tagList:** Specifies a set of tags to apply to the item. TagList consists of a list of tag names, which replace any existing tags for the item. TagList may be an empty list.

Image Items

Items of type image are used to display images on a canvas. Images are created with methods of the following form: :

The **TkcImage.new(canvas,x, y, ?option, value, option, value, ...?)** method will be used to create an image.

The arguments x and y specify the coordinates of a point used to position the image on the display. Here is the description of other options:

- **anchor => anchorPos:** AnchorPos tells how to position the bitmap relative to the positioning point for the item. For example, if anchorPos is center then the bitmap is centered on the point; if anchorPos is n then the bitmap will be drawn so that its top center point is at the positioning point. This option defaults to center.
- **image => name:** Specifies the name of the image to display in the item. This image must have been created previously with the image create command.
- **tags => tagList:** Specifies a set of tags to apply to the item. TagList consists of a list of tag names, which replace any existing tags for the item. TagList may be an empty list.

Line items

Items of type line appear on the display as one or more connected line segments or curves. Lines are created with methods of the following form:

The **TkcLine.new(canvas, x1, y1..., xn, yn, ?option, value, ...?)** method will be used to create a line.

The arguments x1 through yn give the coordinates for a series of two or more points that describe a series of connected line segments. Here is the description of other options:

- **arrow => where:** Indicates whether or not arrowheads are to be drawn at one or both ends of the line. *Where* must have one of the values **none** (for no arrowheads), **first** (for an arrowhead at the first point of the line), **last** (for an arrowhead at the last point of the line), or **both** (for arrowheads at both ends). This option defaults to **none**.
- **arrowshape => shape:** This option indicates how to draw arrowheads. If this option isn't specified then Tk picks a reasonable shape.
- **dash => pattern:** Specifies a pattern to draw the line.
- **capstyle => style:** Specifies the ways in which caps are to be drawn at the endpoints of the line. Possible values are butt, projecting, or round.
- **fill => color:** Color specifies a color to use for drawing the line.
- **joinstyle => style:** Specifies the ways in which joints are to be drawn at the vertices of the line. Possible values are bevel, miter, or round.
- **smooth => boolean:** It indicates whether or not the line should be drawn as a curve.
- **splinesteps => number:** Specifies the degree of smoothness desired for curves: each spline will be approximated with number line segments. This option is ignored unless the *smooth* option is true.
- **stipple => bitmap:** Indicates that the line should be filled in a stipple pattern; bitmap specifies the stipple pattern to use.
- **tags => tagList:** Specifies a set of tags to apply to the item. TagList consists of a list of tag names, which replace any existing tags for the item. TagList may be an empty list.
- **width => lineWidth:** Specifies the width of the line.

Rectangle Items

Items of type rectangle appear as rectangular regions on the display. Each rectangle may have an outline, a fill, or both. Rectangles are created with methods of the following form:

The **TkcRectangle.new(canvas, x1, y1, x2, y2, ?option, value,...?)** method will be used to create a Rectangle.

The arguments x1, y1, x2, and y2 give the coordinates of two diagonally opposite corners of the rectangle. Here is the description of other options:

- **fill => color:** Fills the area of the rectangle with color.

- **outline => color:** Draws an outline around the edge of the rectangle in color.
- **stipple => bitmap:** Indicates that the rectangle should be filled in a stipple pattern; bitmap specifies the stipple pattern to use.
- **tags => tagList:** Specifies a set of tags to apply to the item. TagList consists of a list of tag names, which replace any existing tags for the item. TagList may be an empty list.
- **width => outlineWidth:** Specifies the width of the outline to be drawn around the rectangle.

Event Bindings

Canvas has the default bindings to allow scrolling if necessary: <Up>, <Down>, <Left> and <Right> (and their <Control-*> counter parts). Further <Prior>, <Next>, <Home> and <End>. These bindings allow you to navigate the same way as in other widgets that can scroll.

Example 1

```
require "tk"


canvas = TkCanvas.new


TkcRectangle.new(canvas, '1c', '2c', '3c', '3c',
                 'outline' => 'black', 'fill' => 'blue')


TkcLine.new(canvas, 0, 0, 100, 100,
                 'width' => '2', 'fill' => 'red')
canvas.pack


Tk.mainloop
```

This will produce the following result:

Example 2

```
require 'tk'

root = TkRoot.new
root.title = "Window"

canvas = TkCanvas.new(root) do
   place('height' => 170, 'width' => 100,
          'x' => 10, 'y' => 10)
end

TkcLine.new(canvas, 0, 5, 100, 5)
TkcLine.new(canvas, 0, 15, 100, 15, 'width' => 2)
TkcLine.new(canvas, 0, 25, 100, 25, 'width' => 3)
TkcLine.new(canvas, 0, 35, 100, 35, 'width' => 4)
TkcLine.new(canvas, 0, 55, 100, 55, 'width' => 3,
                    'dash' => ".")
TkcLine.new(canvas, 0, 65, 100, 65, 'width' => 3,
                    'dash' => "-")
TkcLine.new(canvas, 0, 75, 100, 75, 'width' => 3,
                    'dash' => "-.")
TkcLine.new(canvas, 0, 85, 100, 85, 'width' => 3,
                    'dash' => "-..")
TkcLine.new(canvas, 0, 105, 100, 105, 'width' => 2,
                    'arrow' => "first")
TkcLine.new(canvas, 0, 115, 100, 115, 'width' => 2,
```

```
                    'arrow' => "last")
TkcLine.new(canvas, 0, 125, 100, 125, 'width' => 2,
                    'arrow' => "both")
TkcLine.new(canvas, 10, 145, 90, 145, 'width' => 15,
                    'capstyle' => "round")
Tk.mainloop
```

This will produce the following result:

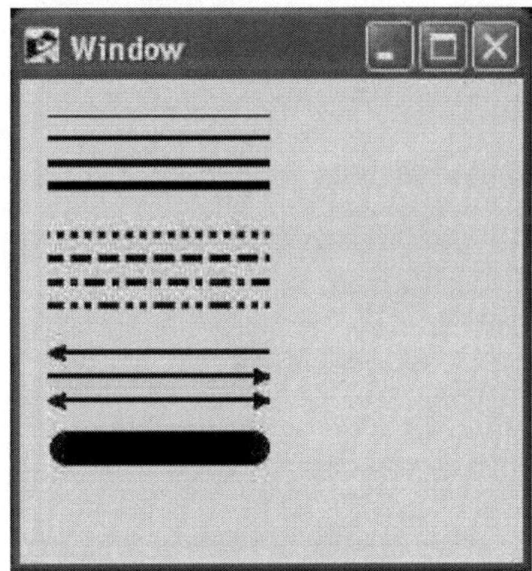

Example 3

```
require 'tk'

root = TkRoot.new
root.title = "Window"

canvas = TkCanvas.new(root) do
   place('height' => 170, 'width' => 100,
          'x' => 10, 'y' => 10)
end

TkcRectangle.new(canvas, 10,  5,    55,  50,
                         'width' => 1)
TkcRectangle.new(canvas, 10,  65,  55, 110,
                         'width' => 5)
TkcRectangle.new(canvas, 10,  125, 55, 170,
```

```
                              'width' => 1, 'fill'  => "red")


Tk.mainloop
```

This will produce the following result:

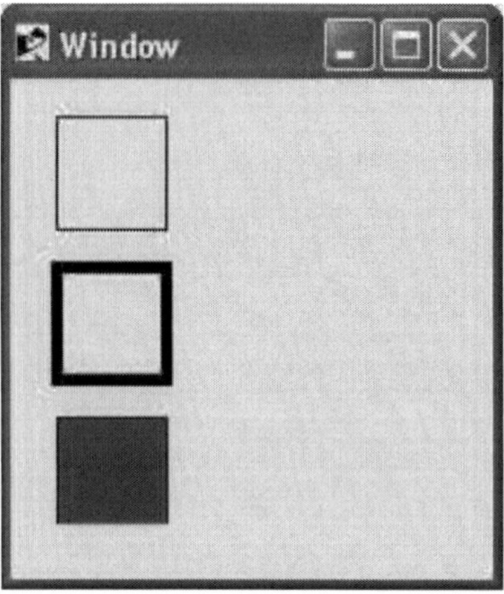

Example 4

```
require 'tk'


root = TkRoot.new
root.title = "Window"


canvas = TkCanvas.new(root) do
   place('height' => 170, 'width' => 100,
          'x' => 10, 'y' => 10)
end


TkcLine.new(canvas, 0,  10, 100,  10,
                    'width' => 10, 'fill' => "blue")
TkcLine.new(canvas, 0,  30, 100,  30,
                    'width' => 10, 'fill' => "red")
TkcLine.new(canvas, 0,  50, 100,  50,
                    'width' => 10, 'fill' => "green")
TkcLine.new(canvas, 0,  70, 100,  70,
                    'width' => 10, 'fill' => "violet")
```

```
TkcLine.new(canvas, 0,  90, 100,  90,
                    'width' => 10, 'fill' => "yellow")
TkcLine.new(canvas, 0, 110, 100, 110,
                    'width' => 10, 'fill' => "pink")
TkcLine.new(canvas, 0, 130, 100, 130,
                    'width' => 10, 'fill' => "orange")
TkcLine.new(canvas, 0, 150, 100, 150,
                    'width' => 10, 'fill' => "grey")
Tk.mainloop
```

This will produce the following result:

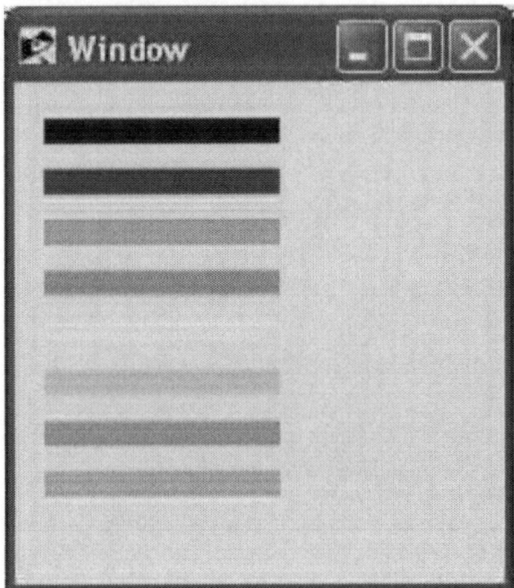

TkScale

Description

A **Scale** is a widget that displays a rectangular trough and a small slider. The trough corresponds to a range of real values (determined by the from, to, and resolution options), and the position of the slider selects a particular real value.

Three annotations may be displayed in a scale widget:

- A label appearing at the top right of the widget (top left for horizontal scales).
- A number displayed just to the left of the slider (just above the slider for horizontal scales).
- A collection of numerical tick marks just to the left of the current value (just below the trough for horizontal scales).

Each of these three annotations may be enabled or disabled using the configuration options.

Syntax

Here is a simple syntax to create this widget:

```
TkScale.new{
  .....Standard Options....
  .....Widget-specific Options....
}
```

Standard Options

- activebackground
- background
- borderwidth
- cursor
- font
- foreground
- highlightbackground
- highlightcolor
- highlightthickness
- orient
- relief
- repeatdelay
- repeatinterval
- takefocus
- troughcolor

These options have been described in the previous chapter.

Widget-Specific Options

SN	Options with Description

1	**bigincrement** =>Integer Some interactions with the scale cause its value to change by *large* increments; this option specifies the size of the large increments. If specified as 0, the large increments default to 1/10 the range of the scale.
2	**command** =>String Specifies the prefix of a Ruby/Tk callback to invoke whenever the scale's value is changed via a method.
3	**digits** =>Integer An integer specifying how many significant digits should be retained when converting the value of the scale to a string. If the number is less than or equal to zero, then the scale picks the smallest value that guarantees that every possible slider position prints as a different string.
4	**from** =>Integer A real value corresponding to the left or top end of the scale.
5	**label** =>String A string to display as a label for the scale. For vertical scales the label is displayed just to the right of the top end of the scale. For horizontal scales the label is displayed just above the left end of the scale.
6	**length** =>Integer Specifies the desired long dimension of the scale in screen units
7	**resolution** =>Integer A real value specifying the resolution for the scale. If this value is greater than zero then the scale's value will always be rounded to an even multiple of this value, as will tick marks and the endpoints of the scale. If the value is less than zero then no rounding occurs. Defaults to 1
8	**showvalue** =>Boolean Specifies a boolean value indicating whether or not the current value of the scale is to be displayed.

9	**sliderlength** =>Integer Specfies the size of the slider, measured in screen units along the slider's long dimension.
10	**sliderrelief** =>String Specifies the relief to use when drawing the slider, such as **raised** or **sunken**.
11	**state** =>String Specifies one of three states for the scale: **normal**, **active**, or **disabled**.
12	**tickinterval** =>Integer Must be a real value. Determines the spacing between numerical tick marks displayed below or to the left of the slider. If 0, no tick marks will be displayed.
13	**to** =>Integer Specifies a real value corresponding to the right or bottom end of the scale. This value may be either less than or greater than the **from** option.
14	**variable** =>Variable Specifies the name of a global variable to link to the scale. Whenever the value of the variable changes, the scale will update to reflect this value. Whenever the scale is manipulated interactively, the variable will be modified to reflect the scale's new value.
15	**width** =>Integer Specifies the desired narrow dimension of the trough in screen units

Manipulating Scales

The following methods are available for scale widgets:

- **coords(?value?)** Returns a list whose elements are the x and y coordinates of the point along the centerline of the trough that corresponds to value. If value is omitted then the scale's current value is used.

- **get(?x, y?)** If x and y are omitted, returns the current value of the scale. If x and y are specified, they give pixel coordinates within the widget; the command returns the scale value corresponding to the given pixel.
- **identify(x, y)** Returns a string indicating what part of the scale lies under the coordinates given by *x* and *y*. A return value of **slider** means that the point is over the slider; **trough1** means that the point is over the portion of the slider above or to the left of the slider; and **trough2** means that the point is over the portion of the slider below or to the right of the slider.
- **set(value)** This command is invoked to change the current value of the scale, and hence the position at which the slider is displayed. Value gives the new value for the scale. The command has no effect if the scale is disabled.

Event Bindings

Ruby/Tk automatically creates class bindings for scales that give them the following default behavior. Where the behavior is different for vertical and horizontal scales, the horizontal behavior is described in parentheses.

- If button 1 is pressed in the trough, the scale's value will be incremented or decremented by the value of the resolution option so that the slider moves in the direction of the cursor. If the button is held down, the action auto-repeats.
- If button 1 is pressed over the slider, the slider can be dragged with the mouse.
- If button 1 is pressed in the trough with the Control key down, the slider moves all the way to the end of its range, in the direction towards the mouse cursor.
- If button 2 is pressed, the scale's value is set to the mouse position. If the mouse is dragged with button 2 down, the scale's value changes with the drag.
- The Up and Left keys move the slider up (left) by the value of the resolution option.
- The Down and Right keys move the slider down (right) by the value of the resolution option.
- Control-Up and Control-Left move the slider up (left) by the value of the bigIncrement option.
- Control-Down and Control-Right move the slider down (right) by the value of the bigIncrement option.
- Home moves the slider to the top (left) end of its range.
- End moves the slider to the bottom (right) end of its range.

If the scale is disabled using the state option, then none of the above bindings have any effect.

Examples

```
require "tk"

$scale = TkScale.new {
  orient 'horizontal'
  length 280
  from 0
  to 250
  command (proc {printheight})
  tickinterval 50
  pack
}

def printheight
  height = $scale.get()
  print height, "\n"
end

Tk.mainloop
```

This will produce the following result:

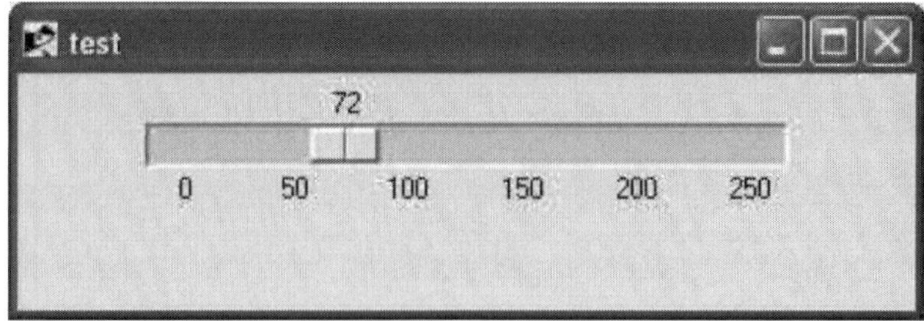

TkText

Description

A **Text** widget provides users with an area so that they can enter multiple lines of text. Text widgets are part of the classic Tk widgets, not the themed Tk widgets.

Text widgets support three different kinds of annotations on the text:

- **Tags** - allow different portions of the text to be displayed with different fonts and colors. In addition, Tcl commands can be associated with tags so that scripts are invoked when particular actions such as keystrokes and mouse button presses occur in particular ranges of the text.

- **Marks** - The second form of annotation consists of marks, which are floating markers in the text. Marks are used to keep track of various interesting positions in the text as it is edited.

- **Embedded windows** - The third form of annotation allows arbitrary windows to be embedded in a text widget.

A label can display a textual string, bitmap or image. If text is displayed, it must all be in a single font, but it can occupy multiple lines on the screen (if it contains newlines or if wrapping occurs because of the *wraplength* option) and one of the characters may optionally be underlined using the *underline* option.

Syntax

Here is a simple syntax to create this widget:

```
TkText.new(root) {
   .....Standard Options....
   .....Widget-specific Options....
}
```

Standard Options

- background
- borderwidth
- cursor
- exportselection
- font
- foreground

- highlightbackground
- highlightcolor
- highlightthickness
- insertbackground
- insertborderwidth
- insertofftime
- insertontime
- insertwidth
- padx
- pady
- relief
- selectbackground
- selectborderwidth
- selectforeground
- setgrid
- takefocus
- xscrollcommand
- yscrollcommand

These options have been described in previous chapter.

Widget-Specific Options

SN	Options with Description
1	**height** => Integer Specifies the desired height for the window, in units of characters. Must be at least one.
2	**spacing1** => Integer Requests additional space above each text line in the widget, using any of the standard forms for screen distances. If a line wraps, this option only applies to the first line on the display. This option may be overriden with **spacing1** options in tags.

3	**spacing2** => Integer For lines that wrap (so that they cover more than one line on the display) this option specifies additional space to provide between the display lines that represent a single line of text. The value may have any of the standard forms for screen distances. This option may be overriden with **spacing** options in tags.
4	**spacing3** => Integer Requests additional space below each text line in the widget, using any of the standard forms for screen distances. If a line wraps, this option only applies to the last line on the display. This option may be overriden with **spacing3** options in tags.
5	**state** => String Specifies one of two states for the text: **normal** or **disabled**. If the text is disabled then characters may not be inserted or deleted and no insertion cursor will be displayed, even if the input focus is in the widget.
6	**tabs** => String Specifies a set of tab stops for the window. The option's value consists of a list of screen distances giving the positions of the tab stops. Each position may optionally be followed in the next list element by one of the keywords **left**, **right**, **center**, or**numeric**, which specifies how to justify text relative to the tab stop. **Left** is the default.
7	**width** => Integer Specifies the desired width for the window in units of characters. If the font doesn't have a uniform width then the width of the character "0" is used in translating from character units to screen units.
8	**wrap** => String Specifies how to handle lines in the text that are too long to be displayed in a single line of the text's window. The value must be **none** or **char** or **word**.

Manipulating Test

The following useful methods are available to manipulate the content of a text:

- **delete(index1, ?index2?):** Deletes a range of characters from the text. If both index1 and index2 are specified, then deletes all the characters starting with the one given by index1 and stopping just before index2. If *index2* doesn't specify a position later in the text than *index1* then no characters are deleted. If *index2* isn't specified then the single character at *index1* is deleted.

- **get(index1, ?index2?)**: Returns a range of characters from the text. The return value will be all the characters in the text starting with the one whose index is *index1* and ending just before the one whose index is *index2* (the character at *index2* will not be returned). If *index2* is omitted then the single character at *index1* is returned.

- **index(index)** : Returns the position corresponding to *index* in the form *line.char*where *line* is the line number and *char* is the character number.

- **insert(index, chars, ?tagList, chars, tagList, ...?)** : Inserts all of the *chars* arguments just before the character at *index*. If *index* refers to the end of the text (the character after the last newline) then the new text is inserted just before the last newline instead. If there is a single *chars* argument and no *tagList*, then the new text will receive any tags that are present on both the character before and the character after the insertion point; if a tag is present on only one of these characters then it will not be applied to the new text. If *tagList* is specified then it consists of a list of tag names; the new characters will receive all of the tags in this list and no others, regardless of the tags present around the insertion point. If multiple *chars-tagList* argument pairs are present, they produce the same effect as if a separate **insert** widget command had been issued for each pair, in order. The last *tagList* argument may be omitted.

- **xview(option, args)** : This command is used to query and change the horizontal position of the text in the widget's window.

- **yview(?args?)** : This command is used to query and change the vertical position of the text in the widget's window.

Event Bindings

Ruby/Tk automatically creates class bindings for texts. Here are few important bindings listed.

- Clicking mouse button 1 positions the insertion cursor just before the character underneath the mouse cursor, sets the input focus to this widget, and clears any selection in the widget. Dragging with mouse button 1 strokes out a selection between the insertion cursor and the character under the mouse.

- Double-clicking with mouse button 1 selects the word under the mouse and positions the insertion cursor at the beginning of the word. Dragging after a double click will stroke out a selection consisting of whole words.
- Triple-clicking with mouse button 1 selects the line under the mouse and positions the insertion cursor at the beginning of the line. Dragging after a triple click will stroke out a selection consisting of whole lines.
- Clicking mouse button 1 with the Control key down will reposition the insertion cursor without affecting the selection.
- The Left and Right keys move the insertion cursor one character to the left or right; they also clear any selection in the text.
- The Up and Down keys move the insertion cursor one line up or down and clear any selection in the text. If Up or Right is typed with the Shift key down, then the insertion cursor moves and the selection is extended to include the new character.
- Control-x deletes whatever is selected in the text widget.
- Control-o opens a new line by inserting a newline character in front of the insertion cursor without moving the insertion cursor.
- Control-d deletes the character to the right of the insertion cursor.

Examples

```
require 'tk'


root = TkRoot.new
root.title = "Window"


text = TkText.new(root) do
  width 30
  height 20
  borderwidth 1
  font TkFont.new('times 12 bold')
   pack("side" => "right",  "padx"=> "5", "pady"=> "5")
end
text.insert 'end', "Hello!\n\ntext widget example"
Tk.mainloop
```

This will produce the following result:

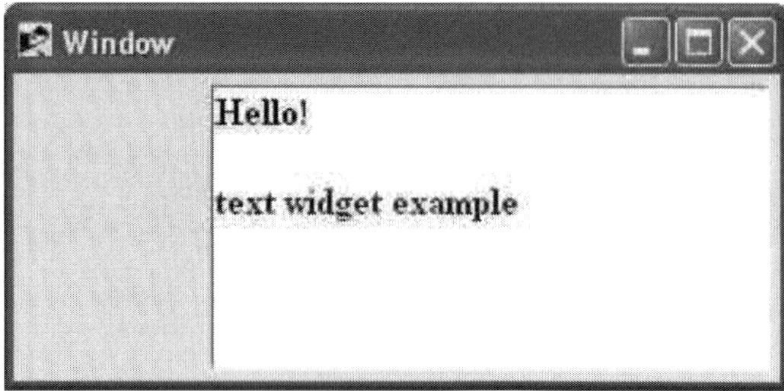

TkToplevel

Description

A **Toplevel** is similar to a frame except that it is created as a top-level window. Its X parent is the root window of a screen rather than the logical parent from its path name.

The primary purpose of a toplevel is to serve as a container for dialog boxes and other collections of widgets. The only visible features of a toplevel are its background color and an optional 3-D border to make the toplevel appear raised or sunken.

Syntax

Here is a simple syntax to create this widget:

```
TkToplevel.new(root) {
  .....Standard Options....
  .....Widget-specific Options....
}
```

Standard Options

- borderwidth
- cursor
- highlightbackground
- highlightcolor
- highlightthickness
- relief

- takefocus

These options have been described in the previous chapter.

Widget-Specific Options

SN	Options with Description
1	**background** => String This option is the same as the standard **background** option except that its value may also be specified as an empty string. In this case, the widget will display no background or border, and no colors will be consumed from its colormap for its background and border.
2	**class** => String Specifies a class for the window. This class will be used when querying the option database for the window's other options, and it will also be used later for other purposes such as bindings. The **class** option may not be changed with the**configure** method.
3	**colormap** => String Specifies a colormap to use for the window. The value may be either **new**, in which case a new colormap is created for the window and its children, or the name of another window.
4	**height** => Integer Specifies the desired height for the window.
5	**width** => Integer Specifies the desired width for the window.

Event Bindings

When a new toplevel is created, it has no default event bindings: toplevels are not intended to be interactive.

Examples

```
require 'tk'
```

```
def make_win
  begin
    $win.destroy
  rescue
  end
  $win = TkToplevel.new
  TkButton.new($win) {
    text 'Window Dismiss'
    command "$win.destroy"
    pack
  }
end

TkButton.new {
  text 'make Window'
  command 'make_win'
  pack('fill' => 'x')
}

Tk.mainloop
```

This will produce the following result:

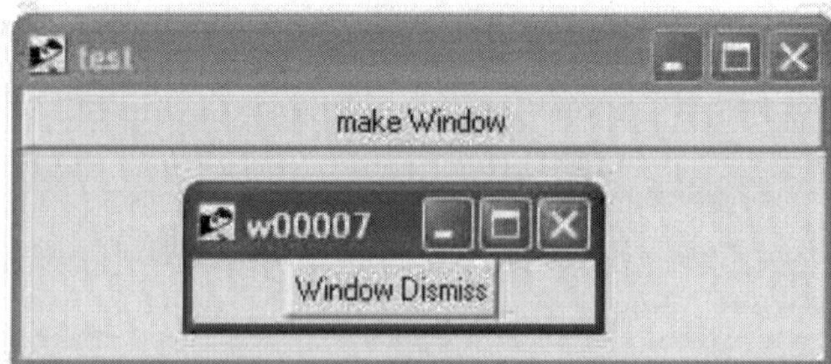

TkSpinbox

Description

A **Spinbox** widget allows users to choose numbers (or in fact, items from an arbitrary list). It does this by combining an entry-like widget showing the current value with a pair of small up/down arrows which can be used to step through the range of possible choices.

Spinboxes are capable of displaying strings that are too long to fit entirely within the widget's window. In this case, only a portion of the string will be displayed; commands described below may be used to change the view in the window.

Spinboxes use the standard **xscrollcommand** mechanism for interacting with scrollbars.

Syntax

Here is a simple syntax to create this widget:

```
TkSpinbox.new(root) {
  .....Standard Options....
  .....Widget-specific Options....
}
```

Standard Options

- activebackground
- background
- borderwidth
- cursor
- exportselection
- font
- foreground
- highlightbackground
- highlightcolor
- highlightthickness
- justify
- relief
- repeatdelay
- repeatinterval
- selectbackground
- selectborderwidth

- selectforeground
- takefocus
- textvariable
- xscrollcommand

These options have been described in the previous chapter.

Widget-Specific Options

SN	Options with Description
1	**buttonbackground** => String The background color to be used for the spin buttons.
2	**buttoncursor** => String The cursor to be used for over the spin buttons. If this is empty (the default), a default cursor will be used.
3	**buttondownrelief** => String The relief to be used for the upper spin button.
4	**command** => String Specifies a Ruby/Tk callback to invoke whenever a Spinbutton is invoked. The callback has these two arguments *appended* to any existing callback arguments: the current value of the widget and the direction of the button press (**up** or **down**).
5	**disabledbackground** => String Specifies the background color to use when the Spinbox is disabled. If this option is the empty string, the normal background color is used.
6	**disabledforeground** => String Specifies the foreground color to use when the Spinbox is disabled. If this option is the empty string, the normal foreground color is used.
7	**format** => String Specifies an alternate format to use when setting the string value when

	using the **from** and **to** range.
8	**from** => Integer A floating-point value corresponding to the lowest value for a Spinbox, to be used in conjunction with **to** and **increment**.
9	**increment** => String A floating-point value specifying the increment. When used with **from** and **to**, the value in the widget will be adjusted by **increment** when a spin button is pressed (up adds the value, down subtracts the value).
10	**state** => String Specifies one of three states for the Spinbox: **normal**, **disabled**, or **readonly**.
11	**to** => Integer A floating-point value corresponding to the highest value for the Spinbox, to be used in conjunction with **from** and **increment**. When all are specified correctly, the Spinbox will use these values to control its contents. This value must be greater than the **from** option. If **values** is specified, it supercedes this option.
12	**validate** => String Specifies the mode in which validation should operate: **none**, **focus**, **focusin**,**focusout**, **key**, or **all**. It defaults to **none**. When you want validation, you must explicitly state which mode you wish to use.
13	**validatecommand** => String Specifies a script to evaluate when you want to validate the input in the widget.
14	**values** => Integer Must be a proper list value. If specified, the Spinbox will use these values as to control its contents, starting with the first value. This option has precedence over the **from** and **to** range.
15	**width** => Integer

	Specifies an integer value indicating the desired width of the Spinbox window, in average-size characters of the widget's font.
16	**wrap** => Boolean Must be a proper boolean value. If on, the Spinbox will wrap around the values of data in the widget.

Validation Stages

Validation works by setting the **validatecommand** option to a callback, which will be evaluated according to the validate option as follows:

- **none:** Default. This means no validation will occur.
- **focus:** *validatecommand* will be called when the Spinbox receives or loses focus.
- **focusin:** *validatecommand* will be called when the Spinbox receives focus.
- **focusout:** *validatecommand* will be called when the Spinbox loses focus.
- **key:** *validatecommand* will be called when the Spinbox is edited.
- **all:** *validatecommand* will be called for all above conditions.

Manipulating Spinbox

Here is a list of few important methods to play with Spinbox:

- **delete(first, ?last?)** : Deletes one or more elements of the Spinbox. *First* is the index of the first character to delete, and *last* is the index of the character just after the last one to delete. If *last* isn't specified it defaults to *first*+1, i.e. a single character is deleted. This command returns an empty string.
- **get** : Returns the Spinbox's string.
- **icursor(index)** : Arrange for the insertion cursor to be displayed just before the character given by index. Returns an empty string.
- **identify(x, y)** : Returns the name of the window element corresponding to coordinates *x* and *y* in the Spinbox. Return value is one of: **none**, **buttondown**,**buttonup**, **entry**.
- **index(index)** : Returns the numerical index corresponding to index.
- **insert(index, string)** : Insert the characters of string just before the character indicated by index. Returns an empty string.

- **invoke(element)** : Causes the specified element, either **buttondown** or**buttonup**, to be invoked, triggering the action associated with it.
- **set(?string?)** : f string is specified, the Spinbox will try and set it to this value, otherwise it just returns the Spinbox's string. If validation is on, it will occur when setting the string.
- **validate** : This command is used to force an evaluation of the **validatecommand** independent of the conditions specified by the **validate** option. This is done by temporarily setting the **validate** option to **all**. It returns 0 or 1.
- **xview(args)** : This command is used to query and change the horizontal position of the text in the widget's window.

Event Bindings

Tk automatically creates class bindings for Spinboxes that gives them the default behavior. Few important behaviors are given below:

- Clicking mouse button 1, positions the insertion cursor just before the character underneath the mouse cursor, sets the input focus to this widget, and clears any selection in the widget. Dragging with mouse button 1, strokes out a selection between the insertion cursor and the character under the mouse.
- Double-clicking with mouse button 1, selects the word under the mouse and positions the insertion cursor at the beginning of the word. Dragging after a double click will stroke out a selection consisting of whole words.
- Triple-clicking with mouse button 1, selects all of the text in the Spinbox and positions the insertion cursor before the first character.
- The ends of the selection can be adjusted by dragging with mouse button 1, while the Shift key is down; this will adjust the end of the selection that was nearest to the mouse cursor when button 1 was pressed. If the button is double-clicked before dragging then the selection will be adjusted in units of whole words.
- Clicking mouse button 1 with the Control key down, will position the insertion cursor in the Spinbox without affecting the selection.
- If any normal printing characters are typed in a Spinbox, they are inserted at the point of the insertion cursor.
- The view in the Spinbox can be adjusted by dragging with mouse button 2. If mouse button 2 is clicked without moving the mouse, the selection is copied into the Spinbox at the position of the mouse cursor.
- If the mouse is dragged out of the Spinbox on the left or right sides while button 1 is pressed, the Spinbox will automatically scroll to make more

text visible (if there is more text off-screen on the side where the mouse left the window).

- The End key, or Control-e, will move the insertion cursor to the end of the Spinbox and clear any selection in the Spinbox. Shift-End moves the cursor to the end and extends the selection to that point.
- The Home key, or Control-a, will move the insertion cursor to the beginning of the Spinbox and clear any selection in the Spinbox. Shift-Home moves the insertion cursor to the beginning of the Spinbox and also extends the selection to that point.
- Control-/ selects all the text in the Spinbox.
- Control-\ clears any selection in the Spinbox.
- The Delete key deletes the selection, if there is one in the Spinbox. If there is no selection, it deletes the character to the right of the insertion cursor.
- The BackSpace key and Control-h delete the selection, if there is one in the Spinbox. If there is no selection, it deletes the character to the left of the insertion cursor.
- Control-d deletes the character to the right of the insertion cursor.
- Meta-d deletes the word to the right of the insertion cursor.
- Control-k deletes all the characters to the right of the insertion cursor.

Examples

```
require 'tk'


root = TkRoot.new
root.title = "Window"
Sb = TkSpinbox.new(root) do
  to 100
  from 5
  increment 5
  pack("side" => "left",  "padx"=> "50", "pady"=> "50")
end


Tk.mainloop
```

This will produce the following result:

TkProgressBar

Description

A **ProgressBar** provides a widget, which will show a graphical representation of a value, given maximum and minimum reference values.

Syntax

Here is a simple syntax to create this widget:

```
Tk::ProgressBar.new(root) {
  .....Standard Options....
  .....Widget-specific Options....
}
```

Standard Options

- borderwidth
- highlightthickness
- padx
- pady
- relief
- troughcolor

These options have been described in the previous chapter.

Widget-Specific Options

SN	Options with Description

1	**anchor** => String This can be used to position the start point of the bar. Default is 'w' (horizontal bar starting from the left). A vertical bar can be configured by using either 's' or 'n'.
2	**blocks** => Integer This controls the number of blocks to be used to construct the progress bar. The default is to break the bar into 10 blocks.
3	**colors** => String Controls the colors to be used for different positions of the progress bar.
4	**from** => Integer This sets the lower limit of the progress bar. If the bar is set to a value below the lower limit no bar will be displayed. Defaults to 0.
5	**gap** => Integer This is the spacing (in pixels) between each block. Defaults to 1. Use 0 to get a continuous bar.
6	**length** => Integer Specifies the desired long dimension of the ProgressBar in screen units.
7	**resolution** => Integer A real value specifying the resolution for the scale. If this value is greater than zero, then the scale's value will always be rounded to an even multiple of this value, as will tick marks and the endpoints of the scale. Defaults to 1.
8	**to** => Integer This sets the upper limit of the progress bar. If a value is specified (for example, using the value method) that lies above this value the full progress bar will be displayed. Defaults to 100.
9	**variable** => Variable Specifies the reference to a scalar variable to link to the ProgressBar. Whenever the value of the variable changes, the ProgressBar will update

	to reflect this value.
10	**value** => Integer The can be used to set the current position of the progress bar when used in conjunction with the standard `configure`. It is usually recommended to use the**value** method instead.
11	**width** => Integer Specifies the desired narrow dimension of the ProgressBar in screen units

Manipulating Progress Bar

You can use **value(?value?)** method along with ProgressBar instance to get current value of the ProgressBar. If value is given, the value of the ProgressBar is set.

Examples

```
require 'tk'
require 'tkextlib/bwidget'

root = TkRoot.new
root.title = "Window"

progressBar = Tk::BWidget::ProgressBar.new(root)

variable = TkVariable.new
progressBar.variable = variable

variable.value = 33

progressBar.maximum = 100
progressBar.place('height' => 25,
                  'width'  => 100,
                  'x'      => 10,
                  'y'      => 10)
```

```
Tk.mainloop
```

This will produce the following result:

Dialog Box

Description

Dialog boxes are a type of window used in applications to get some information from the user, inform them that some event has occurred, confirm an action and more.

The appearance and usage of dialog boxes is usually quite specifically detailed in a platform's style guide. Tk comes with a number of dialog boxes built-in for common tasks, and which help you conform to platform specific style guidelines.

File, Directory and Color Dialog Box

Ruby/Tk provides several dialogs to let the user select files or directories. The *open* variant on the dialog is used when you want the user to select an existing file, while the *save* variant is used to choose a file to save. There are four variants, which can be used:

- **Tk.getOpenFile:** To have one open file dialog box.
- **Tk.getSaveFile:** To have one save file dialog box.
- **Tk.chooseDirectory** To have one choose directory dialog box.
- **Tk.chooseColor** To have one choose color dialog box.

Examples

Following example will explain how to create *Open* file dialog box.

```
require 'tk'


root = TkRoot.new
```

```
root.title = "Window"

button_click = Proc.new {
  Tk.getOpenFile
}

button = TkButton.new(root) do
  text "button"
  pack("side" => "left",  "padx"=> "50", "pady"=> "50")
end

button.comman = button_click

Tk.mainloop
```

This will produce the following result:

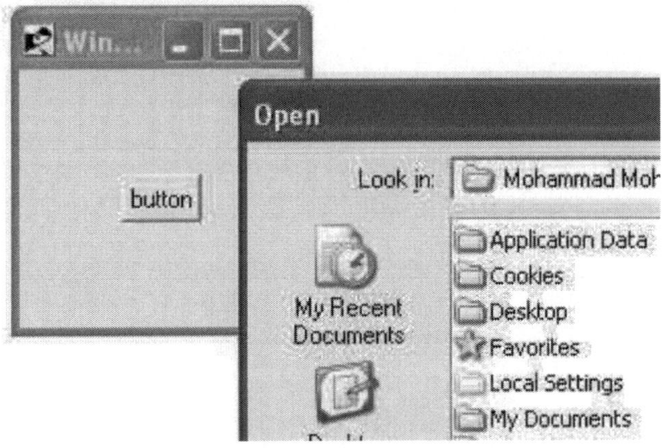

Following example will explain how to create *Choose Color* dialog box.

```
require 'tk'

root = TkRoot.new
root.title = "Window"

button_click = Proc.new {
  Tk.chooseColor
}
```

```
button = TkButton.new(root) do
  text "button"
  pack("side" => "left",  "padx"=> "50", "pady"=> "50")
end

button.comman = button_click

Tk.mainloop
```

This will produce the following result:

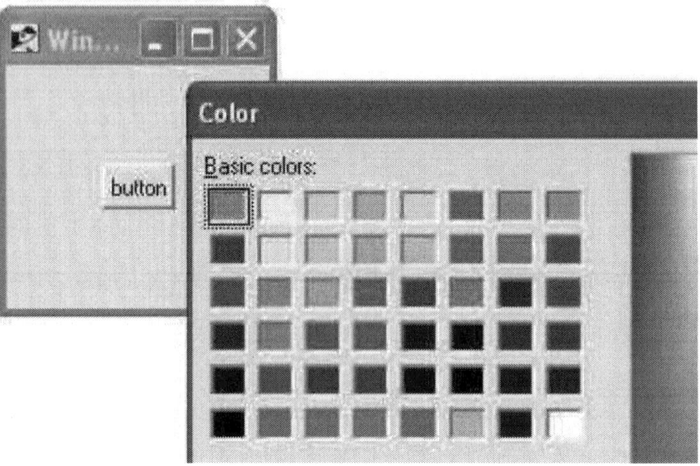

Tk::Tile::Notebook

The NoteBook widget provides a notebook metaphor to display several windows in limited space. The notebook is divided into a stack of pages of which only one is displayed at any time.

The other pages can be selected by means of choosing the visual *tabs* at the top of the widget. Additionally, the <Tab> key may be used to traverse the pages. If **underline** option is used, *Alt-bindings* will also work.

Syntax

Here is a simple syntax to create this widget:

```
Tk::Tile::Notebook.new(root) {
  .....Standard Options....
  .....Widget Specific Options....
```

```
}
```

Standard Options

- class
- cursor
- state
- style
- takefocus

Widget-Specific Options

SN	Options with Description
1	**height** => Integer If present and greater than zero, specifies the desired height of the pane area (not including internal padding or tabs). Otherwise, the maximum height of all panes is used.
2	**padding** => Integer Specifies the amount of extra space to add around the outside of the notebook. The padding is a list of up to four length specifications *left top right bottom*. If fewer than four elements are specified, *bottom* defaults to *top*, *right* defaults to *left*, and*top* defaults to *left*.
3	**width** => Integer If present and greater than zero, specifies the desired width of the pane area (not including internal padding). Otherwise, the maximum width of all panes is used.

Manipulating Notebook

There are various ways to play with Notebook:

- Each page on a Notebook is typically a frame, a direct child (subwindow) of the notebook itself. A new page and its associated tab are added to the end of the list of tabs with the **"add *subwindow ?option value...?*"** method.

- The **text** tab option is used to set the label on the tab; also useful is the **state** tab option, which can have the value **normal**, **disabled** (not selectable), or **hidden**.
- To insert a tab at somewhere other than the end of the list, you can use the**"insert *position subwindow ?option value...?*"**, and to remove a given tab, use the **forget** method, passing it either the position (0..n-1) or the tab's subwindow. You can retrieve the list of all subwindows contained in the notebook via the **tabs** method.
- To retrieve the subwindow that is currently selected, call the **selected** method, and change the selected tab by calling the **select** method, passing it either the tab's position or the subwindow itself as a parameter.
- To change a tab option you can use the **"itemconfigure tabid, :option => value"**method. Where *tabid* is the tab's position or subwindow. You can use the**"itemcget tabid, :option"** to return the current value of the option.

Examples

```
require 'tk'
require 'tkextlib/tile'

root = TkRoot.new
root.title = "Window"

n = Tk::Tile::Notebook.new(root)do
  height 110
  place('height' => 100, 'width' => 200, 'x' => 10, 'y' => 10)
end

f1 = TkFrame.new(n)
f2 = TkFrame.new(n)
f3 = TkFrame.new(n)

n.add f1, :text => 'One', :state =>'disabled'
n.add f2, :text => 'Two'
n.add f3, :text => 'Three'
```

```
Tk.mainloop
```

This will produce the following result:

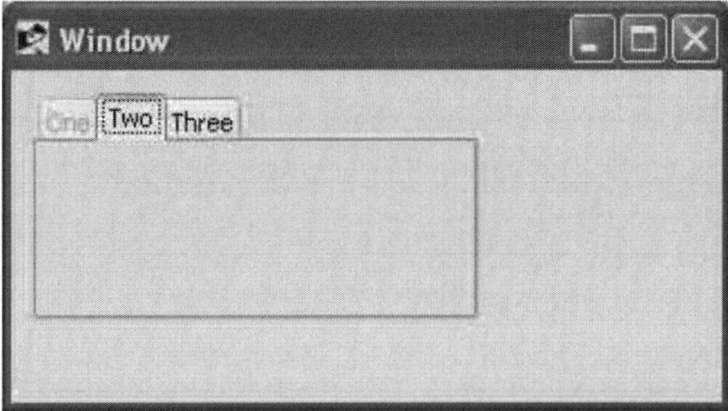

Tk::Tile::Paned

The **Panedwindow** widget lets you stack two or more resizable widgets above and below each other (or to the left and right).

The user can adjust the relative heights (or widths) of each pane by dragging a sash located between them. Typically, the widgets you're adding to a panedwindow will be frames containing many other widgets.

Syntax

Here is a simple syntax to create this widget:

```
Tk::Tile::Paned.new(root) {
  .....Standard Options....
  .....Widget Specific Options....
}
```

Standard Options

- class
- cursor
- style
- takefocus

Widget-Specific Options

SN	Options with Description

1	**orient** => String One of **horizontal** or **vertical**. Specifies the orientation of the separator.
2	**width** => Integer If present and greater than zero, specifies the desired width of the widget in pixels. Otherwise, the requested width is determined by the width of the managed windows.
3	**height** => Integer If present and greater than zero, specifies the desired height of the widget in pixels. Otherwise, the requested height is determined by the height of the managed windows.

Manipulating Paned

- Calling the **"add"** method will add a new pane at the end of the list of panes. The**"insert *position subwindow*"** method allows you to place the pane at the given position in the list of panes (0..n-1); if the pane is already managed by the panedwindow, it will be moved to the new position. You can use the **"forget*subwindow*"** to remove a pane from the panedwindow; you can also pass a position instead of a subwindow.
- Other options let you sign relative weights to each pane so that if the overall panedwindow resizes, certain panes will get more space than others. As well, you can adjust the position of each sash between items in the panedwindow. See the **command reference** for details.

Examples

```
require 'tk'
require 'tkextlib/tile'

$resultsVar = TkVariable.new
root = TkRoot.new
root.title = "Window"

p = Tk::Tile::Paned.new(root)do
  height 110
  place('height' => 100, 'width' => 200, 'x' => 10, 'y' => 10)
```

```
end


f1 = TkFrame.new(p) {
  relief 'groove'
  borderwidth 3
  background "red"
  padx 30
  pady 30
  pack('side' => 'left', 'pady' => 100)
}
f2 = TkFrame.new (p){
  relief 'groove'
  borderwidth 3
  background "yellow"
  padx 30
  pady 30
  pack('side' => 'right', 'pady' => 100)
}


p.add f1, nil
p.add f2, nil


Tk.mainloop
```

This will produce the following result:

Tk::Tile::Separator

The **Separator** widget provides a convenient way of dividing a window into logical parts. You can group widgets in one display using a thin horizontal or vertical rule between groups of widgets.

Syntax

Here is a simple syntax to create this widget:

```
Tk::Tile::Separator.new(root) {
  .....Standard Options....
  .....Widget Specific Options....
}
```

Standard Options

- class
- cursor
- state
- style
- takefocus

Widget-Specific Options

SN	Options with Description
1	**orient** => String One of **horizontal** or **vertical**. Specifies the orientation of the separator.

Examples

```
require 'tk'
require 'tkextlib/tile'

$resultsVar = TkVariable.new
root = TkRoot.new
root.title = "Window"

n = Tk::Tile::Notebook.new(root)do
  height 110
  place('height' => 100, 'width' => 200, 'x' => 10, 'y' => 10)
end

f1 = TkFrame.new(n)
f2 = TkFrame.new(n)
f3 = TkFrame.new(n)

n.add f1, :text => 'One'
n.add f2, :text => 'Two'
n.add f3, :text => 'Three'

s1 = Tk::Tile::Separator.new(f1) do
   orient 'vertical'
   place('height' => 200, 'x' => 40, 'y' => 10)
end

s2 = Tk::Tile::Separator.new(f1) do
   orient 'vertical'
   place('height' => 200, 'x' => 80, 'y' => 10)
end

Tk.mainloop
```

This will produce the following result:

Ruby/Tk Font, Colors, and Images

Ruby/Tk Fonts

Several Tk widgets, such as the label, text, and canvas, allow you to specify the fonts used to display text, typically via a *font* configuration option.

There is already a default list of fonts, which can be used for different requirements:

Font Name	Description
TkDefaultFont	The default for all GUI items not otherwise specified.
TkTextFont	Used for entry widgets, listboxes, etc.
TkFixedFont	A standard fixed-width font.
TkMenuFont	The font used for menu items.
TkHeadingFont	The font typically used for column headings in lists and tables.
TkCaptionFont	A font for window and dialog caption bars.
TkSmallCaptionFont	A smaller caption font for subwindows or tool dialogs
TkIconFont	A font for icon captions.
TkTooltipFont	A font for tooltips.

You can use any of these fonts in the following way:

```
TkLabel.new(root) {text 'Attention!'; font TkCaptionFont}
```

If you are willing to create your new font using different family and font type, then here is a simple syntax to create a font:

```
TkFont.new(
   .....Standard Options....
)
```

Standard Options

You can specify one or more standard option separated by comma.

- Foundry
- Family
- Weight
- Slant
- Swidth
- Pixel
- Point
- Xres
- Yres
- Space
- Avgwidth
- Registry
- Encoding

Ruby/Tk Colors

There are various ways to specify colors. Full details can be found in the **colors command reference**.

The system will provide the right colors for most things. Like with fonts, both Mac and Windows specifies a large number of system-specific color names (see the reference).

You can also specify fonts via RGB, like in HTML, e.g. "#3FF" or "#FF016A".

Finally, Tk recognizes the set of color names defined by X11; normally these are not used, except for very common ones such as "red", "black", etc.

For themed Tk widgets, colors are often used in defining styles that are applied to widgets, rather than applying the color to a widget directly.

Examples

```
require 'tk'


$resultsVar = TkVariable.new
root = TkRoot.new
root.title = "Window"
myFont = TkFont.new("family" => 'Helvetica',
                    "size" => 20,
                    "weight" => 'bold')
Lbl = TkLabel.new(root) do
  textvariable
  borderwidth 5
  font myFont
  foreground  "red"
  relief      "groove"
  pack("side" => "right",  "padx"=> "50", "pady"=> "50")
end


Lbl['textvariable'] = $resultsVar
$resultsVar.value = 'New value to display'


Tk.mainloop
```

This will produce the following result:

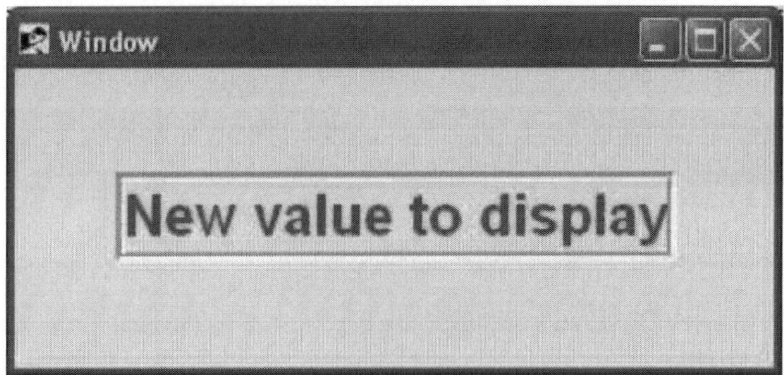

Ruby/Tk Images

Ruby/Tk includes support for GIF and PPM/PNM images. However, there is a Tk extension library called "Img", which adds support for many others: BMP, XBM, XPM, PNG, JPEG, TIFF, etc. Though not included directly in the Tk core, Img is usually included with other packaged distributions.

Here, we will see the basics of how to use images, displaying them in labels or buttons for example. We create an image object, usually from a file on disk.

Examples

```
require 'tk'

$resultsVar = TkVariable.new
root = TkRoot.new
root.title = "Window"

image = TkPhotoImage.new
image.file = "zara.gif"

label = TkLabel.new(root)
label.image = image
label.place('height' => image.height,
            'width' => image.width,
               'x' => 10, 'y' => 10)
Tk.mainloop
```

This will produce the following result:

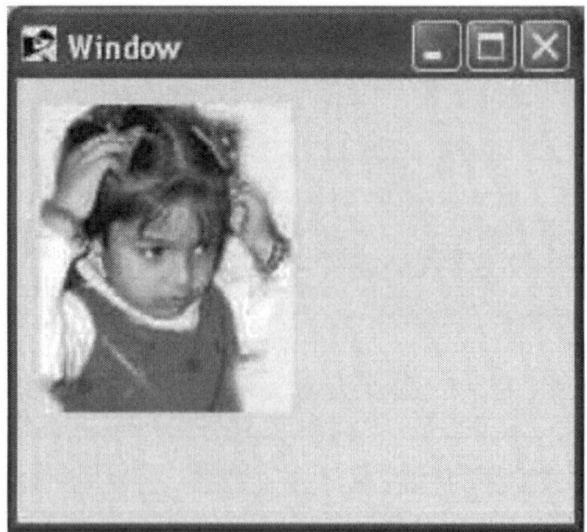

Tk's images are actually quite powerful and sophisticated and provide a wide variety of ways to inspect and modify images. You can find out more from the image command reference and the photo command reference.

Standard Configuration Options

All widgets have a number of different configuration options, which generally control how they are displayed or how they behave. The options that are available depend upon the widget class of course.

Here is a list of all the standard configuration options, which could be applicable to any Ruby/Tk widget. There are other widget specific options also, which would be explained along with widgets.

SN	Options with Description
1	**activebackground** => String Specifies background color to use when drawing active elements. An element is active if the mouse cursor is positioned over the element and pressing a mouse button will cause some action to occur. You can use color names like "red", "blue", "pink", "yellow" etc.
2	**activeborderwidth** => Integer Specifies a non-negative value indicating the width of the 3-D border drawn around active elements.
3	**activeforeground** => String Specifies foreground color to use when drawing active elements.
4	**anchor** => String

	Specifies how the information in a widget (e.g. text or a bitmap) is to be displayed in the widget. Must be one of the values **n**, **ne**, **e**, **se**, **s**, **sw**, **w**, **nw**, or **center**. For example, **nw** means display the information such that its top-left corner is at the top-left corner of the widget.
5	**background or bg** => String Specifies the normal background color to use when displaying the widget.
6	**bitmap** => Bitmap Specifies a bitmap to display in the widget. The exact way in which the bitmap is displayed may be affected by other options such as anchor or justify.
7	**borderwidth or bd** => Integer Specifies a non-negative value indicating the width of the 3-D border to draw around the outside of the widget.
8	**compound** => String Specifies if the widget should display text and bitmaps/images at the same time, and if so, where the bitmap/image should be placed relative to the text. Must be one of the values **none**, **bottom**, **top**, **left**, **right**, or **center**.
9	**cursor** => String Specifies the mouse cursor to be used for the widget. Possible values could be "watch", "arrow" etc.
10	**disabledforeground** => String Specifies foreground color to use when drawing a disabled element.
11	**exportselection** => Boolean Specifies whether or not a selection in the widget should also be the X selection. The value may have any of the **true**, **false**, **0**, **1**, **yes**, or **no**. If the selection is exported, then selecting in the widget deselects the current X selection, selecting outside the widget deselects any widget selection, and the widget will respond to selection retrieval requests when it has a selection.

12	**font** => String Specifies the font to use when drawing text inside the widget.
13	**foreground or fg** => String Specifies the normal foreground color to use when displaying the widget.
14	**highlightbackground** => String Specifies the color to display in the traversal highlight region when the widget does not have the input focus.
15	**highlightcolor** => String Specifies the color to use for the traversal highlight rectangle that is drawn around the widget when it has the input focus.
16	**highlightthickness** => Integer Specifies a non-negative value indicating the width of the highlight rectangle to draw around the outside of the widget when it has the input focus.
17	**image** => Image Specifies an image to display in the widget, which must have been created with an image create. Typically, if the image option is specified then it overrides other options that specify a bitmap or textual value to display in the widget; the image option may be reset to an empty string to re-enable a bitmap or text display.
18	**jump** => String For widgets with a slider that can be dragged to adjust a value, such as scrollbars and scales, this option determines when notifications are made about changes in the value. The option's value must be a boolean. If the value is false, updates are made continuously as the slider is dragged. If the value is true, updates are delayed until the mouse button is released to end the drag; at that point a single notification is made.
19	**justify** => String When there are multiple lines of text displayed in a widget, this option determines how the lines line up with each other. Must be one of **left**, **center**, or **right**. **Left**means that the lines' left edges all line up, **center**

	means that the lines' centers are aligned, and **right** means that the lines' right edges line up.
20	**offset** => String Specifies the offset of tiles (see also **tile** option). It can have two different formats**offset x,y** or **offset side**, where side can be **n**, **ne**, **e**, **se**, **s**, **sw**, **w**, **nw**, or **center**.
21	**orient** => String For widgets that can lay themselves out with either a horizontal or vertical orientation, such as scrollbars, this option specifies which orientation should be used. Must be either **horizontal** or **vertical** or an abbreviation of one of these.
22	**padx** => Integer Specifies a non-negative value indicating how much extra space to request for the widget in the X-direction.
23	**pady** => Integer Specifies a non-negative value indicating how much extra space to request for the widget in the Y-direction.
24	**relief** => Integer Specifies the 3-D effect desired for the widget. Acceptable values are **raised**,**sunken**, **flat**, **ridge**, and **groove**.
25	**repeatdelay** => Integer Specifies the number of milliseconds a button or key must be held down before it begins to auto-repeat. Used, for example, on the up- and down-arrows in scrollbars.
26	**repeatinterval** => Integer Used in conjunction with **repeatdelay**: once auto-repeat begins, this option determines the number of milliseconds between auto-repeats.
27	**selectbackground** => String Specifies the background color to use when displaying selected items.

28	**selectborderwidth** => Integer Specifies a non-negative value indicating the width of the 3-D border to draw around selected items.
29	**selectforeground** => String Specifies the foreground color to use when displaying selected items.
30	**setgrid** => Boolean Specifies a boolean value that determines whether this widget controls the resizing grid for its top-level window. This option is typically used in text widgets, where the information in the widget has a natural size (the size of a character) and it makes sense for the window's dimensions to be integral numbers of these units.
31	**takefocus** => Integer Provides information used when moving the focus from window to window via keyboard traversal (e.g., Tab and Shift-Tab). Before setting the focus to a window, the traversal scripts first check whether the window is viewable (it and all its ancestors are mapped); if not, the window is skipped. A value of 0 means that this window should be skipped entirely during keyboard traversal. 1 means that the this window should always receive the input focus.
32	**text** => String Specifies a string to be displayed inside the widget. The way in which the string is displayed depends on the particular widget and may be determined by other options, such as **anchor** or **justify**.
33	**textvariable** => Variable Specifies the name of a variable. The value of the variable is a text string to be displayed inside the widget; if the variable value changes then the widget will automatically update itself to reflect the new value. The way in which the string is displayed in the widget depends on the particular widget and may be determined by other options, such as **anchor** or **justify**.
34	**tile** => Image Specifies image used to display the widget. If image is the empty string,

	then the normal background color is displayed.
35	**troughcolor** => String Specifies the color to use for the rectangular trough areas in widgets such as scrollbars and scales.
36	**troughtile** => Image Specifies image used to display in the rectangular trough areas in widgets such as scrollbars and scales.
37	**underline** => Integer Specifies the integer index of a character to underline in the widget. This option is used by the default bindings to implement keyboard traversal for menu buttons and menu entries. 0 corresponds to the first character of the text displayed in the widget, 1 to the next character, and so on.
38	**wraplength** => Integer For widgets that can perform word-wrapping, this option specifies the maximum line length.
39	**xscrollcommand** => function Specifies a callback used to communicate with horizontal scrollbars.
40	**yscrollcommand** => function Specifies a callback used to communicate with vertical scrollbars.

Ruby/Tk Geometry Management

Geometry Management deals with positioning different widgets as per requirement. Geometry management in Tk relies on the concept of master and slave widgets.

A master is a widget, typically a top-level window or a frame, which will contain other widgets, which are called slaves. You can think of a geometry manager as taking control of the master widget, and deciding what will be displayed within.

The geometry manager will ask each slave widget for its natural size, or how large it would ideally like to be displayed. It then takes that information and combines it with any parameters provided by the program when it asks the geometry manager to manage that particular slave widget.

There are three geometry managers *place, grid* and *pack* that are responsible for controlling the size and location of each of the widgets in the interface.

- **grid** Geometry manager that arranges widgets in a grid.
- **pack** Geometry manager that packs around edges of cavity.
- **place** Geometry manager for fixed or rubber-sheet placement.

grid

Description

The grid geometry manager is the most flexible and easy-to-use geometry manager. It logically divides the parent window or the widget into rows and columns in a two-dimensional table.

You can then place a widget in an appropriate row and column format by using the *row* and *column* options, respectively. To understand the use of row and column options, consider the following example.

Syntax

Here is a simple syntax to create a grid Widget:

```
grid('row'=>x, 'column'=>y)
```

Examples

Following is the code to display the Label and an Entry widget using the grid geometry manager:

```
require 'tk'


top = TkRoot.new {title "Label and Entry Widget"}


#code to add a label widget
lb1=TkLabel.new(top){
   text 'Hello World'
   background "yellow"
   foreground "blue"
   grid('row'=>0, 'column'=>0)
```

```
}

#code to add an entry widget
e1 = TkEntry.new(top){
   background "red"
   foreground "blue"
   grid('row'=>0, 'column'=>1)
}

Tk.mainloop
```

This will produce the following result:

Pack

Description

The pack geometry manager organizes widgets in rows or columns inside the parent window or the widget. To manage widgets easily, the pack geometry manager provides various options, such as fill, expand, and side.

- **fill:** The fill option is used to specify whether a widget should occupy all the space given to it by the parent window or the widget. Some of the possible values that can be used with this option are none, x, y, or both. By default, the fill option is set to none.
- **expand:** The expand option is used to specify whether a widget should expand to fill any extra space available. The default value is 0, which means that the widget is not expanded. The other value is 1.
- **side:** The side option is used to specify the side against which the widget is to be packed. Some of the possible values that can be used with this option are top, left, bottom, or right. By default, the widgets are packed against the top edge of the parent window.

Syntax

Here is a simple syntax to create a pack Widget:

```
pack('padx'=>10, 'pady'=>10, 'side'=>'left')
```

Examples

Following is the code to display the Label and an Entry widget using the pack geometry manager:

```
require 'tk'

top = TkRoot.new {title "Label and Entry Widget"}

#code to add a label widget
lb1 = TkLabel.new(top){
   text 'Hello World'
   background "yellow"
   foreground "blue"
   pack('padx'=>10, 'pady'=>10, 'side'=>'left')
}

#code to add an entry widget
e1 = TkEntry.new(top){
   background "red"
   foreground "blue"
   pack('padx'=>10, 'pady'=>10, 'side'=>'left')
}

Tk.mainloop
```

This will produce the following result:

Place

Description

The place geometry manager allows you to place a widget at the specified position in the window. You can specify the position either in absolute terms or relative to the parent window or the widget.

To specify an absolute position, use the x and y options. To specify a position relative to the parent window or the widget, use the relx and rely options.

In addition, you can specify the relative size of the widget by using the relwidth and relheight options provided by this geometry manager.

Syntax

Here is a simple syntax to create a place Widget:

```
place(relx'=>x, 'rely'=>y)
```

Examples

Following is the code, which implements the place geometry manager:

```
require 'tk'


top = TkRoot.new {title "Label and Entry Widget"}


#code to add a label widget
lb1=TkLabel.new(top){
   text 'Hello World'
   background "yellow"
   foreground "blue"
   place('relx'=>0.0,'rely'=>0.0)
}


#code to add an entry widget
e1 = TkEntry.new(top){
   background "red"
   foreground "blue"
   place('relx'=>0.4,'rely'=>0.0)
```

```
}

Tk.mainloop
```

This will produce the following result:

Ruby/Tk Event Handling

Ruby/Tk supports *event loop*, which receives events from the operating system. These are things like button presses, keystrokes, mouse movement, window resizing, and so on.

Ruby/Tk takes care of managing this event loop for you. It will figure out what widget the event applies to (did the user click on this button? if a key was pressed, which textbox had the focus?), and dispatch it accordingly. Individual widgets know how to respond to events, so for example a button might change color when the mouse moves over it, and revert back when the mouse leaves.

At a higher level, Ruby/Tk invokes callbacks in your program to indicate that something significant happened to a widget For either case, you can provide a code block or a *Ruby Proc* object that specifies how the application responds to the event or callback.

Let's take a look at how to use the bind method to associate basic window system events with the Ruby procedures that handle them. The simplest form of bind takes as its inputs a string indicating the event name and a code block that Tk uses to handle the event.

For example, to catch the *ButtonRelease* event for the first mouse button on some widget, you'd write:

```
someWidget.bind('ButtonRelease-1') {
    ....code block to handle this event...
}
```

An event name can include additional modifiers and details. A modifier is a string like *Shift*, *Control* or *Alt*, indicating that one of the modifier keys was pressed.

So, for example, to catch the event that's generated when the user holds down the *Ctrl* key and clicks the right mouse button

```
someWidget.bind('Control-ButtonPress-3', proc { puts "Ouch!" })
```

Many Ruby/Tk widgets can trigger *callbacks* when the user activates them, and you can use the *command* callback to specify that a certain code block or procedure is invoked when that happens. As seen earlier, you can specify the command callback procedure when you create the widget:

```
helpButton = TkButton.new(buttonFrame) {
   text "Help"
   command proc { showHelp }
}
```

Or you can assign it later, using the widget's *command* method:

```
helpButton.command proc { showHelp }
```

Since the command method accepts either procedures or code blocks, you could also write the previous code example as:

```
helpButton = TkButton.new(buttonFrame) {
   text "Help"
   command { showHelp }
}
```

You can use the following basic event types in your Ruby/Tk application:

Tag	Event Description
"1" (one)	Clicked left mouse button.

"ButtonPress-1"	Clicked left mouse button.
"Enter"	Moved mouse inside.
"Leave"	Moved mouse outside.
"Double-1"	Double clicked.
"B3-Motion"	Right button drag from one position to another.
Control-ButtonPress-3	Right button is pressed along with *Ctrl* Key.
Alt-ButtonPress-1	Let button is pressed along with *Alt* Key.

The configure Method

The *configure* method can be used to set and retrieve any widget configuration values. For example, to change the width of a button you can call configure method any time as follows:

```
require "tk"


button = TkButton.new {
  text 'Hello World!'
  pack
}
button.configure('activebackground', 'blue')
Tk.mainloop
```

To get the value for a current widget, just supply it without a value as follows:

```
color = button.configure('activebackground')
```

You can also call configure without any options at all, which will give you a listing of all options and their values.

The cget Method

For simply retrieving the value of an option, configure returns more information than you generally want. The cget method returns just the current value.

```
color = button.cget('activebackground')
```

30. LDAP

Ruby/LDAP is an extension library for Ruby. It provides the interface to some LDAP libraries like OpenLDAP, UMich LDAP, Netscape SDK, ActiveDirectory.

The common API for application development is described in RFC1823 and is supported by Ruby/LDAP.

Ruby/LDAP Installation

You can download and install a complete Ruby/LDAP package from **SOURCEFORGE.NET**.

Before installing Ruby/LDAP, make sure you have the following components:

- Ruby 1.8.x (at least 1.8.2 if you want to use ldap/control).
- OpenLDAP, Netscape SDK, Windows 2003 or Windows XP.

Now, you can use standard Ruby Installation method. Before starting, if you'd like to see the available options for extconf.rb, run it with '--help' option.

```
$ ruby extconf.rb [--with-openldap1|--with-openldap2| \
                   --with-netscape|--with-wldap32]
$ make
$ make install
```

NOTE: If you're building the software on Windows, you may need to use *nmake* instead of *make*.

Establish LDAP Connection

This is a two-step process:

Step 1: Create Connection Object

Following is the syntax to create a connection to a LDAP directory.

```
LDAP::Conn.new(host='localhost', port=LDAP_PORT)
```

- **host:** This is the host ID running LDAP directory. We will take it as *localhost*.

- **port:** This is the port being used for LDAP service. Standard LDAP ports are 636 and 389. Make sure which port is being used at your server otherwise you can use LDAP::LDAP_PORT.

This call returns a new *LDAP::Conn* connection to the server, *host*, on port *port*.

Step 2: Binding

This is where we usually specify the username and password we will use for the rest of the session.

Following is the syntax to bind an LDAP connection, using the DN, **dn**, the credential, **pwd**, and the bind method, **method**:

```
conn.bind(dn=nil, password=nil, method=LDAP::LDAP_AUTH_SIMPLE)do
....
end
```

You can use the same method without a code block. In this case, you would need to unbind the connection explicitly as follows:

```
conn.bind(dn=nil, password=nil, method=LDAP::LDAP_AUTH_SIMPLE)
....
conn.unbind
```

If a code block is given, *self* is yielded to the block.

We can now perform search, add, modify or delete operations inside the block of the bind method (between bind and unbind), provided we have the proper permissions.

Example

Assuming we are working on a local server, let's put things together with appropriate host, domain, user id and password, etc.

```
#/usr/bin/ruby -w


require 'ldap'


$HOST =    'localhost'
$PORT =    LDAP::LDAP_PORT
$SSLPORT = LDAP::LDAPS_PORT
```

```
conn = LDAP::Conn.new($HOST, $PORT)
conn.bind('cn=root, dc=localhost, dc=localdomain','secret')
....
conn.unbind
```

Adding an LDAP Entry

Adding an LDPA entry is a two step process:

Step 1: Creating *LDAP::Mod* object

We need *LDAP::Mod* object pass to *conn.add* method to create an entry. Here is a simple syntax to create *LDAP::Mod* object:

```
Mod.new(mod_type, attr, vals)
```

- **mod_type:** One or more option LDAP_MOD_ADD, LDAP_MOD_REPLACE or LDAP_MOD_DELETE.
- **attr:** should be the name of the attribute on which to operate.
- **vals:** is an array of values pertaining to *attr*. If *vals* contains binary data, *mod_type*should be logically OR'ed (|) with LDAP_MOD_BVALUES.

This call returns *LDAP::Mod* object, which can be passed to methods in the LDAP::Conn class, such as Conn#add, Conn#add_ext, Conn#modify and Conn#modify_ext.

Step 2: Calling *conn.add* Method

Once we are ready with *LDAP::Mod* object, we can call *conn.add* method to create an entry. Here is a syntax to call this method:

```
conn.add(dn, attrs)
```

This method adds an entry with the DN, *dn*, and the attributes, *attrs*. Here, *attrs* should be either an array of *LDAP::Mod* objects or a hash of attribute/value array pairs.

Example

Here is a complete example, which will create two directory entries:

```
#/usr/bin/ruby -w

require 'ldap'

$HOST =    'localhost'
$PORT =    LDAP::LDAP_PORT
$SSLPORT = LDAP::LDAPS_PORT

conn = LDAP::Conn.new($HOST, $PORT)
conn.bind('cn=root, dc=localhost, dc=localdomain','secret')

conn.perror("bind")
entry1 = [
  LDAP.mod(LDAP::LDAP_MOD_ADD,'objectclass',['top','domain']),
  LDAP.mod(LDAP::LDAP_MOD_ADD,'o',['TTSKY.NET']),
  LDAP.mod(LDAP::LDAP_MOD_ADD,'dc',['localhost']),
}

entry2 = [
  LDAP.mod(LDAP::LDAP_MOD_ADD,'objectclass',['top','person']),
  LDAP.mod(LDAP::LDAP_MOD_ADD, 'cn', ['Zara Ali']),
  LDAP.mod(LDAP::LDAP_MOD_ADD | LDAP::LDAP_MOD_BVALUES, 'sn',
                     ['ttate','ALI', "zero\000zero"]),
]

begin
  conn.add("dc=localhost, dc=localdomain", entry1)
  conn.add("cn=Zara Ali, dc=localhost, dc=localdomain", entry2)
rescue LDAP::ResultError
  conn.perror("add")
  exit
end
conn.perror("add")
```

```
conn.unbind
```

Modifying an LDAP Entry

Modifying an entry is similar to adding one. Just call the *modify* method instead of *add* with the attributes to modify. Here is a simple syntax of *modify* method.

```
conn.modify(dn, mods)
```

This method modifies an entry with the DN, *dn*, and the attributes, *mods*. Here, *mods* should be either an array of *LDAP::Mod* objects or a hash of attribute/value array pairs.

Example

To modify the surname of the entry, which we added in the previous section, we would write:

```
#/usr/bin/ruby -w

require 'ldap'

$HOST =    'localhost'
$PORT =    LDAP::LDAP_PORT
$SSLPORT = LDAP::LDAPS_PORT

conn = LDAP::Conn.new($HOST, $PORT)
conn.bind('cn=root, dc=localhost, dc=localdomain','secret')

conn.perror("bind")
entry1 = [
  LDAP.mod(LDAP::LDAP_MOD_REPLACE, 'sn', ['Mohtashim']),
]

begin
  conn.modify("cn=Zara Ali, dc=localhost, dc=localdomain", entry1)
rescue LDAP::ResultError
  conn.perror("modify")
  exit
```

```
end
conn.perror("modify")
conn.unbind
```

Deleting an LDAP Entry

To delete an entry, call the *delete* method with the distinguished name as parameter. Here is a simple syntax of *delete* method.

```
conn.delete(dn)
```

This method deletes an entry with the DN, *dn*.

Example

To delete *Zara Mohtashim* entry, which we added in the previous section, we would write:

```
#/usr/bin/ruby -w

require 'ldap'

$HOST =    'localhost'
$PORT =    LDAP::LDAP_PORT
$SSLPORT = LDAP::LDAPS_PORT

conn = LDAP::Conn.new($HOST, $PORT)
conn.bind('cn=root, dc=localhost, dc=localdomain','secret')

conn.perror("bind")
begin
  conn.delete("cn=Zara-Mohtashim, dc=localhost, dc=localdomain")
rescue LDAP::ResultError
  conn.perror("delete")
  exit
end
conn.perror("delete")
conn.unbind
```

Modifying the Distinguished Name

It's not possible to modify the distinguished name of an entry with the *modify* method. Instead, use the *modrdn* method. Here is simple syntax of *modrdn* method:

```
conn.modrdn(dn, new_rdn, delete_old_rdn)
```

This method modifies the RDN of the entry with DN, *dn*, giving it the new RDN, *new_rdn*. If*delete_old_rdn* is *true*, the old RDN value will be deleted from the entry.

Example

Suppose we have the following entry:

```
dn: cn=Zara Ali,dc=localhost,dc=localdomain

cn: Zara Ali

sn: Ali

objectclass: person
```

Then, we can modify its distinguished name with the following code:

```
#/usr/bin/ruby -w


require 'ldap'


$HOST =    'localhost'

$PORT =    LDAP::LDAP_PORT

$SSLPORT = LDAP::LDAPS_PORT


conn = LDAP::Conn.new($HOST, $PORT)

conn.bind('cn=root, dc=localhost, dc=localdomain','secret')


conn.perror("bind")

begin

  conn.modrdn("cn=Zara Ali, dc=localhost, dc=localdomain",

              "cn=Zara Mohtashim", true)

rescue LDAP::ResultError

  conn.perror("modrdn")
```

```
  exit
end
conn.perror("modrdn")
conn.unbind
```

Performing a Search

To perform a search on a LDAP directory, use the *search* method with one of the three different search modes:

- **LDAP_SCOPE_BASEM:** Search only the base node.
- **LDAP_SCOPE_ONELEVEL:** Search all children of the base node.
- **LDAP_SCOPE_SUBTREE:** Search the whole subtree including the base node.

Example

Here, we are going to search the whole subtree of entry *dc=localhost, dc=localdomain* for*person* objects:

```
#/usr/bin/ruby -w

require 'ldap'

$HOST =    'localhost'
$PORT =    LDAP::LDAP_PORT
$SSLPORT = LDAP::LDAPS_PORT

base = 'dc=localhost,dc=localdomain'
scope = LDAP::LDAP_SCOPE_SUBTREE
filter = '(objectclass=person)'
attrs = ['sn', 'cn']

conn = LDAP::Conn.new($HOST, $PORT)
conn.bind('cn=root, dc=localhost, dc=localdomain','secret')

conn.perror("bind")
begin
```

```
  conn.search(base, scope, filter, attrs) { |entry|
     # print distinguished name
     p entry.dn
     # print all attribute names
     p entry.attrs
     # print values of attribute 'sn'
     p entry.vals('sn')
     # print entry as Hash
     p entry.to_hash
  }
rescue LDAP::ResultError
  conn.perror("search")
  exit
end
conn.perror("search")
conn.unbind
```

This invokes the given code block for each matching entry where the LDAP entry is represented by an instance of the LDAP::Entry class. With the last parameter of search, you can specify the attributes in which you are interested, omitting all others. If you pass nil here, all attributes are returned same as "SELECT *" in relational databases.

The dn method (alias for get_dn) of the LDAP::Entry class returns the distinguished name of the entry, and with the to_hash method, you can get a hash representation of its attributes (including the distinguished name). To get a list of an entry's attributes, use the attrs method (alias for get_attributes). Also, to get the list of one specific attribute's values, use the vals method (alias for get_values).

Handling Errors

Ruby/LDAP defines two different exception classes:

- In case of an error, the new, bind or unbind methods raise an LDAP::Error exception.
- In case of add, modify, delete or searching an LDAP directory raise an LDAP::ResultError.

Further Reading

For complete details on LDAP methods, please refer to the standard documentation for **LDAP Documentation**.

31. MULTITHREADING

Traditional programs have a single *thread of execution*: the statements or instructions that comprise the program are executed sequentially until the program terminates.

A multithreaded program has more than one thread of execution. Within each thread, statements are executed sequentially, but the threads themselves may be executed in parallel on a multicore CPU, for example. Often on a single CPU machine, multiple threads are not actually executed in parallel, but parallelism is simulated by interleaving the execution of the threads.

Ruby makes it easy to write multi-threaded programs with the *Thread* class. Ruby threads are a lightweight and efficient way to achieve concurrency in your code.

Creating Ruby Threads

To start a new thread, just associate a block with a call to *Thread.new*. A new thread will be created to execute the code in the block, and the original thread will return from *Thread.new* immediately and resume execution with the next statement:

```
# Thread #1 is running here
Thread.new {
  # Thread #2 runs this code
}
# Thread #1 runs this code
```

Example

Here is an example, which shows how we can use multi-threaded Ruby program.

```
#!/usr/bin/ruby

def func1
   i=0
   while i<=2
      puts "func1 at: #{Time.now}"
      sleep(2)
```

```
      i=i+1
   end
end

def func2
   j=0
   while j<=2
      puts "func2 at: #{Time.now}"
      sleep(1)
      j=j+1
   end
end

puts "Started At #{Time.now}"
t1=Thread.new{func1()}
t2=Thread.new{func2()}
t1.join
t2.join
puts "End at #{Time.now}"
```

This will produce following result:

```
Started At Wed May 14 08:21:54 -0700 2008
func1 at: Wed May 14 08:21:54 -0700 2008
func2 at: Wed May 14 08:21:54 -0700 2008
func2 at: Wed May 14 08:21:55 -0700 2008
func1 at: Wed May 14 08:21:56 -0700 2008
func2 at: Wed May 14 08:21:56 -0700 2008
func1 at: Wed May 14 08:21:58 -0700 2008
End at Wed May 14 08:22:00 -0700 2008
```

Thread Lifecycle

A new threads are created with *Thread.new*. You can also use the synonyms *Thread.start* and *Thread.fork*.

There is no need to start a thread after creating it, it begins running automatically when CPU resources become available.

The Thread class defines a number of methods to query and manipulate the thread while it is running. A thread runs the code in the block associated with the call to *Thread.new* and then it stops running.

The value of the last expression in that block is the value of the thread, and can be obtained by calling the *value* method of the Thread object. If the thread has run to completion, then the value returns the thread's value right away. Otherwise, the *value* method blocks and does not return until the thread has completed.

The class method *Thread.current* returns the Thread object that represents the current thread. This allows threads to manipulate themselves. The class method *Thread.main* returns the Thread object that represents the main thread. This is the initial thread of execution that began when the Ruby program was started.

You can wait for a particular thread to finish by calling that thread's *Thread.join* method. The calling thread will block until the given thread is finished.

Threads and Exceptions

If an exception is raised in the main thread, and is not handled anywhere, the Ruby interpreter prints a message and exits. In threads, other than the main thread, unhandled exceptions cause the thread to stop running.

If a thread **t** exits because of an unhandled exception, and another thread **s** calls *t.join or t.value,* then the exception that occurred in **t** is raised in the thread **s**.

If *Thread.abort_on_exception* is *false*, the default condition, an unhandled exception simply kills the current thread and all the rest continue to run.

If you would like any unhandled exception in any thread to cause the interpreter to exit, set the class method *Thread.abort_on_exception* to *true*.

```
t = Thread.new { ... }

t.abort_on_exception = true
```

Thread Variables

A thread can normally access any variables that are in scope when the thread is created. Variables local to the block of a thread are local to the thread, and are not shared.

Thread class features a special facility that allows thread-local variables to be created and accessed by name. You simply treat the thread object as if it were a Hash, writing to elements using []= and reading them back using [].

In this example, each thread records the current value of the variable count in a threadlocal variable with the key *mycount*.

```
#!/usr/bin/ruby

count = 0
arr = []

10.times do |i|
   arr[i] = Thread.new {
      sleep(rand(0)/10.0)
      Thread.current["mycount"] = count
      count += 1
   }
end

arr.each {|t| t.join; print t["mycount"], ", " }
puts "count = #{count}"
```

This produces the following result:

```
8, 0, 3, 7, 2, 1, 6, 5, 4, 9, count = 10
```

The main thread waits for the subthreads to finish and then prints out the value of *count* captured by each.

Thread Priorities

The first factor that affects the thread scheduling is the thread priority: high-priority threads are scheduled before low-priority threads. More precisely, a thread will only get CPU time if there are no higher-priority threads waiting to run.

You can set and query the priority of a Ruby Thread object with *priority=* and *priority*. A newly created thread starts at the same priority as the thread that created it. The main thread starts off at priority 0.

There is no way to set the priority of a thread before it starts running. A thread can, however, raise or lower its own priority as the first action it takes.

Thread Exclusion

If two threads share access to the same data, and at least one of the threads modifies that data, you must take special care to ensure that no thread can ever see the data in an inconsistent state. This is called *thread exclusion*.

Mutex is a class that implements a simple semaphore lock for mutually exclusive access to some shared resource. That is, only one thread may hold the lock at a given time. Other threads may choose to wait in line for the lock to become available, or may simply choose to get an immediate error indicating that the lock is not available.

By placing all accesses to the shared data under control of a *mutex*, we ensure consistency and atomic operation. Let's try to examples, first one without mutax and second one with mutax:

Example without Mutax

```
#!/usr/bin/ruby
require 'thread'


count1 = count2 = 0
difference = 0
counter = Thread.new do
   loop do
      count1 += 1
      count2 += 1
   end
end
spy = Thread.new do
   loop do
      difference += (count1 - count2).abs
   end
end
sleep 1
puts "count1 :  #{count1}"
puts "count2 :  #{count2}"
puts "difference : #{difference}"
```

This will produce the following result:

```
count1 :  1583766
count2 :  1583766
difference : 0
```

```
#!/usr/bin/ruby
require 'thread'
mutex = Mutex.new

count1 = count2 = 0
difference = 0
counter = Thread.new do
   loop do
      mutex.synchronize do
         count1 += 1
         count2 += 1
      end
    end
end
spy = Thread.new do
   loop do
       mutex.synchronize do
          difference += (count1 - count2).abs
       end
   end
end
sleep 1
mutex.lock
puts "count1 :  #{count1}"
puts "count2 :  #{count2}"
puts "difference : #{difference}"
```

This will produce the following result:

```
count1 :  696591
count2 :  696591
difference : 0
```

Handling Deadlock

When we start using *Mutex* objects for thread exclusion we must be careful to avoid *deadlock*. Deadlock is the condition that occurs when all threads are waiting to acquire a resource held by another thread. Because all threads are blocked, they cannot release the locks they hold. And because they cannot release the locks, no other thread can acquire those locks.

This is where *condition variables* come into picture. A *condition variable* is simply a semaphore that is associated with a resource and is used within the protection of a particular *mutex*. When you need a resource that's unavailable, you wait on a condition variable. That action releases the lock on the corresponding *mutex*. When some other thread signals that the resource is available, the original thread comes off the wait and simultaneously regains the lock on the critical region.

Example

```
#!/usr/bin/ruby
require 'thread'
mutex = Mutex.new

cv = ConditionVariable.new
a = Thread.new {
   mutex.synchronize {
      puts "A: I have critical section, but will wait for cv"
      cv.wait(mutex)
      puts "A: I have critical section again! I rule!"
   }
}

puts "(Later, back at the ranch...)"

b = Thread.new {
   mutex.synchronize {
```

```
        puts "B: Now I am critical, but am done with cv"
        cv.signal
        puts "B: I am still critical, finishing up"
    }
}
a.join
b.join
```

This will produce the following result:

```
A: I have critical section, but will wait for cv
(Later, back at the ranch...)
B: Now I am critical, but am done with cv
B: I am still critical, finishing up
A: I have critical section again! I rule!
```

Thread States

There are five possible return values corresponding to the five possible states as shown in the following table. The *status* method returns the state of the thread.

Thread state	Return value
Runnable	run
Sleeping	Sleeping
Aborting	aborting
Terminated normally	false
Terminated with exception	nil

Thread Class Methods

Following methods are provided by *Thread* class and they are applicable to all the threads available in the program. These methods will be called as using *Thread* class name as follows:

```
Thread.abort_on_exception = true
```

Here is the complete list of all the class methods available:

SN	Methods with Description
1	**Thread.abort_on_exception** Returns the status of the global *abort on exception* condition. The default is *false*. When set to *true*, will cause all threads to abort (the process will exit(0)) if an exception is raised in any thread.
2	**Thread.abort_on_exception=** When set to *true*, all threads will abort if an exception is raised. Returns the new state.
3	**Thread.critical** Returns the status of the global *thread critical* condition.
4	**Thread.critical=** Sets the status of the global *thread critical* condition and returns it. When set to *true*, prohibits scheduling of any existing thread. Does not block new threads from being created and run. Certain thread operations (such as stopping or killing a thread, sleeping in the current thread, and raising an exception) may cause a thread to be scheduled even when in a critical section.
5	**Thread.current** Returns the currently executing thread.
6	**Thread.exit** Terminates the currently running thread and schedules another thread to be run. If this thread is already marked to be killed, *exit* returns the *Thread.* If this is the main thread, or the last thread, exit the process.
7	**Thread.fork { block }** Synonym for Thread.new.

8	**Thread.kill(aThread)** Causes the given *aThread* to exit.
9	**Thread.list** Returns an array of *Thread* objects for all threads that are either runnable or stopped. Thread.
10	**Thread.main** Returns the main thread for the process.
11	**Thread.new([arg]*) {| args | block }** Creates a new thread to execute the instructions given in block, and begins running it. Any arguments passed to *Thread.new* are passed into the block.
12	**Thread.pass** Invokes the thread scheduler to pass execution to another thread.
13	**Thread.start([args]*) {| args | block }** Basically the same as *Thread.new* . However, if class *Thread* is subclassed, then calling *start* in that subclass will not invoke the subclass's *initialize* method.
14	**Thread.stop** Stops execution of the current thread, putting it into a *sleep* state, and schedules execution of another thread. Resets the *critical* condition to false.

Thread Instance Methods

These methods are applicable to an instance of a thread. These methods will be called as using an instance of a *Thread* as follows:

```
#!/usr/bin/ruby


thr = Thread.new do   # Calling a class method new

   puts "In second thread"
```

```
   raise "Raise exception"
end
thr.join   # Calling an instance method join
```

Here is the complete list of all the instance methods available:

SN	Methods with Description
1	**thr[aSymbol]** Attribute Reference - Returns the value of a thread-local variable, using either a symbol or an *aSymbol* name. If the specified variable does not exist, returns *nil*.
2	**thr[aSymbol] =** Attribute Assignment - Sets or creates the value of a thread-local variable, using either a symbol or a string.
3	**thr.abort_on_exception** Returns the status of the *abort on exception* condition for *thr*. The default is *false*.
4	**thr.abort_on_exception=** When set to *true*, causes all threads (including the main program) to abort if an exception is raised in *thr*. The process will effectively *exit(0)*.
5	**thr.alive?** Returns *true* if *thr* is running or sleeping.
6	**thr.exit** Terminates *thr* and schedules another thread to be run. If this thread is already marked to be killed, *exit* returns the *Thread*. If this is the main thread, or the last thread, exits the process.
7	**thr.join** The calling thread will suspend execution and run *thr*. Does not return until *thr* exits. Any threads not joined will be killed when the main

	program exits.
8	**thr.key?** Returns *true* if the given string (or symbol) exists as a thread-local variable.
9	**thr.kill** Synonym for *Thread.exit* .
10	**thr.priority** Returns the priority of *thr*. Default is zero; higher-priority threads will run before lower priority threads.
11	**thr.priority=** Sets the priority of *thr* to an Integer. Higher-priority threads will run before lower priority threads.
12	**thr.raise(anException)** Raises an exception from *thr*. The caller does not have to be *thr*.
13	**thr.run** Wakes up *thr*, making it eligible for scheduling. If not in a critical section, then invokes the scheduler.
14	**thr.safe_level** Returns the safe level in effect for *thr*.
15	**thr.status** Returns the status of *thr*: *sleep* if *thr* is sleeping or waiting on I/O, *run* if *thr* is executing, false if *thr* terminated normally, and *nil* if *thr* terminated with an exception.
16	**thr.stop?** Returns *true* if *thr* is dead or sleeping.

17	**thr.value** Waits for thr to complete via *Thread.join* and returns its value.
18	**thr.wakeup** Marks *thr* as eligible for scheduling, it may still remain blocked on I/O, however.

32. BUILT-IN FUNCTIONS

Since the *Kernel* module is included by *Object* class, its methods are available everywhere in the Ruby program. They can be called without a receiver (functional form). Therefore, they are often called functions.

A complete list of Built-in Functions is given here for your reference:

SN	Methods with Description
1	**abort** Terminates program. If an exception is raised (i.e., $! isn't nil), its error message is displayed.
2	**Array(obj)** Returns obj after converting it to an array using to_ary or to_a.
3	**at_exit {...}** Registers a block for execution when the program exits. Similar to END statement, but END statement registers the block only once.
4	**autoload(classname, file)** Registers a class classname to be loaded from file the first time it's used. classname may be a string or a symbol.
5	**binding** Returns the current variable and method bindings. The *Binding* object that is returned may be passed to the *eval* method as its second argument.
6	**block_given?** Returns true if the method was called with a *block*.
7	**callcc {| c|...}** Passes a *Continuation* object c to the block and executes the block. *callcc* can be used for global exit or loop construct.

8	**caller([n])** Returns the current execution stack in an array of the strings in the form *file:line*. If n is specified, returns stack entries from nth level on down.
9	**catch(tag) {...}** Catches a nonlocal exit by a throw called during the execution of its block.
10	**chomp([rs=$/])** Returns the value of variable $_ with the ending newline removed, assigning the result back to $_. The value of the newline string can be specified with rs.
11	**chomp!([rs=$/])** Removes newline from $_, modifying the string in place.
12	**chop** Returns the value of $_ with its last character (one byte) removed, assigning the result back to $_.
13	**chop!** Removes the last character from $_, modifying the string in place.
14	**eval(str[, scope[, file, line]])** Executes *str* as Ruby code. The binding in which to perform the evaluation may be specified with *scope*. The filename and line number of the code to be compiled may be specified using *file* and line.
15	**exec(cmd[, arg...])** Replaces the current process by running the command *cmd*. If multiple arguments are specified, the command is executed with no shell expansion.
16	**exit([result=0])** Exits program, with *result* as the status code returned.

17	**exit!([result=0])** Kills the program bypassing exit handling such as *ensure*, etc.
18	**fail(...)** See raise(...).
19	**Float(obj)** Returns obj after converting it to a float. Numeric objects are converted directly; nil is converted to 0.0; strings are converted considering 0x, 0b radix prefix. The rest are converted using obj.to_f.
20	**fork** **fork {...}** Creates a child process. *nil* is returned in the child process and the child process' ID (integer) is returned in the parent process. If a block is specified, it's run in the child process.
21	**format(fmt[, arg...])** See sprintf.
22	**gets([rs=$/])** Reads the filename specified in the command line or one line from standard input. The record separator string can be specified explicitly with rs.
23	**global_variables** Returns an array of global variable names.
24	**gsub(x, y)** **gsub(x) {...}** Replaces all strings matching x in $_ with y. If a block is specified, matched strings are replaced with the result of the block. The modified result is assigned to $_.
25	**gsub!(x, y)** **gsub!(x) {...}** Performs the same substitution as gsub, except the string is changed in

	place.
26	**Integer(obj)** Returns obj after converting it to an integer. Numeric objects are converted directly; nil is converted to 0; strings are converted considering 0x, 0b radix prefix. The rest are converted using obj.to_i.
27	**lambda {| x|...}** **proc {| x|...}** **lambda** proc Converts a block into a *Proc* object. If no block is specified, the block associated with the calling method is converted.
28	**load(file[, private=false])** Loads a Ruby program from *file*. Unlike *require*, it doesn't load extension libraries. If *private* is *true*, the program is loaded into an anonymous module, thus protecting the namespace of the calling program.
29	**local_variables** Returns an array of local variable names.
30	**loop {...}** Repeats a block of code.
31	**open(path[, mode="r"])** **open(path[, mode="r"]) {| f|...}** Opens a *file*. If a block is specified, the block is executed with the opened stream passed as an argument. The file is closed automatically when the block exits. If *path*begins with a pipe |, the following string is run as a command, and the stream associated with that process is returned.
32	**p(obj)** Displays obj using its inspect method (often used for debugging).

33	**print([arg...])** Prints arg to *$defout*. If no arguments are specified, the value of $_ is printed.
34	**printf(fmt[, arg...])** Formats arg according to *fmt* using *sprintf* and prints the result to *$defout*. For formatting specifications, see sprintf for detail.
35	**proc {| x|...}** **proc** See lamda.
36	**putc(c)** Prints one character to the default output (*$defout*).
37	**puts([str])** Prints string to the default output (*$defout*). If the string doesn't end with a newline, a newline is appended to the string.
38	**raise(...)** **fail(...)** Raises an exception. Assumes *RuntimeError* if no exception class is specified. Calling *raise* without arguments in a *rescue* clause re-raises the exception. Doing so outside a rescue clause raises a message-less *RuntimeError*. **fail** is an obsolete name for raise.
39	**rand([max=0])** Generates a pseudo-random number greater than or equal to 0 and less than max. If max is either not specified or is set to 0, a random number is returned as a floating-point number greater than or equal to 0 and less than 1. *srand* may be used to initialize pseudo-random stream.
40	**readline([rs=$/])** Equivalent to gets except it raises an EOFError exception on reading EOF.
41	**readlines([rs=$/])**

	Returns an array of strings holding either the filenames specified as command-line arguments or the contents of standard input.
42	**require(lib)** Loads the library (including extension libraries) *lib* when it's first called. require will not load the same library more than once. If no extension is specified in *lib*, require tries to add .rb,.so, etc., to it.
43	**scan(re)** **scan(re) {|x|...}** Equivalent to $_.scan.
44	**select(reads[, writes=nil[, excepts=nil[, timeout=nil]]])** Checks for changes in the status of three types of IO objects input, output, and exceptions which are passed as arrays of IO objects. *nil* is passed for arguments that don't need checking. A three-element array containing arrays of the IO objects for which there were changes in status is returned. *nil* is returned on timeout.
45	**set_trace_func(proc)** Sets a handler for tracing. *proc* may be a string or *proc* object. *set_trace_func* is used by the debugger and profiler.
46	**sleep([sec])** Suspends program execution for sec seconds. If sec isn't specified, the program is suspended forever.
47	**split([sep[, max]])** Equivalent to $_.split.
48	**sprintf(fmt[, arg...])** **format(fmt[, arg...])** Returns a string in which arg is formatted according to fmt. Formatting specifications are essentially the same as those for sprintf in the C programming language. Conversion specifiers (% followed by conversion field specifier) in *fmt* are replaced by formatted string of corresponding argument. A list of conversion filed is given below in next section.

49	**srand([seed])** Initializes an array of random numbers. If *seed* isn't specified, initialization is performed using the time and other system information for the seed.
50	**String(obj)** Returns obj after converting it to a string using obj.to_s.
51	**syscall(sys[, arg...])** Calls an operating system call function specified by number *sys*. The numbers and meaning of *sys* is system-dependant.
52	**system(cmd[, arg...])** Executes *cmd* as a call to the command line. If multiple arguments are specified, the command is run directly with no shell expansion. Returns *true* if the return status is 0 (success).
53	**sub(x, y)** **sub(x) {...}** Replaces the first string matching x in $_ with y. If a block is specified, matched strings are replaced with the result of the block. The modified result is assigned to $_.
54	**sub!(x, y)** **sub!(x) {...}** Performs the same replacement as sub, except the string is changed in place.
55	**test(test, f1[, f2])** Performs various file tests specified by the character *test*. In order to improve readability, you should use File class methods (for example File::readable?) rather than this function. A list of arguments is given below in next section.
56	**throw(tag[, value=nil])** Jumps to the catch function waiting with the symbol or string *tag*. value is

	the return value to be used by *catch*.
57	**trace_var(var, cmd)** **trace_var(var) {...}** Sets tracing for a global variable. The variable name is specified as a symbol. *cmd*may be a string or Proc object.
58	**trap(sig, cmd)** **trap(sig) {...}** Sets a signal handler. sig may be a string (like SIGUSR1) or an integer. SIG may be omitted from signal name. Signal handler for EXIT signal or signal number 0 is invoked just before process termination.
59	**untrace_var(var[, cmd])** Removes tracing for a global variable. If *cmd* is specified, only that command is removed.

Functions for Numbers

Here is a list of Built-in Functions related to number. They should be used as follows:

```
#!/usr/bin/ruby


num = 12.40
puts num.floor      # 12
puts num + 10       # 22.40
puts num.integer?   # false  as num is a float.
```

This will produce the following result:

```
12
22.4
false
```

Assuming, **n** is a number:

SN	Methods with Description
1	**n + num** **n - num** **n * num** n / num Performs arithmetic operations: addition, subtraction, multiplication, and division.
2	**n % num** Returns the modulus of n.
3	**n ** num** Exponentiation.
4	**n.abs** Returns the absolute value of n.
5	**n.ceil** Returns the smallest integer greater than or equal to n.
6	**n.coerce(num)** Returns an array containing num and n both possibly converted to a type that allows them to be operated on mutually. Used in automatic type conversion in numeric operators.
7	**n.divmod(num)** Returns an array containing the quotient and modulus from dividing n by num.
8	**n.floor** Returns the largest integer less than or equal to n.

9	**n.integer?** Returns true if n is an integer.
10	**n.modulo(num)** Returns the modulus obtained by dividing n by num and rounding the quotient with *floor*
11	**n.nonzero?** Returns n if it isn't zero, otherwise nil.
12	**n.remainder(num)** Returns the remainder obtained by dividing **n** by **num** and removing decimals from the quotient. The **result** and **n** always have same sign.
13	**n.round** Returns n rounded to the nearest integer.
14	**n.truncate** Returns n as an integer with decimals removed.
15	**n.zero?** Returns zero if n is 0.
16	**n & numn | num** **n ^ num** Bitwise operations: AND, OR, XOR, and inversion.
17	**n << num** n >> num Bitwise left shift and right shift.
18	**n[num]** Returns the value of the **num**th bit from the least significant bit, which is n[0].

19	**n.chr** Returns a string containing the character for the character code **n**.
20	**n.next** **n.succ** Returns the next integer following n. Equivalent to n + 1.
21	**n.size** Returns the number of bytes in the machine representation of **n**.
22	**n.step(upto, step) {|n| ...}** Iterates the block from **n** to **upto**, incrementing by **step** each time.
23	**n.times {|n| ...}** Iterates the block **n** times.
24	**n.to_f** Converts **n** into a floating point number. Float conversion may lose precision information.
25	**n.to_int** Returns **n** after converting into interger number.

Functions for Float

Here is a list of Ruby Built-in functions especially for float numbers. Assuming we have a float number **f**:

SN	Methods with Description
1	**Float::induced_from(num)** Returns the result of converting *num* to a floating-point number.
2	**f.finite?**

	Returns true if *f* isn't infinite and f.nan is false.
3	**f.infinite?** Returns 1 if *f* is positive infinity, -1 if negative infinity, or nil if anything else.
4	**f.nan?** Returns true if *f* isn't a valid IEEE floating point number.

Functions for Math

Here is a list of Ruby Built-in math functions:

SN	Methods with Description
1	**atan2(x, y)** Calculates the arc tangent.
2	**cos(x)** Calculates the cosine of x.
3	**exp(x)** Calculates an exponential function (e raised to the power of x).
4	**frexp(x)** Returns a two-element array containing the nominalized fraction and exponent of x.
5	**ldexp(x, exp)** Returns the value of x times 2 to the power of exp.
6	**log(x)** Calculates the natural logarithm of x.
7	**log10(x)**

	Calculates the base 10 logarithm of x.
8	**sin(x)** Calculates the sine of x.
9	**sqrt(x)** Returns the square root of x. x must be positive.
10	**tan(x)** Calculates the tangent of x.

Conversion Field Specifier

The function *sprintf(fmt[, arg...]) and format(fmt[, arg...])* returns a string in which arg is formatted according to fmt. Formatting specifications are essentially the same as those for sprintf in the C programming language. Conversion specifiers (% followed by conversion field specifier) in *fmt* are replaced by formatted string of corresponding argument.

The following conversion specifiers are supported by Ruby's format:

Specifier	Description
b	Binary integer
c	Single character
d,i	Decimal integer
e	Exponential notation (e.g., 2.44e6)
E	Exponential notation (e.g., 2.44E6)
f	Floating-point number (e.g., 2.44)
g	use %e if exponent is less than -4, %f otherwise

G	use %E if exponent is less than -4, %f otherwise
o	Octal integer
s	String or any object converted using to_s
u	Unsigned decimal integer
x	Hexadecimal integer (e.g., 39ff)
X	Hexadecimal integer (e.g., 39FF)

Following is the usage example:

```
#!/usr/bin/ruby

str = sprintf("%s\n", "abc")   # => "abc\n" (simplest form)
puts str

str = sprintf("d=%d", 42)      # => "d=42" (decimal output)
puts str

str = sprintf("%04x", 255)     # => "00ff" (width 4, zero padded)
puts str

str = sprintf("%8s", "hello")  # => " hello" (space padded)
puts str

str = sprintf("%.2s", "hello") # => "he" (trimmed by precision)
puts str
```

This will produce the following result:

```
abc
d=42
00ff
   hello
he
```

Test Function Arguments

The function *test (test, f1[, f2])* performs one of the following file tests specified by the character *test*. In order to improve readability, you should use File class methods (for example, File::readable?) rather than this function. Here are the file tests with one argument:

Argument	Description
?r	Is f1 readable by the effective uid of caller?
?w	Is f1 writable by the effective uid of caller?
?x	Is f1 executable by the effective uid of caller?
?o	Is f1 owned by the effective uid of caller?
?R	Is f1 readable by the real uid of caller?
?W	Is f1 writable by the real uid of caller?
?X	Is f1 executable by the real uid of caller?
?O	Is f1 owned by the real uid of caller?
?e	Does f1 exist?
?z	Does f1 have zero length?
?s	File size of f1(nil if 0)

?f	Is f1 a regular file?
?d	Is f1 a directory?
?l	Is f1 a symbolic link?
?p	Is f1 a named pipe (FIFO)?
?S	Is f1 a socket?
?b	Is f1 a block device?
?c	Is f1 a character device?
?u	Does f1 have the setuid bit set?
?g	Does f1 have the setgid bit set?
?k	Does f1 have the sticky bit set?
?M	Last modification time for f1.
?A	Last access time for f1.
?C	Last inode change time for f1.

File tests with two arguments are as follows:

Argument	Description
?=	Are modification times of f1 and f2 equal?
?>	Is the modification time of f1 more recent than f2 ?
?<	Is the modification time of f1 older than f2 ?

?-	Is f1 a hard link to f2 ?

Following is the usage example. Assuming main.rb exist with read, write and not execute permissions:

```
#!/usr/bin/ruby


puts test(?r, "main.rb" )   # => true
puts test(?w, "main.rb" )   # => true
puts test(?x, "main.rb" )   # => false
```

This will produce the following result:

```
true
true
false
```

33. PREDEFINED VARIABLES

Ruby's predefined variables affect the behavior of the entire program, so their use in libraries is not recommended.

The values in most predefined variables can be accessed by alternative means.

Following table lists all the Ruby's predefined variables.

Variable Name	Description
$!	The last exception object raised. The exception object can also be accessed using => in *rescue* clause.
$@	The *stack backtrace* for the last exception raised. The *stack backtrace* information can retrieved by Exception#backtrace method of the last exception.
$/	The input record separator (newline by default). *gets, readline,* etc., take their input record separator as optional argument.
$\	The output record separator (nil by default).
$,	The output separator between the arguments to print and Array#join (nil by default). You can specify separator explicitly to Array#join.
$;	The default separator for split (nil by default). You can specify separator explicitly for String#split.
$.	The number of the last line read from the current input file. Equivalent to ARGF.lineno.
$<	Synonym for ARGF.
$>	Synonym for $defout.
$0	The name of the current Ruby program being executed.

$$	The process pid of the current Ruby program being executed.
$?	The exit status of the last process terminated.
$:	Synonym for $LOAD_PATH.
$DEBUG	True if the -d or --debug command-line option is specified.
$defout	The destination output for *print* and *printf* (*$stdout* by default).
$F	The variable that receives the output from *split* when -a is specified. This variable is set if the -a command-line option is specified along with the -p or -n option.
$FILENAME	The name of the file currently being read from ARGF. Equivalent to ARGF.filename.
$LOAD_PATH	An array holding the directories to be searched when loading files with the load and require methods.
$SAFE	The security level 0 --> No checks are performed on externally supplied (tainted) data. (default) 1 --> Potentially dangerous operations using tainted data are forbidden. 2 --> Potentially dangerous operations on processes and files are forbidden. 3 --> All newly created objects are considered tainted. 4 --> Modification of global data is forbidden.
$stdin	Standard input (STDIN by default).
$stdout	Standard output (STDOUT by default).
$stderr	Standard error (STDERR by default).

$VERBOSE	True if the -v, -w, or --verbose command-line option is specified.
$- x	The value of interpreter option -x (x=0, a, d, F, i, K, l, p, v). These options are listed below
$-0	The value of interpreter option -x and alias of $/.
$-a	The value of interpreter option -x and true if option -a is set. Read-only.
$-d	The value of interpreter option -x and alias of $DEBUG
$-F	The value of interpreter option -x and alias of $;.
$-i	The value of interpreter option -x and in in-place-edit mode, holds the extension, otherwise nil. Can enable or disable in-place-edit mode.
$-I	The value of interpreter option -x and alias of $:.
$-l	The value of interpreter option -x and true if option -lis set. Read-only.
$-p	The value of interpreter option -x and true if option -pis set. Read-only.
$_	The local variable, last string read by gets or readline in the current scope.
$~	The local variable, *MatchData* relating to the last match. Regex#match method returns the last match information.
$ n ($1, $2, $3...)	The string matched in the nth group of the last pattern match. Equivalent to m[n], where m is a *MatchData* object.
$&	The string matched in the last pattern match. Equivalent to m[0], where m is a *MatchData* object.

$`	The string preceding the match in the last pattern match. Equivalent to m.pre_match, where m is a *MatchData* object.
$'	The string following the match in the last pattern match. Equivalent to m.post_match, where m is a MatchData object.
$+	The string corresponding to the last successfully matched group in the last pattern match.

34. PREDEFINED CONSTANTS

The following table lists all the Ruby's Predefined Constants:

NOTE: TRUE, FALSE, and NIL are backward-compatible. It's preferable to use true, false, and nil.

Constant Name	Description
TRUE	Synonym for true.
FALSE	Synonym for false.
NIL	Synonym for nil.
ARGF	An object providing access to virtual concatenation of files passed as command-line arguments or standard input if there are no command-line arguments. A synonym for $<.
ARGV	An array containing the command-line arguments passed to the program. A synonym for $*.
DATA	An input stream for reading the lines of code following the __END__ directive. Not defined if __END__ isn't present in code.
ENV	A hash-like object containing the program's environment variables. ENV can be handled as a hash.
RUBY_PLATFORM	A string indicating the platform of the Ruby interpreter.
RUBY_RELEASE_DATE	A string indicating the release date of the Ruby interpreter
RUBY_VERSION	A string indicating the version of the Ruby interpreter.

STDERR	Standard error output stream. Default value of *$stderr*.
STDIN	Standard input stream. Default value of $stdin.
STDOUT	Standard output stream. Default value of $stdout.
TOPLEVEL_BINDING	A binding object at Ruby's top level.

35. ASSOCIATED TOOLS

Standard Ruby Tools

The standard Ruby distribution contains useful tools along with the interpreter and standard libraries:

These tools help you debug and improve your Ruby programs without spending much effort. This book will give you a very good start with these tools.

- **RubyGems:**
  RubyGems is a package utility for Ruby, which installs Ruby software packages and keeps them up-to-date.

- **Ruby Debugger:**
  To help deal with bugs, the standard distribution of Ruby includes a debugger. This is very similar to *gdb* utility, which can be used to debug complex programs.

- **Interactive Ruby (irb):**
  irb (Interactive Ruby) was developed by Keiju Ishitsuka. It allows you to enter commands at the prompt and have the interpreter respond as if you were executing a program. irb is useful to experiment with or to explore Ruby.

- **Ruby Profiler:**
  Ruby profiler helps you to improve the performance of a slow program by finding the bottleneck.

RubyGems

RubyGems is a package utility for Ruby, which installs Ruby software packages and keeps them up-to-date.

Usage Syntax

```
$ gem command [arguments...] [options...]
```

Example

Check to see whether RubyGems is installed:

```
$ gem --version
0.9.0
```

RubyGems Commands

Here is a list of all important commands for RubyGems:

SN	Command with Description
1	**build** Builds a gem from a gemspec.
2	**cert** Adjusts RubyGems certificate settings.
3	**check** Checks installed gems.
4	**cleanup** Cleans up old versions of installed gems in the local repository.
5	**contents** Displays the contents of the installed gems.
6	**dependency** Shows the dependencies of an installed gem.
7	**environment** Displays RubyGems environmental information.
8	**help** Provides help on the 'gem' command.
9	**install** Installs a gem into the local repository.
10	**list** Displays all gems whose name starts with STRING.
11	**query** Queries gem information in local or remote repositories.
12	**rdoc** Generates RDoc for pre-installed gems.
13	**search** Displays all gems whose name contains STRING.

14	**specification** Displays gem specification (in yaml).
15	**uninstall** Uninstalls a gem from the local repository.
16	**unpack** Unpacks an installed gem to the current directory.
17	**update** Updates the named gem (or all installed gems) in the local repository.

RubyGems Common Command Options

Following is the list of common options:

SN	Command with Description
1	**--source URL** Uses URL as the remote source for gems.
2	**-p, --[no-]http-proxy [URL]** Uses HTTP proxy for remote operations.
3	**-h, --help** Gets help on this command.
4	**--config-file FILE** Uses this config file instead of default.
5	**--backtrace** Shows stack backtrace on errors.
6	**--debug** Turns on Ruby debugging.

RubyGems Install Command Options

This is a list of the options, which use most of the time when you use RubyGems while installing any Ruby package:

SN	Command with Description
1	**-v, --version VERSION** Specifies version of gem to install.
2	**-l, --local** Restricts operations to the LOCAL domain (default).
3	**-r, --remote** Restricts operations to the REMOTE domain.
4	**-b, --both** Allows LOCAL and REMOTE operations.
5	**-i, --install-dir DIR** Where to install.
6	**-d, --[no-]rdoc** Generates RDoc documentation for the gem on install.
7	**-f, --[no-]force** Forces gem to install, bypassing dependency checks.
8	**-t, --[no-]test** Runs unit tests prior to installation.
9	**-w, --[no-]wrappers** Uses bin wrappers for executables.
10	**-P, --trust-policy POLICY** Specifies gem trust policy.
11	**--ignore-dependencies** Do not install any required dependent gems.
12	**-y, --include-dependencies** Unconditionally installs the required dependent gems.

Examples

This will install 'SOAP4R', either from local directory or remote server including all the dependencies:

```
gem install soap4r --include-dependencies
```

This will install 'rake', only from remote server:

```
gem install rake --remote
```

This will install 'rake' from remote server, and run unit tests, and generate RDocs:

```
gem install --remote rake --test --rdoc --ri
```

Further Readings

- The **RubyGems User Guide** gives you almost everything you need to know about using RubyGems.
- The **RubyGems Command Reference** for RubyGems.

Ruby Debugger

It doesn't matter how easy a language is to use, it usually contains some bugs if it is more than a few lines long. To help deal with bugs, the standard distribution of Ruby includes a debugger.

In order to start the Ruby debugger, load the debug library using the command-line option *-r debug*. The debugger stops before the first line of executable code and asks for the input of user commands.

Usage Syntax

Here is the usage syntax to use ruby debugger:

```
$ ruby -r debug filename[, ...]
```

Ruby Debugger Commands

Here is a complete list of commands, which you can use while debugging your program. Here, it is not necessary to use complete keyword to give a command, part given inside [...] is option.

SN	Command with Description
1	**b[reak] [< file| class>:]< line| method>** Sets breakpoint to some position. Breakpoint is a place where you want to pause program execution for debugging purpose.

<table>
<tr><td>2</td><td>wat[ch] expression

Sets watchpoints.</td></tr>
<tr><td>3</td><td>cat[ch] (exception|off)

Sets catchpoint to an exception.</td></tr>
<tr><td>4</td><td>b[reak]

Displays breakpoints and watchpoints.</td></tr>
<tr><td>5</td><td>del[ete] [n]

Deletes breakpoints.</td></tr>
<tr><td>6</td><td>disp[lay] expression

Displays value of expression.</td></tr>
<tr><td>7</td><td>undisp[lay] [n]

Removes display of n.</td></tr>
<tr><td>8</td><td>c[ont]

Continues execution.</td></tr>
<tr><td>9</td><td>s[tep] [n]

Executes next n lines stepping into methods.</td></tr>
<tr><td>10</td><td>n[ext] [n]

Executes next n lines stepping over methods.</td></tr>
<tr><td>11</td><td>w[here]

Displays stack frame.</td></tr>
<tr><td>12</td><td>f[rame]

Synonym for where.</td></tr>
<tr><td>13</td><td>l[ist][<-| n- m>]</td></tr>
</table>

	Displays source lines from n to m.
14	**up [n]** Moves up n levels in the stack frame.
15	**down [n]** Moves down n levels in the stack frame.
16	**fin[ish]** Finishes execution of the current method.
17	**tr[ace] [on|off]** Toggles trace mode on and off.
18	**q[uit]** Exits debugger.
19	**v[ar] g[lobal]** Displays global variables.
20	**v[ar] l[ocal]** Displays local variables.
21	**v[ar] i[instance] *object*** Displays instance variables of *object.*
22	**v[ar] c[onst] *object*** Displays constants of *object.*
23	**m[ethod] i[instance] *object*** Displays instance methods of *object.*
24	**m[ethod] *class| module*** Displays instance methods of the *class or module.*

25	**th[read] l[ist]** Displays threads.
26	**th[read] c[ur[rent]]** Displays current thread.
27	**th[read] n** Stops specified thread.
28	**th[read] stop >** Synonym for th[read] n.
29	**th[read] c[ur[rent]] n>** Synonym for th[read] n.
30	**th[read] resume >** Resumes thread n.
31	**p *expression*** Evaluates the *expression.*
32	**h[elp]** Displays help message.
33	**everything else** Evaluates.

Example

Consider the following file *hello.rb*, which needs to be debugged:

```
#!/usr/bin/env ruby
class Hello
   def initialize( hello )
      @hello = hello
   end
```

```
    def hello
        @hello
    end
end

salute = Hello.new( "Hello, Mac!" )
puts salute.hello
```

Here is one interactive session captured. Given commands are written in bold:

```
[root@ruby]# ruby -r debug hello.rb
Debug.rb
Emacs support available.

hello.rb:3:class Hello
(rdb:1) v l
  salute => nil
(rdb:1) b 10
Set breakpoint 1 at hello.rb:10
(rdb:1) c
Hello, Mac!
[root@ruby]#
```

Interactive Ruby

Interactive Ruby or irb is an interactive programming environment that comes with Ruby. It was written by Keiju Ishitsuka.

Usage Syntax

To invoke it, type irb at a shell or command prompt, and begin entering Ruby statements and expressions. Use *exit* or *quit* to exit *irb*.

```
$ irb[.rb] [options] [programfile] [arguments]
```

Here is a complete list of options:

SN	Command with Description
1	**-f** Suppress reading of the file ~/.irbrc.
2	**-m** bc mode (load mathn library so fractions or matrix are available).
3	**-d** Sets $DEBUG to true (same as ruby -d).
4	**-r load-module** Same as ruby -r.
5	**-I path** Specifies $LOAD_PATH directory.
6	**--inspect** Uses inspect for output (default except for bc mode).
7	**--noinspect** Doesn't use inspect for output.
8	**--readline** Uses Readline extension module.
9	**--noreadline** Doesn't use Readline extension module.
10	**--prompt prompt-mode (--prompt-mode prompt-mode)** Switches prompt mode. Predefined prompt modes are *default, simple, xmp,* and *inf-ruby.*
11	**--inf-ruby-mode**

	Uses prompt appropriate for *inf-ruby-mode* on Emacs. Suppresses --*readline*.
12	**--simple-prompt** Simple prompt mode.
13	**--noprompt** No prompt mode.
14	**--tracer** Displays trace for each execution of commands.
15	**--back-trace-limit n** Displays backtrace top n and tail n. The default value is 16.
16	**--irb_debug n** Sets internal debug level to n (not for popular use).
17	**-v (--version).** Prints the version of irb.

Example

Here is a sample of irb evaluating a variety of expressions::

```
$ irb

irb(main):001:0> 23 + 27

=> 50

irb(main):002:0> 50 - 23

=> 27

irb(main):003:0> 10 * 5

=> 50

irb(main):004:0> 10**5

=> 100000

irb(main):006:0> x = 1

=> 1
```

```
irb(main):007:0> x + 59
=> 60
irb(main):005:0> 50 / 5
=> 10
irb(main):008:0> hi = "Hello, Mac!"
=> "Hello, Mac!"
```

You can also invoke a single program with *irb*. After running the program, *irb* exits. Let's call our hello.rb program:

```
$ irb hello.rb
hello.rb(main):001:0> #!/usr/bin/env ruby
hello.rb(main):002:0*
hello.rb(main):003:0* class Hello
hello.rb(main):004:1> def initialize( hello )
hello.rb(main):005:2> @hello = hello
hello.rb(main):006:2> end
hello.rb(main):007:1> def hello
hello.rb(main):008:2> @hello
hello.rb(main):009:2> end
hello.rb(main):010:1> end
=> nil
hello.rb(main):011:0>
hello.rb(main):012:0* salute = Hello.new( "Hello, Mac!" )
=> #<Hello:0x319f20 @hello="Hello, Mac!">
hello.rb(main):013:0> puts salute.hello
Hello, Mac!
=> nil
hello.rb(main):014:0> $
```

Ruby Profiler

In most cases, you can improve the performance of a slow program by removing the bottleneck. The profiler is a tool that finds the bottleneck.

In order to add profiling to your Ruby program, you need to first load the *Profile* library using the command-line option *-r profile*.

Usage Syntax

```
$ ruby -r profile [programfile] [arguments]
```

Example

Here is the output generated from *hello.rb* file but this would not give you much idea so, you can try using a bigger program. Output is shown with small font.

```
[root@ruby]# ruby -r profile hello.rb
```

```
Hello, Mac!
  %   cumulative   self              self     total
 time   seconds   seconds    calls  ms/call  ms/call  name
  0.00     0.00      0.00        2     0.00     0.00  IO#write
  0.00     0.00      0.00        2     0.00     0.00
Module#method_added
  0.00     0.00      0.00        1     0.00     0.00  Hello#hello
  0.00     0.00      0.00        1     0.00     0.00  Hello#initialize
  0.00     0.00      0.00        1     0.00     0.00  Class#inherited
  0.00     0.00      0.00        1     0.00     0.00  Kernel.puts
  0.00     0.00      0.00        1     0.00     0.00  Class#new
  0.00     0.01      0.00        1     0.00    10.00  #toplevel
```

Additional Ruby Tools

There are other useful tools that don't come bundled with the Ruby standard distribution. However, you do need to install them yourself.

- **eRuby: Embeded Ruby:**
  eRuby stands for embedded Ruby. It's a tool that embeds fragments of Ruby code in other files, such as HTML files similar to ASP, JSP and PHP.

- **ri: Ruby Interactive Reference:**
  When you have a question about the behavior of a certain method, you can invoke ri to read the brief explanation of the method.

eRuby: Embeded Ruby

eRuby stands for *embedded Ruby*. It's a tool that embeds fragments of Ruby code in other files such as HTML files similar to ASP, JSP and PHP.

eRuby allows Ruby code to be embedded within (delimited by) a pair of <% and %> delimiters. These embedded code blocks are then evaluated in-place, i.e., they are replaced by the result of their evaluation.

Syntax

Here is a syntax to write single line of *eRuby* code:

```
<% ruby code %>
```

They function like blocks in Ruby and are terminated by <% end %>.

```
<ul>
<% 3.times do %>

  <li>list item</li>

<% end %>
</ul>
```

All Ruby code after the # is ignored and treated as comments.

```
<%# ruby code %>
```

Example

Here's a sample eRuby file:

```
This is sample eRuby file<br>
The current time here is <%=Time.now%>.
<%[1,2,3].each{|x|print x,"<br>\n"}%>
```

Here's the output from this sample file:

```
This is sample eRuby file<br>
The current time here is Wed Aug 29 18:54:45 JST 2001.
1
2
3
```

For complete details on *eRuby*, refer to **eRuby Home**.

ri: Ruby Interactive Reference

ri is an online reference tool developed by Dave Thomas, the famous pragmatic programmer.

When you have a question about the behavior of a certain method, you can invoke *ri* to read the brief explanation of the method.

You can get ri from **ri: Ruby Interactive**

Usage Syntax

Here is simple syntax to use *ri*

```
ri [ options ] [ methodname... ]
```

Here is a complete list of options:

SN	Command with Description
1	**--version,** **-v** Displays version and exits.
2	**--line-length=n** **-l n** Sets the line length for the output (minimum is 30 characters).
3	**--synopsis** **-s** Displays just a synopsis.
4	**--format= name** **-f name** Uses the *name* module (default is *Plain*) for output formatting. Here are the available modules: *Tagged:* Simple tagged output *Plain:* Default plain output *name* should be specified in any of the following forms: Class

	Class::method Class#method Class.method Method.

Index

A

B

C

D

E

M

N

O

P

R

S

T

U

V

X

Y

Made in the USA
Middletown, DE
05 September 2021